A WORLD OF DIFFERENCE

BARBARA JOHNSON

A World of Difference

The Johns Hopkins University Press

Baltimore and London

© 1987 The Johns Hopkins University Press
All rights reserved
Printed in the United States of America

Second printing, hardcover, 1989
Johns Hopkins Paperbacks edition, 1989

The Johns Hopkins University Press
701 West 40th Street
Baltimore, Maryland 21211
The Johns Hopkins Press Ltd., London

Library of Congress Cataloging-in-Publication Data
Johnson, Barbara, 1947–
  A world of difference.
  Bibliography: p.
  Includes index.
  1. Criticism. I. Title.
PN85.J5 1987   801'.95   86-46286
ISBN 0-8018-2651-9
ISBN 0-8018-3745-6 (pbk.)

In memory of Paul de Man and Linda Miller

When the most basic concepts—the concepts, as it is said, from which we begin—are suddenly seen to be not concepts but problems, not analytic problems either but historical movements that are still unresolved, there is no sense in listening to their sonorous summons or their resounding clashes. We have only, if we can, to recover the substance from which their forms were cast.

—Raymond Williams, *Marxism and Literature*

We are, I am, you are
by cowardice or courage
the one who find our way
back to this scene
carrying a knife, a camera
a book of myths
in which
our names do not appear.

—Adrienne Rich, *Diving into the Wreck*

Contents

Preface to the Paperback Edition

A Note on the Wartime Writings of Paul de Man

The Surprise of Otherness

If I perceive my ignorance as a gap in knowledge instead of an imperative that changes the very nature of what I think I know, then I do not truly experience my ignorance. The surprise of otherness is that moment when a new form of ignorance is suddenly activated as an imperative.

—Barbara Johnson, "Nothing Fails Like Success"

As the dedication of this book will attest, Paul de Man was extremely important to me both intellectually and personally. When Jonathan Culler first informed me of the existence of over 150 articles written by de Man between 1940 and 1942 for a Belgian newspaper whose regular editorial staff had been replaced by collaborators and whose editorial line was distinctly anti-Semitic and pro-Nazi, my first impulse was a desire to rename my dogs (Nietzschie and Wagner). That is, my reaction was symptomatic of a logic of purification, expulsion, the vomiting of the name. Yet the logic of contamination and purification is the very logic of Nazism. Surely this "good breast/bad breast" split was too simplistic a way of dealing with what amounted to an urgent imperative to historicize.

If the quantity and intensity of the articles already published on the subject are any indication, there is clearly something at stake in this bibliographical discovery. Beyond the fact that Nazism is always news and that people love a fall, what is it that transforms this archival revelation into an *event*? I will begin a rather roundabout approach to these questions by quoting from one of de Man's last discussions of the nature of historical occurrences:

> When I speak of irreversibility and insist on irreversibility, it is because in all those texts and those juxtapositions of texts, we have been aware of something which one could call a progression though it shouldn't be, a movement from cognition, from acts of knowledge, from states of cognition, to something which is no longer a cognition but which is

to some extent an occurrence, which has the materiality of something that actually happens, that actually occurs. And there, the sort of material occurrence . . . that . . . leaves a trace on the world, that does something to the world as such, that notion of occurrence is not opposed in any sense to the notion of writing.[1]

It is a fitting illustration of Paul de Man's theory of history as the disruption of a cognitive progression that his wartime writings should have been unearthed not by a critic but by an admirer, Ortwin de Graef, a Belgian graduate student. Although de Man had referred to his *Le Soir* articles in several contexts in the course of his life (in a letter to the chairman of Harvard's Society of Fellows, in a conversation with Harold Bloom), they had remained, like the purloined letter, exposed but invisible, open but unread, until the relentless progress of archival devotion delivered them from sufferance. Whether or not those articles contributed in any way to the wartime history of Belgium, the arrival of this long-delayed letter strikes us *now* with the full disruptive force of an event. It is an event that is structured *like* what de Man describes in the above quotation as an "occurrence"—an irreversible disruption of cognition—but it is a disruption that is happening *to* his own acts of cognition. It is as though de Man had tried to theorize the disruption of his own acts of theorizing, had tried to include the theory's own outside within it. But that theory's outside was precisely, we now know, always already within. And he could not, of course, control the very loss of control he outlined as inevitable and defined as irony. "Irony comes into being precisely when self-consciousness loses its control over itself," he told Robert Moynihan. "For me, at least, the way I think of it now, irony is not a figure of self-consciousness. It's a break, an interruption, a disruption. It is a moment of loss of control, and not just for the author but for the reader as well."[2] The arrival of this purloined letter, then, is an event not only for de Man but also for his readers, however uncannily his theory might have predicted its inevitability. His death makes it necessary to face the letter without him, but in any case he could not have served as guide to its interpretation. All the wisdom he had on the subject, he had already delivered. Indeed, this is one of the things that has become newly readable in his late work. As Christopher Norris, Cynthia Chase, and doubtless many others are in the process of arguing, the critic to whom de Man was most polemically and mercilessly opposed was his own former self. But who *was* that masked de Man?

National Literatures, Genre Theory, and Racial Hygiene

Thus, in the framework of three lectures, Professor Domini has given us a complete overview of Italian poetry, which seems to be

realizing most felicitously the hope expressed by Mussolini when he declared that "It is especially at the present time that poetry is necessary to the life of a people."
—Paul de Man, *Le Soir*, February 18, 1941

Paul de Man was born in Antwerp on December 6, 1919, to a rather well-to-do family that was both patriotically Flemish and cultivatedly cosmopolitan.[3] One of his strongest early influences seems to have been his uncle Hendrik de Man, a prominent socialist theorist, president of the Belgian Labor Party, and a minister in several governments. Hendrik de Man was the only important member of the Belgian government who agreed with the timing and mode of King Leopold's decision to capitulate to the Germans in May 1940. In a manifesto to the members of the Belgian Labor Party, published in July 1940, Hendrik wrote:

> Be among the first rank of those who struggle against poverty and demoralization, for the resumption of work and the return to normal life.
>
> But do not believe that it is necessary to resist the occupying power; accept the fact of his victory and try rather to draw lessons therefrom so as to make of this the starting point for new social progress.
>
> The war has led to the debacle of the parliamentary regime and of the capitalist plutocracy in the so-called democracies.
>
> For the working classes and for socialism, this collapse of a decrepit world is, far from a disaster, a deliverance.[4]

As minister of finance in the prewar years, Hendrik de Man had been appalled by the power wielded by high finance in the Belgian political process. He was indeed so disgusted by the "sleaze factor" that he was ready to abandon the democratic process altogether. His mistake in 1940 was to see capitalism as a worse evil than Nazism. Hendrik's enthusiasm for the new "revolution," however, did not last. In his struggle on behalf of the working classes, he fell increasingly out of favor with the German authorities until he left Belgium in late 1941 for an Alpine retreat in France. The book he published in 1942 was immediately seized by the Nazis. In 1944 he took refuge in Switzerland, where he learned of his conviction for treason, *in absentia*, by a Belgian military court. He died in a car accident in 1953.

The impact of Hendrik's intellectually and politically picaresque career on Paul—both the Paul of 1940–42 and the Paul of 1953–83—is incalculable. It is tempting to see the young Paul as beguiled into profascist sympathies by his uncle's utopian hopes, just as it is tempting to see the older Paul's warnings against the "unwarranted hopeful solutions"[5] of idealistic political activists as stemming from his uncle's catastrophic misjudgment. But these suppositions are at once impossible to verify and fundamentally inadequate in the sense that they reduce a complex political and ideological overdetermination to a personal and psychological "case." Paul de Man's early writings are part of a much larger intellectual and literary configuration, most of whose sinister consequences would have been hard to predict. Let us look briefly now at those writings.

Between December 1940 and November 1942, Paul de Man wrote 169 book and music reviews for the Brussels French-language newspaper *Le Soir*, and contributed another 10 articles to the Flemish newspaper *Het Vlaamsche Land*. Most of the essays have little apparent relation to politics beyond a vague assent to the new order. Their aim is rather to develop and practice a kind of literary criticism that is best summed up in a review of René Lalou's *Histoire de la littérature Française contemporaine*. After criticizing Lalou for spending too much time on the specificity of individual authors, de Man writes:

> By thus excessively multiplying his differentiations (*différencier à outrance*), he ends up giving the impression of a jungle of trees and creeping vines. And he will have missed the principal goal of any critical exposé: to give an image of the spirit, a synthesis of the thought, of a century.
>
> For what matters most is not the subtle differences of expression between two authors but their common submission to implacable rules. It is manifest that each period forges, sometimes unconsciously, its own aesthetic law. There may perhaps exist some eternal and immutable Beauty but it is nonetheless true that that Beauty is illuminated, in each era, from a different angle. A conscious critic must determine what that angle is and deduce his criteria from it.[6]

De Man's general concern in these reviews is with the orderly development of different literary genres and national traditions. This makes for rather repetitive reading. Indeed, while slogging my way through the pile of eye-straining photocopies of the young de Man's chronicles, I began to wonder why *Le Soir* itself didn't send out the hook for him. What good is a book review that tells you only about the place a novel holds in the evolution of the genre and never gives you a clue about the plot? Did de Man seriously think his readers were going to run out and buy the latest novel because it had timidly begun the necessary synthesis of French rationalism and German mysticism?

More to the point, for our purposes, is the question of the politics of this kind of literary history. The following quotation from one of the articles in *Het Vlaamsche Land* begins to show the sinister side of the notion of "proper traditions":

When we investigate the post-war literary production in Germany, we are immediately struck by the contrast between two groups, which moreover were also materially separated by the events of 1933. The first of these groups celebrates an art with a strongly cerebral disposition, founded upon some abstract principles and very remote from all naturalness. The in themselves very remarkable theses of expressionism were used in this group as tricks, as skillful artifices calculated at easy effects. The very legitimate basic rule of artistic transformation, inspired by the personal vision of the creator, served here as a pretext for a forced, caricatured representation of reality. Thus, [the artists of this group] came into an open conflict with the proper traditions of German art which had always and before everything else clung to a deep spiritual sincerity. Small wonder, then, that it was mainly non-Germans, and in specific Jews, that went in this direction.[7]

In the notorious essay "Jews in Contemporary Literature" (the only other one of the 179 articles that mentions Jews), de Man pushes these ideas to their appalling conclusion:

The fact that they [Western intellectuals] have been able to preserve themselves from Jewish influence in as representative a cultural domain as literature is proof of their vitality. One would not be able to hold out much hope for the future of our civilization if it had let itself be invaded, without resistance, by a foreign force. In keeping, despite Semitic interference in all aspects of European life, an intact originality and character, it [our civilization] has shown that its profound nature was healthy. In addition, one can thus see that a solution to the Jewish problem that would aim toward the creation of a Jewish colony far from Europe would not entail, for the literary life of the West, any deplorable consequences.[8]

How can one avoid feeling rage and disgust at a person who could write such a thing? How can I not understand and share the impulse to throw this man away? The fact that "Jews in Contemporary Literature" was written for a special issue of *Le Soir* on anti-Semitism does not excuse it. The fact that it is the only example of such a sentiment expressed in 179 articles does not erase it. The fact that de Man seems not to have been anti-Semitic in his personal life in 1940–42 (and certainly showed no trace of it in later years) only points up a too limited notion of what anti-Semitism is. And the fact that, as Derrida puts it, "de Man wants especially to propose a thesis on literature that visibly interests him more here than either anti-Semitism or the Jews"[9] is also no comfort. If there had not been people who, without any particular personal anti-Semitism, found the idea of deportation *reasonable*, there could have been no Holocaust. In his eagerness to preserve differences *between* European national traditions (including Flemish) and to allow for productive cross-fertilization and exchange among them, de Man judges as extraneous and distracting any "foreign" differences *within*, which might blur the picture of the organic development of forms. Never has the repression of "differences within" had such horrible consequences. But is genre theory therefore fascist? Is comparative literature Volkish?[10] Things can hardly be so simple.

The Question of Deconstruction

> *The de-construction of a text does not proceed by random doubt or arbitrary subversion, but by the careful teasing out of warring forces of signification within the text itself.*
> —Barbara Johnson, "The Critical Difference: BartheS/BalZac"

Whatever Paul de Man is doing in these early essays, it is certainly not deconstruction. Indeed, deconstruction is precisely the dismantling of these notions of evolutionary continuity, totalization, organicism, and "proper" traditions. No one could be more different from *Le Soir*'s suave synthesizer than the de Man who wrote:

> *Allegories of Reading* started out as a historical study and ended up as a theory of reading. I began to read Rousseau seriously in preparation for a historical reflection on Romanticism and found myself unable to progress beyond local difficulties of interpretation.[11]

Indeed, the later de Man's work exhibits all the negative characteristics cited by the young Paul: cerebrality, abstraction, a tendency to "*différencier à outrance.* . . ." But if de Man was not doing deconstruction in 1940–42, why have the deconstructors become so defensive?

One answer, of course, is that some critics of deconstruction have taken this occasion to conflate the early and late work of de Man and to proclaim, as reported in *Newsweek*, that "the movement is finished. As one Ivy League professor gleefully exclaims, 'deconstruction turned out to be the thousand-year Reich that lasted 12 years' " (February 15, 1988). This "gleeful" joy in annihilation clearly draws on the energies of the evil that opponents think they are combating. The recent spate of publicity has produced somewhat contradictory capsule descriptions of deconstruction ("a crucial tenet of deconstruction is that the relation between words and what they mean is sometimes arbitrary and always indeterminate") [*Newsweek*]; "Deconstruction views language as a slippery and inherently false medium that always reflects the biases of its users" [*New York Times*, December 1, 1987]). It is no wonder that deconstructors should want to set the record straight. But what seems clearer than ever in the extreme violence and "glee" of the recent attacks on deconstruction is the extent to which any questioning of the reliability of language, any suggestion that meaning cannot be taken for granted, violates a powerful taboo in our culture. To say that deconstruction is "hostile to the very principles of Western thought" (*Newsweek*) is like saying that quantum mechanics is hostile to the notion of substances. No one could have been a more enthusiastic upholder of the integrity of Western thought than the Paul de Man of 1940–42. It is not a question of hostility but of analysis.

In the absence of any guarantee as to Paul de Man's moral character, why are his writings still useful and, perhaps, necessary? On the one hand, as Christopher Norris, Cynthia Chase, and others have argued, because there is probably no literary critic who has sought as rigorously to dismantle the philosophical and literary roots of fascist ideology. On the other hand, because he dared to pursue the consequences of paying close attention to language even beyond the point of "moral good conscience." His work was not an attempt at reparation, but an attempt to deal with the irreparable.

If it were easy to remain grounded in the morally good, the history of the twentieth century would look quite different. Although deconstruction cannot be reduced to an outcome of one individual's biography, it may well be that it has arisen as an attempt to come to terms with the Holocaust as a radical disruption produced as a logical extention of Western thinking. If idealism can turn out to be terroristic, if the defense of Western civilization can become the annihilation of otherness, and if the desire for a beautiful and orderly society should require the tidying action of cattle cars and gas chambers, it is not enough to decide that we now recognize evil in order to locate ourselves comfortably in the good. In Nazi Germany, the seduction of an image of the good was precisely the road to evil.

It is thus not out of "hostility" to the moral values of Western civilization that deconstruction has arisen, but out of a desire to understand how those values are potentially already different from *themselves*. By rereading the texts of writers and philosophers that have made a difference to Western history, it might be possible to become aware of the repressions, the elisions, the contradictions, and the linguistic slippages that have functioned unnoticed and that undercut the certainties those texts have been read as upholding. If certainty had never produced anything but just and life-affirming results, there would be no need to analyze it. It is because of the self-contradictions and ambiguities already present within the text and the history of even the clearest and most admirable statements that careful reading is essential. Such a reading does not aim to eliminate or dismiss texts or values, but rather to see them in a more complex, more *constructed,* less idealized light. And this applies as much to the work and life of Paul de Man as it does to any of the texts he deconstructed.

Notes

1. Paul de Man, "Kant and Schiller," in "Aesthetic Ideology," ed. Andrzej War-minski (forthcoming).
2. Robert Moynihan, *A Recent Imagining: Interviews with Harold Bloom, Geoffrey Hartman, J. Hillis Miller, and Paul de Man* (Hamden, Conn.: Archon, 1986), p. 137.
3. Factual support for this section comes from the following sources: Ortwin de Graef, "Paul de Man's Proleptic 'Nachlass' " (forthcoming); Peter Dodge, *A Documentary Study of Hendrik de Man, Socialist Critic of Marxism* (Princeton: Princeton University Press, 1979); and Henri de Man, *Cavalier Seul* (Geneva: Les Editions du Cheval Ailé, 1948).
4. Dodge, *Documentary Study of Hendrik de Man*, p. 326.
5. Paul de Man, "Image and Emblem in Yeats," in *The Rhetoric of Romanticism* (New York: Columbia University Press, 1984), p. 238.
6. Paul de Man, *Le Soir*, April 8, 1941 (translation mine).
7. Paul de Man, "A View on Contemporary German Fiction," *Het Vlaamsche Land*, August 20, 1942 (translated from Flemish by Ortwin de Graef).
8. Paul de Man, *Le Soir*, March 4, 1941 (translation mine).
9. Jacques Derrida, "Like the Sound of the Sea Deep within a Shell: Paul de Man's War," *Critical Inquiry* 14 (Spring 1988): 626.
10. Volkish thinking, on which Adolph Hitler based many of his ideas, is described by a scholar of Nazism, George L. Mosse, in his book *The Crisis of German Ideology: Intellectual Origins of the Third Reich* (New York: Schocken, 1964), as the conflation of soil, blood (race), and culture: "According to many Volkist theorists, the nature of the soul of a Volk is determined by the native landscape. Thus the Jews, being a desert people, are viewed as shallow, arid, 'dry' people, devoid of profundity and totally lacking in creativity. Because of the barrenness of the desert landscape, the Jews are a spiritually barren people. They thus contrast markedly with the Germans, who, living in the dark, mist-shrouded forests, are deep, mysterious, profound. Because they are so constantly shrouded in darkness, they strive toward the sun, and are truly *Lichtmenschen*" (pp. 4–5). A desert is only a desert, but darkness is also light. One glimpses here the dangers not only of an ahistorical essentialism but also of allowing a contradiction to appear logical and natural.
11. Paul de Man, *Allegories of Reading* (New Haven: Yale University Press, 1979), p. ix.

Acknowledgments

This book could never have been written without the aid of two fellowships which allowed me the time to reflect in a more concentrated way than is ever possible during a year of teaching. In 1982–83, I spent a year in Cambridge on a Bunting Fellowship, and in 1985–86, I was able to complete work on the manuscript with the support of a Guggenheim Fellowship.

Many of the essays in this volume have appeared elsewhere. I wish to acknowledge permission to reprint from the following original sources:

"Nothing Fails Like Success," *SCE Reports 8*, Fall 1980.

"Rigorous Unreliability," *Critical Inquiry*, December 1984.

"Gender Theory and the Yale School," *Genre*, Summer 1984.

"Teaching Ignorance," *Yale French Studies* 63 (1982).

"Disfiguring Poetic Language," in *The Prose Poem in France*, ed. Mary Ann Caws and Hermine Riffaterre (New York: Columbia University Press, 1983).

"Les Fleurs du Mal Armé" first appeared in *Michigan Romance Studies* 2 (1981), then was revised for inclusion in *Lyric Poetry: Beyond New Criticism*, ed. Chaviva Hošek and Patricia Parker (Ithaca, N.Y.: Cornell University Press, 1985). The present version has been further revised.

"Mallarmé as Mother," *Denver Quarterly*, Spring 1984.

"My Monster/My Self," *Diacritics*, Summer 1982.

"Metaphor, Metonymy, and Voice in *Their Eyes Were Watching God*," in *Black Literature and Literary Theory*, ed. Henry Louis Gates, Jr. (New York: Methuen, 1984).

"Thresholds of Difference: Structures of Address in Zora Neale Hurston," *Critical Inquiry,* Autumn 1985.

"Apostrophe, Animation, and Abortion," *Diacritics,* Spring 1986.

No book springs fully armed from the head of a single creator. Among those who have most shaped my writing and thinking in the past, no one is more important than Shoshana Felman, whose generous refusal to indulge my desire to avoid criticism was relentless, and whose insight and brilliance have always pushed my thinking farther than it would ever have gone on its own. Others whose impact on this book is probably greater than they suspect are Henry Louis Gates, Jr., Martha Collins, Marjorie Garber, Rachel Jacoff, and the members of the two study groups in which I participated in 1982–83: Ellen Bassuk, Diane Middlebrook, Joan Landes, Linda Williams, and Sumie Jones; and Susan Suleiman, Susan Gubar, Dee Morris, Wendy Deutelbaum, Alice Jardine, and Naomi Schor. To all, warm thanks.

Introduction

At this point it seems impossible to think difference without thinking it aggressively or defensively. But think it we must, because if we don't, it will continue to think us, as it has since Genesis at the very least.
—Alice Jardine, *The Future of Difference*

The truth is that, with the fading of the Renaissance ideal through progressive stages of specialism, leading to intellectual emptiness, we are left with a potentially suicidal movement among "leaders of the profession," while, at the same time, the profession sprawls, without its old center, in helpless disarray.

One quickly cited example is the professional organization, the Modern Language Association. . . . A glance at its thick program for its last meeting shows a massive increase and fragmentation into more than 500 categories! I cite a few examples: "Deconstruction as Politics," "Lesbian Feminist Poetry in Texas," "The Trickster Figure in Chicano and Black Literature," or (astonishingly) "The Absent Father in Fact, Metaphor, and Metaphysics in the Middle Generation of American Poets." . . . Naturally, the progressive trivialization of topics has made these meetings a laughingstock in the national press.
—Walter Jackson Bate, "The Crisis in English Studies"

*Those of us who stand outside the circle of this society's definition of acceptable women; those of us who have been forged in the crucibles of difference—those of us who are poor, who are lesbians, who are Black, who are older—*know that survival is not an academic skill. It is *learning how to stand alone, unpopular and sometimes reviled, and how to make common cause with those others identified as outside the structures in order to define and seek a world in which we can all flourish. It is learning how to take our differences and make them*

strengths. For the master's tools will never dismantle the
master's house.
—Audre Lorde, *Sister Outsider*

Critical Differences

The essays in this book are united by a common aim, diversely conceived and executed, but relatively easy to describe. They all attempt, in
one way or another, to transfer the analysis of difference (as pursued in
such studies as my earlier book, *The Critical Difference*) out of the realm of
linguistic universality or deconstructive allegory and into contexts in
which difference is very much at issue in the "real world." This book
begins, in other words, from two very different starting points at once:
(1) a reading strategy designed to uncover the workings of "differences
within" and (2) a subject matter that asks the question of difference *as if*
"differences between" had referential validity.

In the introduction to *The Critical Difference*, I had described the
differential reading strategy I was attempting to employ as follows:

> Reading, here, proceeds by identifying and dismantling differences
> by means of other differences that cannot be fully identified or dis-
> mantled. The starting point is often a binary difference that is subse-
> quently shown to be an illusion created by the workings of differences
> much harder to pin down. The differences *between* entities (prose and
> poetry, man and woman, literature and theory, guilt and innocence)
> are shown to be based on a repression of differences *within* entities,
> ways in which an entity differs from itself. But the way in which a text
> thus differs from itself is never simple: it has a certain rigorous, con-
> tradictory logic whose effects can, up to a certain point, be read.[1]

What strikes me now about this passage is the heterogeneity of the
elements included in the parenthetical list. Each pair operates with very
different stakes in the world. It was when I realized that my discussion
of such differences was taking place entirely within the sameness of the
white male Euro-American literary, philosophical, psychoanalytical,
and critical canon that I began to ask myself what differences I was really
talking about. To say, for instance, that the difference *between* man and
woman is an illusion created by the repression of differences *within* each
may to some extent be true, but it does not account for the historical
exclusion of women from the canon. Jacques Derrida may sometimes
see himself as *philosophically* positioned as a woman, but he is not *politically* positioned as a woman. Being positioned as a woman is not something that is entirely voluntary. Or, to put it another way, if you tell a

member of the Ku Klux Klan that racism is a repression of self-difference, you are likely to learn a thing or two about repression.

There is, of course, no guarantee that to speak of the gender or race of an author (including one's own) is to situate the literary-theoretical activity in the "real world." But then, the very prevalence of the view that "theory" is a turning away from the world needs to be reexamined. Nothing indeed could be more commonplace than to hear academics speak of the "real world" as something lying outside their own sphere of operations. The following sentence from Duncan Kennedy's *Legal Education and the Reproduction of Hierarchy,* although it concerns legal rather than literary theory, depicts a typical view of the relations between academic "theory" and the "real world":

> There is a distinct lawyers' mystique of the irrelevance of the "theoretical" material learned in school, and of the crucial importance of abilities that cannot be known or developed until one is out in the "real world," "on the firing line," and "in the trenches."[2]

Implicit in the figurative language of this "mystique" is the assumption that violence is more real than safety, the physical more real than the intellectual, war more real than school. So ordinary are these assumptions that I was recently startled to come across (in some waiting-room reading I can no longer retrieve) a reference to "the 'real world,' as the G.I.'s used to say." Suddenly it became clear to me that the "real world" was constantly being put in quotation marks, always being defined as where "we" are not. "La vraie vie est ailleurs," wrote Rimbaud, before he left to go elsewhere. Yet these differing perceptions of the real are nothing other than perceptions of the boundaries of institutions. Whether one is in the university or in the army, the real world seems to be the world outside the institution. It is as though institutions existed precisely to create boundaries between the unreal and the real, to assure docility, paradoxically, through the assumption of unreality. Yet institutions are nothing if not *real* articulations of power. They are strategies of containment (to use Jameson's phrase) designed to mobilize some impulses and to deactivate others. Always ideological, they are also heuristically, if not existentially, inescapable.

It is toward a critique of the fallacious naturalness and blindered focus of certain institutional boundaries that this book attempts to move. It therefore generally concentrates on thresholds where an inside/outside opposition can be shown to be in a state of crisis, both within the text and between the text and the context of its reading or writing. While *The Critical Difference* seemed to say, "Here is a text; let me read it"; the present volume adds: "Why am I reading *this* text? What

4 / A World of Difference

kind of act was the writing of it? What question about it does it itself *not* raise? What am I participating in when I read it?" The institution whose boundaries are most insistently interrogated in this book is the literary canon, particularly in terms of its sexual and racial exclusions and efface- ments. Yet to "include" or to "claim an identity they taught me to de- spise" (to cite the title of Michelle Cliff's powerful book) is by no means a simple operation. If identities are lost through acts of negation, they are also acquired thereby, and the restoration of what has been denied cannot be accomplished through simple affirmation. What emerges from these readings is that the constraints and opportunities afforded by gender, race, literary genre, or institutional context, for both writer and reader, can be located neither inside nor outside the texts but are rather effects of the complex dynamism of an interaction.

Dialogism

Parts of a World

It would be falsely progressivist, however, to see in these essays an itinerary that could be labeled "From Deconstruction to Feminism" or "From White Mythology to Black Mythology." Some essays remain within a deconstructive frame reminiscent of *The Critical Difference;* oth- ers attempt a much messier form of bricolage. The book as a whole moves back and forth among positions that remain skeptical of each other, though perhaps not always skeptical enough. Yet, some sem- blance of a progression does exist within the book as a whole, within each section, and sometimes within a single essay, in the move from white male long-standingly canonical authors to white or black female authors who are rapidly being canonized even as I write. Whether this is in any sense progress is something I am not in a position to judge.

Part One consists of a series of occasional pieces that respond to some of the polemics surrounding deconstruction in its North Ameri- can context. Given in slightly altered chronological order, they also mark various phases of mourning for the death of Paul de Man. Chapter 1 is without suspicion, though it is an advance mourning; in Chapter 2, the death occurs in anecdotal fact (I was informed of it while writing about "the eclipse of the subject"); in Chapter 3, deconstruction is seen as the politics of the penultimate; in Chapter 4, deconstruction acquires gender; in Chapter 5, it is set in a pedagogical context.

Part Two returns to a less polemical, more analytical mode of literary analysis, going back to three highly canonical authors in order to rethink a question central to *The Critical Difference:* "the functioning of *what is not known* in literature or theory." In Chapter 6, what is not known is called "obscurity"; in Chapter 7, it is called "erasure"; in Chapter 8, "teaching." The essays on Thoreau and Mallarmé are attempts to complicate received notions of the difference between textuality and the real world, or between symbol and referent. The essay on Molière is a meditation on Western pedagogy as the repression of the knowledge of (sexual) difference. Socrates, in a sense, becomes Tiresias.

In Part Three (which should be read together with Chapter 16), the question of difference arises as a structuring principle of poetic language. "Strange Fits" juxtaposes a defense of poetry as the "real language of real men" (Wordsworth) alongside a defense of poetry as exhibiting "the rigid consequence of a mathematical problem" (Poe), in order to show that it is just as difficult to keep the signifier empty as it is to reach the fullness of the signified. "Disfiguring Poetic Language" (most of which was written in 1974, but which anticipates what is worked out in Chapter 16) demonstrates the inextricability of poetic figuration from violence. And "Les Fleurs du Mal Armé" charts difference as the force of unconsciousness and displacement that engenders literary history.

In Part Four, difference is explicitly dramatized in sexual and racial terms. The psychogenesis of difference is first explored in terms of differentiation and separation from the mother. Motherhood as image and as function, which had already arisen in Chapter 11, occurs in Chapter 12 as an explanation of ambivalence toward Mallarmé, and in Chapter 13 as a figure for the ambivalence of female authorship. Dorothy Dinnerstein, Nancy Friday, and Mary Shelley all seem to be writing critiques of motherhood as a way of overcoming their own repression of autobiography. In Chapter 14, Zora Neale Hurston's ways of articulating racial and sexual difference are analyzed in rhetorical terms, while in Chapter 15, what is analyzed is the rhetoric of her ways of *baffling* the desire for an answer to the question of difference. Chapter 16, "Apostrophe, Animation, and Abortion," is an attempt to pull many threads together out of the disparate fabrics unraveled by the previous essays. Rhetoric, violence, mourning, motherhood, and the lyric are woven into patterns of problematized address and of revised literary history. The proper names recapitulate the itinerary of the book as a whole: Baudelaire, Mallarmé, Thoreau, Percy Bysshe Shelley, Gwendolyn Brooks, Anne Sexton, Lucille Clifton, Adrienne Rich. And language here *is* the relation between life and death.

On the threshold between the animate and the inanimate, the physical and the intelligible, the internal and the external, language is always also an articulation of power relations inscribed by, within, or upon the speaker. As such, it can only be studied as rhetoric. Whether one defines rhetoric as "language that says one thing and means another" (as I do in Chapter 16), as "the study of misunderstanding and its remedies" (as I. A. Richards does), or as "the faculty of observing in any given case the available means of persuasion" (as Aristotle and most teachers of composition do),[3] it is clear that the study of rhetoric has everything to do with human politics. As de Man frequently notes, however, there are two seemingly distinct branches of the study of rhetoric: the study of tropes and the study of persuasion, or the cognitive and the performative dimensions of language. Many of the essays here are attempts to carry the implications of one branch over to the other: to show, for example, the violence inherent in as tranquil a notion as metaphor; or to demonstrate that political issues can be structured like, and by, the contours of figurative language. For local historical reasons, metaphor and metonymy get star billing, with a supporting cast of catachresis, apostrophe, chiasmus, anacoluthon, hendiadys, repetition, ellipsis, and personification.

While this book has many agendas (some of which are probably still not clear to me), its most conscious preoccupation has thus been the attempt to recontextualize a certain way of reading. Central to this project, clearly, is the work of Paul de Man. My dedication and epigraphs are meant to situate this book in complex relation to de Man's death.

I am always startled by the vehemence of de Man's critics. His work is viewed, both from the left and from the right, not just as misguided or useless, but somehow almost as evil. Radicals see in his writing a conservative plot to talk literary critics out of participating in social change. Conservatives see in it a nihilistic desire to cancel out human meaning altogether. Both positions are responses to de Man's central insight: that language, since it is (to use Raymond Williams' term) *constitutive* of the human, cannot itself be entirely "human." It is neither inside nor outside the subject, but both at once. As the ground of possibility of expressive intentionality, language cannot itself be entirely reduced to interpretability. This does not mean that language *never* means, but rather that beyond the apparent meaning, and even beyond the suppressed or hidden meanings (unconscious, poetic, ideological, counterdiscursive), there can always be a residue of functioning—which produces effects—that is not a *sign* of anything, but merely the outcome of linguistic rules, or even of "the absolute randomness of language."[4] Not that language is always absolutely random, but that we can never be sure that it isn't. Why is this theory of the resistance of language to intentionality so hotly resisted? Why is it always absolutized into nihilism or quietism?

The problem, it seems to me, is not whether or not language is problematic as a medium of understanding, but rather what use we can make of the perception that it is. What do we *do* with the knowledge that we cannot be sure that any given language pattern isn't random? Any utterance, if scrutinized sufficiently, *does* become problematic, like the dots in a newspaper photograph. But if one turns one's attention to other questions, it is easy to forget that the road to understanding is paved with the potholes of *différance* (indeed, that forgetting is essential for life), and to fall into a purely representational view of how language functions. This is why ideological or political criticism so often concentrates on prose rather than poetry, and why poetry so often seems to be either propagandistic or beside the point. Poetry, it seems to me, is precisely the repository of knowledge about the resistance of language to intentional dissolution. And "absolute randomness" is the outer limit of that resistance.

The questions toward which this book moves, then, are as follows. What are the political consequences of the fact that language is not a transparently expressive medium? What role does literature's radicalization of this fact play? How can the study of suppressed, disseminated, or marginalized messages within texts equip us to intervene against oppression and injustice in the world? Is a willingness to carry an inquiry to the point of undecidability necessarily at odds with political engagement? Is the exploration of logics other than the logic of binary opposition necessarily a way of avoiding participation in the process of change? The essays collected in this volume are attempts to show that these are not merely rhetorical questions.

I

THE FATE OF DECONSTRUCTION

1

Nothing Fails Like Success

As soon as any radically innovative thought becomes an *ism*, its specific groundbreaking force diminishes, its historical notoriety increases, and its disciples tend to become more simplistic, more dogmatic, and ultimately more conservative, at which time its power becomes institutional rather than analytical. The fact that what is loosely called deconstructionism is now being widely institutionalized in the United States seems to me both intriguing and paradoxical, but also a bit unsettling, although not for the reasons advanced by most of its opponents. The questions I shall ask are the following: How can the deconstructive impulse retain its *critical* energy in the face of its own success? What can a reader who has felt the surprise of intellectual discovery in a work by Jacques Derrida or Paul de Man do to remain in touch not so much with the content of the discovery as with the intellectual upheaval of the surprise? How can that surprise be put to *work* in new ways?

I would like to begin by examining briefly two types of accusations commonly directed *against* deconstruction: the literarily conservative, which accuses deconstruction of going too far, and the politically radical, which accuses deconstruction of not going far enough. The first type comes from well-established men of letters who attempt to defend their belief in the basic communicability of meanings and values against what is said to be the deconstructionists' relativism, nihilism, or self-indulgent love of meaninglessness. What I shall try to determine is not whether misunderstanding is a mere accident or the inevitable fate of reading, but rather what the relation is between deconstruction and the type of logic on which these opponents' accusations of relativism and solipsism are based. Consider the following sentences taken from well-known critiques of deconstruction:

> In revisionist criticism the first consequence of calling discourse itself into question is the proposition that all criticism amounts to misreading, and thus one reading is as legitimate as another.

But if all interpretation is misinterpretation, and if all criticism (like all history) of texts can engage only with a critic's own misconstruction, why bother to carry on the activities of interpretation and criticism?

In the absence of any appeal to such a coercive reality to which the plurality of subjectivities can be referred, all perspectives become equally valid.

Certainty and piety of all kinds are systematically undermined in favor of a universal relativism of values and judgment. Just as the revisionists are led to reduce the act of criticism to a given critic's subjective preference, so do professors relegate judgment of all sorts to the students' subjective preferences.

What Deconstruction urges is not a new system of thought but skepticism toward all the old ways, which are construed as really only one way.[1]

The logic behind such utterances is the logic of binary opposition, the principle of noncontradiction, often thought of as the very essence of Logic as such. The arguments can be reduced to the following logical formulas:

1. If all readings are misreadings, then all readings are equally valid.
2. If there is no such thing as an objective reading, then all readings are based on subjective preferences.
3. If there is no absolute truth, then everything is relative.
4. To criticize is to be skeptical; to put in question is to dismiss.

In other words, if not absolute, then relative; if not objective, then subjective; if you are not for something, you are against it. Now, my understanding of what is most radical in deconstruction is precisely that it questions this basic logic of binary opposition, but not in a simple, binary, antagonistic way. Consider the following passage from Derrida's *Dissemination:*

It is thus not simply false to say that Mallarmé is a Platonist or a Hegelian. But it is above all not true. And vice versa.[2]

Instead of a simple "either/or" structure, deconstruction attempts to elaborate a discourse that says *neither* "either/or", *nor* "both/and" nor even "neither/nor", while at the same time not totally abandoning these logics either. The very word *deconstruction* is meant to undermine the either/or logic of the opposition "construction/destruction." Deconstruction is both, it is neither, and it reveals the way in which both construction and destruction are themselves not what they appear to be. Deconstruction both opposes and redefines; it both reverses an opposition and reworks the terms of that opposition so that what was formerly understood by them is no longer tenable. In the case of the much-publicized opposition between speech and writing, deconstruction *both* appears to grant to writing the priority traditionally assigned to speech *and* redefines "writing" as *différance* (difference/deferment) so that it can no longer simply mean "marks on a page" but can very well also refer to those aspects of spoken speech (nonimmediacy, the non-transparency of meaning, the gap between signifier and signified) that are normally occulted by traditional notions of what speech is. In the case of the opposition between objectivity and subjectivity, deconstruction *seems* to locate the moment of meaning-making in the nonobjectivity of the act of reading rather than in the inherent givens of a text, but then the text seems already to anticipate the reading it engenders, and at the same time the reader's "subjectivity" is discovered to function something like a text, that is, something whose conscious awareness of meaning and desire is only one aspect of a complex unconscious signifying system which determines consciousness as one of its several effects. To imply that subjectivity is structured like a machine, as Paul de Man does in his essay "The Purloined Ribbon,"[3] is both to subvert the opposition between subject and object (since a machine is considered to be an object) and to displace the traditional notion of what a subject is. If the original opposition between subject and object corresponds, as Gerald Graff would have it, to the opposition between the pleasure principle and the reality principle,[4] what deconstruction shows is that there is *something else involved* that puts in question the very separability of the pleasure principle and the reality principle, something that continuously generates effects that can be explained by neither. Freud called this something the death instinct, but this death instinct is to be understood as what ceaselessly escapes the mastery of understanding and the logic of binary opposition by exhibiting some "other" logic one can neither totally comprehend nor exclude. It is the attempt to *write with* this "other" logic that produces the appearance of obscurity in many deconstructive texts. Any statement that *affirms* while using a logic different from the logic of binary opposition will necessarily not conform to binary notions of "clarity."

Hence, if deconstruction focuses on the act of reading rather than on the objective meaning of a text, this in no way entails any greater degree of self-indulgence than the belief in conventional values does: on the contrary, at its best it undoes the very comforts of mastery and consensus that underlie the illusion that objectivity is situated somewhere outside the self. Thus, the incompatibility between deconstruction and its conservative detractors is an incompatibility of logics. While traditionalists say that a thing cannot be both A and not-A, deconstructors open up ways in which A is necessarily but unpredictably already different from A.

Now we come to the second type of critique of deconstruction, which accuses it of not living up to its own claims of radicality, of working with too limited a notion of textuality, and of applying its critical energy only within an institutional structure that it does not question and therefore confirms.[5] This charge, which judges deconstruction against its own claims to an unflagging critical stance, is one which deconstruction must in fact continuously make against itself. Any discourse that is based on the questioning of boundary lines must never stop questioning its own. To reserve the deconstructive stance solely for literary criticism without analyzing its institutional underpinnings and economic and social relations with the world is to decide where the boundaries of the very critique of boundaries lie. To read a text apart from the historical and biographical conditions and writings that participate in its textual network is to limit a priori the kinds of questions that can be asked. Why, therefore, do some deconstructors tend to avoid going beyond the limits of the literary text?

There are, I think, three reasons for this unwarranted restriction. The first is entailed by the current institutionalization of deconstruction: the more it becomes entrenched as the self-definition of some literary critics in their opposition to other literary critics, the more it will resist problematizing the institutional conditions of literary criticism as such. The other two reasons spring out of an oversimplified understanding of certain aspects of deconstructive theory. To say, as Derrida has said, that there is nothing outside the text is not to say that the reader should read only one piece of literature in isolation from history, biography, and so on. It is to say that *nothing* can be said to be *not* a text, subject to the différance, the nonimmediacy, of presence or meaning. Even the statement that there is nothing outside the text cannot be taken to be the absolute certainty it appears to be, since it has to include itself in its own consequences. If there is nothing outside the text, then how can *any* locus of research or action be considered a priori as illegitimate?

The final reason for the conservatism of some forms of deconstruction is more pervasive: in questioning the nature of knowledge and causality, deconstruction has often given nothing but negative help in the attempt to read literature or philosophy *with* history and biography. In saying that history is a fiction, a text subject to ideological skewings and mystifications, and that it cannot be relied upon as a source of objective knowledge, deconstructive theory sometimes seems to block all access to the possibility of reading explicitly "referential" documents in conjunction with literary or speculative texts. Yet in practice, we find Derrida drawing upon Freud's life and letters in his analysis of *Beyond the Pleasure Principle* (in *La Carte Postale*), and de Man often beginning an article with a historical account that in some way doubles the rhetorical problem he is about to discuss. The question, then, is how to use history and biography *deconstructively,* how to seek in them not answers, causes, explanations, or origins, but new questions and new ways in which the literary and nonliterary texts alike can be made to read and rework each other.

I would now like to outline a few general remarks about how to avoid becoming too comfortable in the abyss. To go back to the original objection that "if all readings are misreadings, then all readings are equally valid," how is it possible to maintain that some readings are better than others in a way that cannot be entirely reduced to a binary opposition? Since it is obvious that no deconstructor actually thinks all readings are equally valid, what kind of evaluation does deconstruction permit?

The sentence "all readings are misreadings" does not *simply* deny the notion of truth. Truth is preserved in vestigial form in the notion of error. This does not mean that there is, somewhere out there, forever unattainable, the one true reading against which all others will be tried and found wanting. Rather, it implies (1) that the reasons a reading might consider itself *right* are motivated and undercut by its own interests, blindnesses, desires, and fatigue, and (2) that the *role* of truth cannot be so simply eliminated. Even if truth is but a fantasy of the will to power, *something* still marks the point from which the imperatives of the not-self make themselves felt. To reject objective truth is to make it harder to avoid setting oneself up as an arbitrary arbiter. Therefore, the one imperative a reading must obey is that it follow, with rigor, what puts in question the kind of reading it thought it was going to be. A reading is strong, I would therefore submit, to the extent that it encounters and propagates the surprise of otherness. The impossible but necessary task of the reader is to set herself up to be surprised.

No methodology can be relied on to generate surprise. On the contrary, it is usually surprise that engenders methodology. Derrida brings to his reader the surprise of a nonbinary, undecidable logic. Yet comfortable undecidability needs to be surprised by its own conservatism. My emphasis on the word *surprise* is designed to counter the idea that a good deconstructor must constantly put his own enterprise into question. This is true, but it is not enough. It can lead to a kind of infinite regress of demystification, in which ever more sophisticated subtleties are elaborated within an unchanging field of questions.

How, then, can one set oneself up to be surprised by otherness?

Obviously, in a sense, one cannot. Yet one can begin by transgressing one's own usual practices, by indulging in some judicious time-wasting with what one does not know how to use, or what has fallen into disrepute. What the surprise encounter with otherness should do is lay bare some hint of an ignorance one never knew one had. Much has been made of the fact that "knowledge" cannot be taken for granted. But perhaps rather than simply questioning the nature of knowledge, we should today reevaluate the static, inert concept we have always had of ignorance. Ignorance, far more than knowledge, is what can never be taken for granted. If I perceive my ignorance as a gap in knowledge instead of an imperative that changes the very nature of what I think I know, then I do not truly experience my ignorance. The surprise of otherness is that moment when a new form of ignorance is suddenly activated as an imperative. If the deconstructive impulse is to retain its vital, subversive power, we must therefore become ignorant of it again and again. It is only by forgetting what we know how to do, by setting aside the thoughts that have most changed us, that those thoughts and that knowledge can go on making accessible to us the surprise of an otherness we can only encounter in the moment of suddenly discovering we are ignorant of it.

2

Rigorous Unreliability

It might seem paradoxical to speak of an implicit evaluative system underlying the practice of deconstruction. Deconstructors, after all, are far more likely to speak of "valorization" than of "evaluation," far more likely to engage in a *critique* of value systems than to elaborate a value system of their own. Yet however "extramoral" a critique of "truth" and "beauty" might consider itself to be, it carries with it a sense of urgency that cannot help but imply that the critiquing of value systems is itself a valuable activity. Even if the deconstructive hand is always quicker than the evaluative eye, the card trick of insight can only be appreciated by the blindness of understanding. As Paul de Man says of the word *deconstruction* itself: "No other word states so economically the impossibility to evaluate positively or negatively the inescapable evaluation it implies."[1]

This chapter can be understood as a gloss on the following sentence by Paul de Man, in which evaluative terms flicker in and out, up and down, without reaching a stable resolution, but also without enabling one to envisage a stance beyond evaluation:

> Literature as well as criticism—the difference between them being delusive—is condemned (or privileged) to be forever the most rigorous and, consequently, the most unreliable language in terms of which man names and transforms himself. (P. 19)

Wrinkles in a Whale's Brow

As a critique of a certain Western conception of the nature of signification, deconstruction focuses on the functioning of claim-making and claim-subverting structures within texts. A deconstructive reading is an attempt to show how the conspicuously foregrounded statements in a text are systematically related to discordant signifying elements that the text has thrown into its shadows or margins, an attempt both to recover what is lost and to analyze what happens when a text is read solely in function of intentionality, meaningfulness, and representativity. Deconstruction thus confers a new kind of readability on those elements in a text that readers have traditionally been trained to disregard, overcome, explain away, or edit out—contradictions, obscurities, ambiguities, incoherences, discontinuities, ellipses, interruptions, repetitions, and plays of the signifier. In this sense it involves a reversal of values, a revaluation of the signifying function of everything that, in a signified-based theory of meaning, would constitute "noise." Derrida has chosen to speak of the values involved in this reversal in terms of "speech" and "writing," in which "speech" stands for the privilege accorded to meaning as immediacy, unity, identity, truth, and presence, while "writing" stands for the devalued functions of distance, difference, dissimulation, and deferment.

This transvaluation has a number of consequences for the appreciation of literature. By shifting the attention from intentional meaning to writing as such, deconstruction has enabled readers to become sensitive to a number of recurrent literary topoi in a new way. Texts have been seen as commentaries on their own production or reception through their pervasive thematizations of textuality—the myriad letters, books, tombstones, wills, inscriptions, road signs, maps, birthmarks, tracks, footprints, textiles, tapestries, veils, sheets, brown stockings, and self-abolishing laces that serve in one way or another as figures for the text to be deciphered or unraveled or embroidered upon. Thus, a deconstructor finds new delight in a Shakespearean character named Sir Oliver Martext or in Melville's catalog of whales as books in *Moby Dick*, or makes jokes about the opposition between speech and writing by citing the encounter between Little Red Riding Hood and the phony grammy.

In addition, by seeing interpretation itself as a fiction-making activity, deconstruction has both reversed and displaced the narrative categories of "showing" and "telling," mimesis and diegesis. Instead of according moments of textual self-interpretation an authoritative metalinguistic status, deconstruction considers anything the text says about itself to be another fiction, an allegory of the reading process. Hence, the privilege traditionally granted to showing over telling is reversed: "telling" becomes a more sophisticated form of "showing," in which what is "shown" is the breakdown of the show/tell distinction. Far from doing the reader's work for her, the text's self-commentary only gives the reader more to do. Indeed, it is the way in which a text subverts the possibility of any authoritative reading by inscribing the reader's strat-

Inscribing the reader.

egies into its own structures that often, for de Man, ends up being constitutive of literature as such.

Deconstructors, therefore, tend to privilege texts that are self-reflexive in interestingly and rigorously unreliable ways. Since self-reflexive texts often explicitly posit themselves as belated or revolutionary with respect to a tradition on which they comment, deconstruction can both reinstate the self-consciously outmoded or overwritten (such as Melville's *Pierre*) and canonize the experimental or avant-garde. But because deconstruction has focused on the ways in which the Western white male philosophico-literary tradition subverts itself *from within*, it has often tended to remain within the confines of the established literary and philosophical canon. In the above quotation from Paul de Man, for example, it is still "man" who is naming and transforming "himself." If it has questioned the boundary lines of literature, it has done so not with respect to the noncanonical but with respect to the line between literature and philosophy or between literature and criticism. It is as a rethinking of those distinctions that deconstruction most radically displaces certain traditional evaluative assumptions.

Hendiadys

Consider the following typical de Manian shift in the usage of the terms *philosophy* and *literature*.

> The question of the relationship between philosophical and literary discourse is linked, in Nietzsche, to his critique of the main concepts underlying Western metaphysics: the concept of the one [*hen*], the good [*agathon*] and the true [*aletheia*]. This critique is not conducted in the tone and by means of the arguments usually associated with classical critical philosophy. It is often carried out by means of such pragmatic and demagogical value-oppositions as weakness and strength, disease and health, herd and the "happy few," terms so arbitrarily valorized that it becomes difficult to take them seriously. But since it is commonly admitted that value-seductions are tolerated (and even admired) in so-called literary texts in a manner that would not pass muster in "philosophical" writings, the value of these values is itself linked to the possibility of distinguishing philosophical from literary texts. This is also the crudely empirical level on which one first encounters the specific difficulty of Nietzsche's works: the patent literariness of texts that keep making claims usually associated with philosophy rather than with literature. Nietzsche's work raises the

perennial question of the distinction between philosophy and literature by way of a deconstruction of the value of values. (P. 119)

Rather than asking the question of the evaluation of literary texts, de
Man is here taking value itself as a characteristic *of* the literary: literature is that discourse in which arbitrarily valorized value-seductions
are tolerated or even admired. What this says about philosophy is
more complicated: philosophy would seem to be a discourse in which
values are not arbitrary, or are not seductive, or in which arbitrary
seductions are not tolerated or admired. Values in a philosophical text
have to be taken seriously or they do not pass muster and the text is
transformed into literature. Yet Nietzsche's deconstruction of the value
of values leads precisely to the discovery that philosophy *is* always
already literature. As de Man puts it, "The critical deconstruction . . . leads to the discovery of the literary, rhetorical nature of the
philosophical claim to truth . . . : literature turns out to be the main
topic of philosophy and the model for the kind of truth to which it
aspires. . . . Philosophy turns out to be an endless reflection on its
own destruction at the hands of literature. . . . What seems to be most
difficult to admit is that this allegory of errors is the very model of
philosophical rigor" (pp. 115, 118).

Thus the relation between literature and philosophy involves the
repetitive set-up and collapse of their difference: philosophy's self-definition relies on a claim to rigor that is subverted by the literarity of its
rhetoric of truth, but it is precisely that literarity that turns out to be the
very model for philosophical rigor. Philosophy is defined by its refusal
to recognize itself as literature; literature is defined as the rhetorical self-
transgression of philosophy. This positing and erasing of difference,
this fluctuation between two and one, could perhaps be called a hendiadys (a figure in which, for example, "Deconstruction and Criticism"
substitutes for "Deconstructive Criticism," as Geoffrey Hartman has
suggested),[2] the rhetorical figure that most aptly names such versions of
the question of the chicken and the egg. What is at stake in the hendiadys "philosophy and literature" is precisely the status of values: if
literature resorts to philosophically inadmissible value-seductions in
order to out-philosophize philosophy, then the distinction between the
"serious" and the "arbitrary" breaks down. But what has happened to
the attendant functions of tolerance and admiration? And what of that
most seductive de Manian hendiadys, the conjunction between rigor
and unreliability? If the hendiaditic relation between literature and criticism confers the privilege or curse of being forever most rigorous *and*
most unreliable, how is this conjunction enacted in de Man's own
writing?

The "Real Mystery"

The opening essay of *Allegories of Reading*, entitled "Semiology and Rhetoric," begins with the analysis of a fact of literary studies:

> On the one hand, literature cannot merely be received as a definite unit of referential meaning that can be decoded without leaving a residue. The code is unusually conspicuous, complex, and enigmatic; it attracts an inordinate amount of attention to itself, and this attention has to acquire the rigor of a method. The structural moment of concentration on the code for its own sake cannot be avoided, and literature necessarily breeds its own formalism.
>
> On the other hand—and this is the real mystery—no literary formalism, no matter how accurate and enriching in its analytic powers, is ever allowed to come into being without seeming reductive. . . . Like the grandmother in Proust's novel ceaselessly driving the young Marcel out into the garden, away from the unhealthy inwardness of his closeted reading, critics cry out for the fresh air of referential meaning. (P. 4)

The existence of these two stances breeds "a highly respectable moral imperative that strives to reconcile the internal, formal, private structures of literary language with their external, referential, and public effects" (p. 3). But de Man hastens to assert that "the attraction of reconciliation is the elective breeding ground of false models and metaphors"—here, the model of literature as a box with an inside and an outside. The remainder of the essay is a deconstruction of the inside/outside opposition through a speculation on the terms *grammar* and *rhetoric*. The essay concludes with the sentence cited earlier: "Literature as well as criticism—the difference between them being delusive—is condemned (or privileged) to be forever the most rigorous and, consequently, the most unreliable language in terms of which man names and transforms himself."

In an effort to capture the rigor and unreliability of de Man's own enactment of the deconstruction of the opposition between literature and criticism, I shall begin by attempting to situate its "literarity." Included in de Man's list of arbitrary and therefore literary Nietzschean value-seductions, you will recall, was the opposition between disease and health. That opposition appears in de Man's description of those who try to drive readers of literature out of the unhealthy inwardness of the prison-house of language. But the fresh air of referentiality seems to spawn diseases of its own, which de Man, later in the essay, proposes to combat by introducing some "preventative semiological hygiene" (p. 6). On one level, then, de Man is employing, quite ironically, the value-seductions of a vocabulary of sickness and health in order, literarily, to reverse the value-seductions of a certain sort of literary criticism. But the literarity of the essay does not stop there. For the literary passage on which de Man's essay primarily focuses is a passage from Proust that precisely duplicates the figures through which the essay's polemical situation is described. Marcel is in his room reading while the grandmotherly forces are trying to shoo him into the healthy outdoors. In order to overcome the guilt of inwardness, Proust's text strives to reconcile the outdoor values of light, warmth, and activity with the indoor values of darkness, coolness, and passivity. The reconciliation depends for its success on the privileging of metaphor as necessity. De Man's reading of the passage shows that the reconciliation cannot in fact be accomplished without recourse to metonymy, which thus subverts the ground on which the erasure of guilt was to be founded.[3] Yet if the reconciliation is not achieved, then Marcel—and by implication, close(ted) reading—is still guilty. What then are the consequences for de Man's semiological hygiene?

The situation is in fact even more complex than this. In order to deconstruct the seduction of reconciliation, de Man focuses on the way in which the Proust passage privileges metaphor as necessity at the expense of metonymy as contingency. By showing that the metaphorical reconciliation occurs through a hidden metonymical accident, de Man deconstructs the rhetorical privilege accorded the notion of necessity. But necessity and contingency are precisely the terms in which the distinction between formalism and referentiality were initially described. Literature was said to "necessarily" breed its own formalism just as summer in the Proust passage "necessarily" bred flies, while the "real mystery" consisted in the seemingly contingent fact that such an apparent necessity is never allowed to stand without seeming reductive. The moral imperative always occurs as an imperative to move "beyond formalism," beyond the questions necessarily raised by the language of the text. Yet the final irony lies in the fact that in his close reading of the Proust passage, de Man deconstructs the very value ("necessity") that he says makes close reading unavoidable. The "real mystery" for de Man would seem to be the eternal return of the moral imperative to resist reading. But only by resisting reading the contradiction between necessity as the object of deconstruction and necessity as the imperative to deconstruct.could we assert that de Man is simply attempting to plead in favor of formalism. His text is, rather, enacting the very unreliability of the rigor any formalism might wish to posit.

But so much for the philosophical grammar of de Man's literary rhetoric. What about the philosophical rhetoric of de Man's often bizarre grammar?

Demanding Anacoluthons

The question of guilt serves as one of de Man's favorite tropes for the resistance to reading. In two separate essays, de Man uses "guilt" as a way of reversing the relations between textuality and subjectivity.

> One should not conclude that the subjective feelings of guilt motivate the rhetorical strategies as causes determine effects. It is not more legitimate to say that the ethical interests of the subject determine the invention of figures than to say that the rhetorical potential of language engenders the choice of guilt as theme; no one can decide whether Proust invented metaphors because he felt guilty or whether he had to declare himself guilty in order to find a use for his metaphors. Since the only irreducible "intention" of a text is that of its constitution, the second hypothesis is in fact less unlikely than the first. The problem has to be left suspended in its own indecision. (Pp. 64–65)

> The text as body, with all its implications of substitutive tropes ultimately always retraceable to metaphor, is displaced by the text as machine and, in the process, it suffers the loss of the illusion of meaning. The deconstruction of the figural dimension is a process that takes place independently of any desire; as such it is not unconscious but mechanical, systematic in its performance but arbitrary in its principle, like a grammar. . . . Any guilt, including the guilty pleasure of writing the *Fourth Rêverie*, can always be dismissed as the gratuitous product of a textual grammar or a radical fiction: there can never be enough guilt around to match the text-machine's infinite power to excuse. (Pp. 298–99)

By locating the text-generating agency in the text's own desire to constitute itself independently of any human subject, de Man sees subjectivity itself as a rhetorical effect rather than a cause. If the one irreducible force at work is the machinelike grammar of textuality, this amounts, ultimately, to a definition of the subject's function in language as a potential for ellipsis. In Rousseau's story of the false accusation of Marion as the stealer of a ribbon, de Man describes the incompatibility between Rousseau's description of his choice of the name Marion as motivated by his desire for her, on the one hand, and Rousseau's explanation that the name came to him by accident, on the other, in terms of the figure of anacoluthon—a syntactical interruption or discontinuity. What is revealed by Rousseau's anacoluthon, says de Man, is the eclipse of the subject ("Rousseau") by the textual machine. De Man goes on to conclude:

> Far from seeing language as an instrument in the service of a psychic energy, the possibility now arises that the entire construction of drives, substitutions, repressions, and representations is the aberrant, metaphorical correlative of the absolute randomness of language, prior to any figuration or meaning. (P. 299)

What is striking about this sentence is that it is itself a grammatical anacoluthon: the participle "seeing" in the introductory subordinate clause demands a corresponding subject in the main clause, but in the main clause that subject is replaced by an abstraction: "Far from seeing X, the possibility now arises that Y." The grammar of the anacoluthon thus *enacts* the eclipse of the interpreting subject that it describes. The "we" that would situate *us* as readers who are far from seeing drops out of the sentence that describes that very dropping out.

If the machine of textuality functions like a grammar through which subjectivity can indifferently be produced or erased, what is one to say about a grammatical error? Does de Man's dangling participle stand as the eclipse or rather as the inscription of a subject? Couldn't subjectivity be defined as a grammatical mistake? Consider another anacoluthonic de Manian sentence in which a whole intersubjective drama is caught in the discontinuities of the apparent awkwardness of the grammar: "Thus, with the structure of the code so opaque, but the meaning so anxious to blot out the obstacle of form, no wonder that the reconciliation of form and meaning would be so attractive" (pp. 4–5). In the floating functions of anxiousness, wonder, and attraction, de Man's text inscribes signs of subjectivity in the absence of any grammatical subject. As de Man says elsewhere, "By calling the subject a text, the text calls itself, to some extent, a subject" (p. 112). It is in the irreducible incompatibility between a code whose structure is opaque and a will to erase through which meaning exists as an anxiousness to blot out the obstacle of form that the "real mystery" of reading is always inscribed. But it is a mystery about which no moral imperative to leap from textuality to subjectivity or history can tell us more than de Man's stubborn labyrinths of rigor, resistance, and profoundly meaningful unreliability.

3

Is Writerliness Conservative?

Is writerliness conservative? It will probably come as no surprise that I don't have a clear yes-or-no answer to this question. It may well be that, asked in these terms, the question is undecidable. But, as I hope to make clear, it is precisely the status of the undecidable that is, for me, at issue *in* the question. For in recent "Left" criticism of recent "Left" criticism, undecidability, described as an outgrowth of certain critical theorists' privileging of language, has repeatedly been deemed politically suspect as an oppositional strategy.[1] What I would like to analyze briefly in this chapter are some of the possible political functions of undecidability.

First, some definitions. On the contemporary political resonance of the word *conservative*, I quote first Frank Lentricchia's handy and representative four-level mapping of political possibilities. Lentricchia begins his introduction to *Criticism and Social Change* with John Dewey's distinction between "education as a function of society" and "society as a function of education." He then goes on to gloss the distinction as follows:

> If you are at home in society, you will accept it, and you will want education to perform the function of preparing the minds of the young and the not-so-young to maintain society's principles and directives. . . . If you hold such a theory of education, you are a conservative. Insofar as you think the order should be reversed, that society should be a function of education, you are a radical, or that strange, impossible utopian, the radical in reverse gear we call a reactionary. (To complete the picture: liberals, in this scheme, are nervous conservatives governed by an irresistible urge to tinker, though when the chips are down, they usually find a way to resist their need to mess with the machine.)[2] . . . Now, if the social project of the reactionary can't be taken seriously on its own terms, and if liberalism is mainly an illusion, we are left with two political choices: conservatism or radicalism (Pp. 1–2)

For a second version of this distinction, I turn to Charles Sanders Peirce's essay "The Scientific Attitude and Fallibilism." Peirce sees the opposition between conservative and radical as follows: "Conservatism, in the sense of a dread of consequences, is altogether out of place in science, which has, on the contrary, always been forwarded by radicals and radicalism, in the sense of the eagerness to carry consequences to their extreme."[3] Conservatives, for Peirce, ask "Where will it all end?" while radicals counter with "Why stop there?"

But what does it mean to carry consequences to their extreme? In science, it involves the testing of new hypotheses, the collecting of new data. Without a passage through the otherness of the material, any pursuit of consequences is simply the following out of existing laws—an activity which does not transform but only refines. What then is the *literary* equivalent of a passage through the otherness of the material? What kinds of consequences can literary criticism carry to their extreme? Or, in Lentricchia's phrase, "Can a literary intellectual . . . do radical work *as* a literary intellectual?" (p. 2).

I will leave these questions hanging for a moment in order to return to the task of definition. What is writerliness? While the ordinary resonance of the word is not irrelevant to my purpose, I have taken the term *writerly* from Richard Miller's translation of Roland Barthes's *S/Z*, where it is meant to render Barthes's term *le scriptible*—literally, "the writable."[4] Barthes's book begins with a theoretical introduction in which an opposition is set up between *le scriptible* and *le lisible*—"the readable," or, in Miller's translation, "the readerly." The readerly is the aspect of a text through which it is assimilated to ideological norms of meaning, while the writerly is a hypothetical state of textual resistance to such assimilation. The readerly is a product to be consumed by the reader; the writerly is a process of production in which the reader becomes a producer. It is, says Barthes, "ourselves writing." The readerly is constrained by considerations of representation: it is irreversible, "natural," decidable, continuous, totalizable, and unified into a coherent whole based on the signified. The writerly is infinitely plural and open to the free play of signifiers and of difference, unconstrained by representative considerations, and transgressive of any desire for decidable, unified, totalized meaning.

The rhetoric of liberation perceptible in *S/Z* is typical of the Marxist (or even Maoist) phase of the Tel Quel group in the years surrounding the events of May 1968 in France. A parallel was then being drawn between the materiality of the signifier and historical materialism, through which it seemed possible to bring about radical change by freeing the signifier from its subordination to the signified. If the signified was the site and the prerogative of dominant ideology, the signifier was the guardian of a resistance, or at least an *in*sistance, of the work and discourse of the Other. It soon became apparent, however, that the analogy between linguistic materiality and historical materialism was not enough to guarantee that to concentrate on the play of the signifier was to do anything radical at all: indeed, the privileging of language entailed by such an approach seemed to confirm fetishized structures of literary value and canonical authority. In recent critiques of the liberating claims of writing-based theory, the writerly has been toppled from its stance of radicality and come to seem one more do-nothing confirmation of the cultural status quo. Writerliness is therefore something that can take on diametrically opposed political valences, but it is something about which it is somehow not irrelevant—indeed, it seems urgent—to *raise* political questions.

What does literature have to say about the political status of its own writerliness? What kinds of claims does poetry make about the possibility of *poetically* intervening in the world? Any answer to this question would clearly depend on a particular historical and political context. Pending a more encompassing treatment of these issues, I would like here to examine briefly some nineteenth-century French responses from the two poets whose work has most informed my own understanding of the nature of poetry: Baudelaire and Mallarmé. It is surprising, indeed, how insistently the late poetic prose of both writers takes up the question of the political valence of the poetic stance. That question is often worried in terms of allegorical encounters between a poet figure and a worker figure. Baudelaire does this with violent irony; Mallarmé with grandiose mildness. In "Le Mauvais vitrier," for example, Baudelaire drops a flower pot on the back of a poor glazier, shattering his fragile merchandise, while shouting, "La vie en beau! La vie en beau!" In "La Corde," he describes a Manet figure buying a young boy from his poor parents to serve as a model for his painting. When the model later hangs himself, the boy's mother requests the rope from the distraught artist, who first sees this as an act of maternal devotion but later realizes, from the number of requests for the rope he receives, that the rope has been fetishized into a commodity, that the mother (unlike the artist, of course) has gone into the business of making the metonymy of suicide pay. In the most explicit of such allegories of art as interclass violence, "Assommons les pauvres" ["Let's Beat Up the Poor"], Baudelaire pictures himself as a philosopher testing out a theory of human dignity by beating up a beggar until the latter begins to defend himself, then signaling to him that the discussion is over, since the two combattants are now equal. The unexamined authority of theory—of language—is here acted out as the power to turn violence into a declaration of equality.

Mallarmé, too, imagines a "fist fight that would illustrate the class struggle," when, in a prose text entitled "Conflit,"[5] he encounters a band of drunken railroad workers inhabiting the country house he habitually rents for the summer. Annoyed at the noise they are making, the fussy poet nevertheless is struck with awe at the archetypal workerliness of shovels, axes, and shoulders:

> Cette cohue entre, part, avec la manche, à l'épaule, de la pioche et de la pelle: or, elle invite, en sa faveur, les émotions de derrière.la tête et force à procéder, directement, d'idées dont on se dit *c'est de la littérature!* (P. 356)

> [This gang comes in, goes out, shouldering the handle of pickaxe or spade: somehow the crew invites, in its favor, emotions from the back of the mind and forces one to proceed, directly, from ideas, about which one tells oneself, *that's literature!*]

C'est de la littérature—a suspicion, a dismissal, or a definition, murmured by a poet encountering a worker as material for the reexamination of the value of his own work. The very rhetorical status of "*c'est de la littérature*" is at the heart of all these issues. Uneasily, the poet pursues an imaginary conversation with the worker, concluding,

> "Peut-être moi, aussi, je travaille..." A quoi, n'eût objecté aucun, admettant, à cause de comptables, l'occupation transférée des bras à la tête. A quoi—tait, dans la conscience seule, un écho—du moins, qui puisse servir, parmi l'échange général. Tristesse que ma production reste, à ceux-ci, par essence, comme les nuages au crépuscule ou des étoiles, vaine. (P. 358)

> ["Maybe I, too, work..." At what? no one would have objected, admitting, because of accountants, that occupations can be transferred from the arms to the head. At what—is silenced, in conscience alone, an echo—at least, what that might serve, within the general system of exchange. Sadness that my production remains, to them, in essence, like evening clouds or stars, vain.]

The suspicion of the vanity of literary work within the system of general exchange echoes unsettlingly in the poet's conscience. In another text, "Confrontation,"[6] a similar nervousness is prompted by a similar imagined conversation with a worker whose presence amounts to a question addressed to the poet: "What are *you* doing here?" It is as though the writer is one whose legitimacy in the world is not a given, one whose work is not, as the laborer's is, "blessed by the security of effort." Yet Mallarmé's stance of self-invalidation is also a stance of exceptionality: "Peut-être, j'ai perçu, dans la différence qui le sépare du travailleur,

l'attitude, exceptionnelle, commise au lettré" ("Perhaps I have perceived, in the difference that separates him from the worker, the attitude—exceptionality—entrusted to the man of letters"). If, as Mallarmé says elsewhere, "La littérature existe—à l'exception de tout" (p.
646; "literature exists—in exception to everything"), what kind of *social*
site does it occupy? Is this a form of elitist separatism, or is separatism
already part of the polity as such? What kind of act is the act of writing—
as self-exception?

   In a text entitled "L'Action restreinte," Mallarmé offers the flip
side of this self-invalidation, making perhaps his grandest political
claims for writerliness. In answer to a young poet who confides to
Mallarmé his desire to act, Mallarmé meditates on two kinds of action,
one characterized by fullness, the other by haste, but both by written-
ness.

> Agir . . . signifia . . . produire sur beaucoup un mouvement qui te
> donne en retour l'émoi que tu en fus le principe, donc existes: dont
> aucun ne se croit, au préalable, sûr. Cette pratique entend deux fa-
> çons; ou par une volonté, à l'insu, qui dure une vie, jusqu'à l'éclat
> multiple—penser, cela: sinon, les déversoirs à portée maintenant
> dans une prévoyance, journaux et leur tourbillon, y déterminer une
> force en un sens, quelconque de divers contrariée, avec l'immunité du
> résultat nul.
>   Au gré, selon la disposition, plénitude, hâte.
>   Ton acte toujours s'applique à du papier; car méditer, sans
> traces, devient évanescent, ni que s'exalte l'instinct en quelque geste
> véhément et perdu que tu cherchas.
>   Ecrire—
>   L'encrier, cristal comme une conscience, avec sa goutte, au
> fond, de ténèbres relative à ce que quelque chose soit: puis, écarte la
> lampe.
>   Tu remarquas, on n'écrit pas, lumineusement, sur champ
> obscur, l'alphabet des astres, seul, ainsi s'indique, ébauché ou inter-
> rompu; l'homme poursuit noir sur blanc.
>   Ce pli de sombre dentelle, qui retient l'infini, tissé par mille,
> chacun selon le fil ou prolongement ignoré son secret, assemble des
> entrelacs distants où dort un luxe à inventorier. (Pp. 369–70)

[To act . . . signified . . . to produce upon many a movement that gives
you back the feeling that *you* originated it, and therefore exist: something no one is sure of. This praxis can be understood in two ways:
either, by will, unbeknownst to others, to spend a whole life toward a
multiple outburst—which would be *thinking:* or else, using the means
available now—journals and their whirlwind—to send a force in

some direction, any direction, which, when countered, gives you immunity from having no result.

At will, according to disposition—fullness, haste.

Your act is always applied to paper; for meditating without a trace is evanescent, nor is the exalting of an instinct in some vehement, lost gesture what you were seeking.

To write—

The inkwell, crystalline like consciousness, with its drop, at bottom, of shadows relative to letting something be: then, take away the lamp.

You noted, one does not write, luminously, on a dark field; the alphabet of stars alone does that, sketched or interrupted; man pursues black upon white.

This fold of dark lace, which retains the infinite, woven by thousands, each according to the thread or extension unknowing a secret, assembles distant spacings in which riches yet to be inventoried sleep.]

Mallarmé is here suggesting that action cannot be defined otherwise than as the capacity to leave a trace—a written trace, a trace not of clarity but of darkness. It is with his obscurity, his nonknowledge, that man writes, and the poet's duty is to stand as guardian of an ignorance that does not know itself, an ignorance that would otherwise be lost: "Le meilleur qui se passe entre deux gens, toujours, leur échappe, en tant qu'interlocuteurs. L'expression, probablement, concerne la littérature" (p. 411; "The best of what happens between two people always escapes them, as interlocutors. This expression, probably, concerns literature.") Mallarmé is thus a sophisticated example of wanting to have it both ways: poetry is beside the point; poetry is the repository of something the world cannot do without. Poetry is outside the political; poetry is the stuff of the political. Poetry makes nothing happen; poetry makes *nothing* happen.

Yet how can the plea for slowness, for the suspension of decision, for the questioning of knowledge, ever function as anything other than a refusal to intervene? Nothing could be more convincing than the idea that political radicality requires decisiveness, not indecision; haste, not hesitation. To the extent that writerliness might exalt obscurity and undecidability as ultimate values, it can always be seen as conserving rather than subverting the existing ideological confines of its own territory. The privileging of ambiguity would always appear to be an avoidance of action. Yet if undecidability is politically suspect, it is so not only to the left, but also to the right. Nothing could be more comforting to the established order than the requirement that everything be assigned a clear meaning or stand. It is precisely because the established order leaves no room for unneutralized (i.e., unestheticized) ambiguity that it seems urgent to meet decisiveness with decisiveness. But for that same reason it also seems urgent not to. I am reminded of a sentence in Adrienne Rich's *On Lies, Secrets, and Silence*, which runs: "Much of what is narrowly termed 'politics' seems to rest on a longing for certainty even at the cost of honesty, for an analysis which, once given, need not be re-examined."[7]

The profound political intervention of feminism has indeed been not simply to enact a radical politics but to redefine the very nature of what is deemed political—to take politics down from its male incarnation as a change-seeking interest in what is *not* nearest to hand, and to bring it into the daily historical texture of the relations between the sexes. The *literary* ramifications of this shift involve the discovery of the rhetorical survival skills of the formerly unvoiced. Lies, secrets, silences, and deflections of all sorts are routes taken by voices or messages not granted full legitimacy in order not to be altogether lost. If writerliness is defined as attention to the trace of otherness in language, as attention to the way in which there is always more than one message, then it is hard to see how a true instatement of the power of other voices is possible without something like a writerly apprenticeship. Where can the world's unread letters be *kept*, other than in writing? "Ce pli de sombre dentelle, qui retient l'infini, tissé par mille, chacun selon le fil ou prolongement ignoré son secret, assemble des entrelacs distants où dort un luxe à inventorier." Isn't each radical theoretical revolution just such an inventorial awakening, a reinvention of what reading is, such that the formerly unvoiced speaks and is heard?

If writerliness cannot be set up as an *ultimate* value without neutralizing itself, it nevertheless seems to stand as the un-bypassable site of the *pen*ultimate—the place where a new passage through otherness can be opened up, if and only if one is attempting to follow an imperative not to stop there. It would thus probably never be false to say that to privilege writerliness is conservative—though I'm not sure it would always be true—but writerliness itself is conservative only in the sense that it is capable of inscribing and conserving messages the radicality of which may not yet have been explored.

4

Gender Theory and the Yale School

I hope that by the end of this paper I will not have bitten off more of the hand that feeds me than I can chew.
—From the original introduction to "Gender Theory and the Yale School"

In January 1984, shortly after the death of Paul de Man, I received a call from Robert Con Davis and Ronald Schleifer inviting me to attempt the painful and obviously impossible task of replacing de Man in a conference entitled "Genre Theory and the Yale School" in which Geoffrey Hartman, Hillis Miller, and Paul de Man had been asked to speak about genre theory in relation to their own work. I was invited to speak, however, not about *my* own work but about de Man's. The reasons for this are certainly understandable. I could easily sympathize with the conference organizers' impulse: there is nothing I could wish more than that de Man had not died. But the invitation to appear as de Man's *supplément*—supplemented in turn by a panel on de Man with participants of my own choosing—gave me pause. For it falls all too neatly into patterns of female effacement already well established by the phenomenon of the Yale School—and indeed, with rare exceptions, by the phenomenon of the critical "school" as such. Like others of its type, the Yale School has always been a Male School.

Would it have been possible for there to have been a female presence in the Yale School? Interestingly, in Jonathan Culler's bibliography to *On Deconstruction*, Shoshana Felman's book *La Folie et la chose littéraire* is described as "a wide-ranging collection of essays by a member of the 'école de Yale.'"[1] Felman, in other words, *was* a member of the Yale School, but only in French. This question of the foreignness of the female language will return, but for now, suffice it to say that there was no reason other than gender why Felman's work—certainly closer to de

Man's and Derrida's than the work of Harold Bloom—should not have been seen as an integral part of the Yale School.

At the time of the publication of the Yale School's nonmanifesto, *Deconstruction and Criticism*, several of us—Shoshana Felman, Gayatri Spivak, Margaret Ferguson, and I—discussed the possibility of writing a companion volume inscribing female deconstructive protest and affirmation centering not on Percy Bysshe Shelley's "The Triumph of Life" (as the existing volume was originally slated to do) but on Mary Shelley's *Frankenstein*. That book might truly have illustrated the Girardian progression "from mimetic desire to the monstrous double." Unfortunately, this *Bride of Deconstruction and Criticism* never quite got off the ground, but it is surely no accident that the project was centered around monstrosity. As Derrida puts it in "The Law of Genre" (which is also, of course, a law of gender), "As soon as genre announces itself, one must respect a norm, one must not cross a line of demarcation, one must not risk impurity, anomaly, or monstrosity."[2] After all, Aristotle, the founder of the law of gender as well as of the law of genre, considered the female the first distortion of the genus "man" en route to becoming a monster. But perhaps it was not *Frankenstein* but rather *The Last Man*, Mary Shelley's grim depiction of the gradual extinction of humanity altogether, that would have made a fit counterpart to "The Triumph of Life." Percy Bysshe Shelley is entombed in both, along with a certain male fantasy of Romantic universality. The only universality that remains in Mary Shelley's last novel is the plague.

It would be easy to accuse the male Yale School theorists of having avoided the issue of gender entirely. What I intend to do, however, is to demonstrate that they have had quite a lot to say about the issue, often without knowing it. Before moving on to a female version of the Yale School, therefore, I will begin by attempting to extract from the essays in *Deconstruction and Criticism* and related texts an implicit theory of the relations between gender and criticism. For the purposes of this paper, I will focus on the four members of the Yale School who have actually taught full time at Yale. Since Derrida, the fifth participant in *Deconstruction and Criticism*, has in contrast consistently and explicitly foregrounded the question of gender, his work would demand far more extensive treatment than is possible here. I will confine myself to the more implicit treatments of the subject detectable in the writings of Bloom, Hartman, Miller, and de Man.

Geoffrey Hartman, ever the master of the throwaway line, has not failed to make some memorable remarks about the genderedness of the reading process. "Much reading," he writes in *The Fate of Reading*, "is indeed, like girl-watching, a simple expense of spirit." And in *Beyond*

Formalism, he claims: "Interpretation is like a football game. You spot a hole and you go through. But first you may have to induce that opening."[3]

In his essay in *Deconstruction and Criticism*, Hartman examines a poem in which Wordsworth, suddenly waylaid by a quotation, addresses his daughter Dora with a line from Milton's Samson that harks back to the figure of blind Oedipus being led by his daughter Antigone:

> A Little onward lend thy guiding hand
> To these dark steps, a little further on![4]

This is certainly a promising start for an investigation of gender relations. Yet Wordsworth and Hartman combine to curb the step of this budding Delilah and to subsume the daughter under the Wordsworthian category of "child," who, as everyone knows, is *Father* of the man. While the poem works out a power reversal between blind father and guiding daughter, restoring the father to his role of natural leader, the commentary works out *its* patterns of reversibility between Wordsworth and Milton. "Let me, thy happy guide, now point thy way / And now precede thee." When Wordsworth leads his daughter to the edge of the abyss, it is the abyss of intertextuality.

While brooding on the abyss in *The Fate of Reading*, Hartman looks back at his own precursor self and says: "In *The Unmediated Vision* the tyranny of sight in the domain of sensory organization is acknowledged, and symbol making is understood as a kind of 'therapeutic alliance' between the eye and other senses through the medium of art. I remember how easy it was to put a woman in the landscape, into every eyescape rather; and it struck me that in works of art there were similar centers, depicted or inferred" (p. 6). Yet the woman in Wordsworth's poemscape is precisely what Hartman does not see. And this may be just what Wordsworth intended. In the short paragraph in which Hartman acknowledges that there may be something oedipal about this Oedipus figure, he describes the daughter as *barred* by the incest prohibition. The poem would then transmit a disguised desire for the daughter, repressed and deflected into literary structures. Yet might it not also be that Wordsworth so often used incest figures in his poetry as a way, precisely, of barring the reality of the woman as other, a way of keeping the woman in and *only* in the eyescape, making a nun out of a nymph? For the danger here is that the daughter will neither follow nor lead, but simply leave:

> the birds salute
> The cheerful dawn, brightening for me the east;
> For me, thy natural leader, once again

Impatient to conduct thee, not as erst
A tottering infant, with compliant stoop
From flower to flower supported; but to curb
Thy nymph-like step swift-bounding o'er the lawn,
Along the loose rocks, or the slippery verge
Of foaming torrents.

The family romance takes a slightly different form in Hillis Miller's essay, "The Critic as Host." In that essay, Miller discusses Booth's and Abrams' image of deconstructive criticism as "parasitical" on the "obvious or univocal reading" of a text. Miller writes:

> "Parasitical"—the word suggests the image of "the obvious or univocal reading" as the mighty oak, rooted in the solid ground, endangered by the insidious twining around it of deconstructive ivy. That ivy is somehow feminine, secondary, defective, or dependent. It is a clinging vine, able to live in no other way but by drawing the life sap of its host, cutting off its light and air. I think of Hardy's *The Ivy-Wife*. . . .
>   Such sad love stories of a domestic affection which introduces the parasitical into the closed economy of the home no doubt describe well enough the way some people feel about the relation of a "deconstructive" interpretation to "the obvious or univocal reading." The parasite is destroying the host. The alien has invaded the house, perhaps to kill the father of the family in an act which does not look like parricide, but is. Is the "obvious" reading, though, so "obvious" or even so "univocal"? May it not itself be the uncanny alien which is so close that it cannot be seen as strange? (*DC*, p. 218)

It is interesting to note how effortlessly the vegetal metaphor is sexualized in Miller's elaboration of it. If the parasite is the feminine, then the feminine must be recognized as that uncanny alien always already in the house—and in the host. What turns out, in Miller's etymological analysis, to be uncanny about the relation between host and parasite— and by extension between male and female—is that each is already inhabited by the other as a difference from itself. Miller then goes on to describe the parasite as invading virus in the following terms: "The genetic pattern of the virus is so coded that it can enter a host cell and violently reprogram all the genetic material in that cell, turning the cell into a little factory for manufacturing copies of itself, so destroying it. This is *The Ivy-Wife*, with a vengeance" (*DC*, p. 222). Miller then goes on to ask, "Is this an allegory, and if so, of what?" Perhaps of the gender codes of literature, or of criticism. But this image of cancerous femininity may be less a fear of takeover than an extreme version of the desire to

Wow!

same as
difference!!

deny difference. There is perhaps something reassuring about total annihilation as opposed to precarious survival. The desire to deny difference is in fact, in a euphoric rather than a nightmarish spirit, the
central desire dramatized by the Shelley poems Miller analyzes. The
obsessive cry for oneness, for sameness, always, however, meets the
same fate: it cannot subsume and erase the trace of its own elaboration.
The story Shelley tells again and again is the story of the failure of the
attempt to abolish difference. As Miller points out, difference is re-
discovered in the linguistic traces of that failure. But a failed erasure of
difference is not the same as a recognition of difference—unless, as
Miller's analysis suggests, difference can be recognized only in the
failure of its erasure.

If the parasite is both feminine and parricidal, then the parasite
can only be a daughter. Miller does not follow up on the implications of a
parricidal daughter, but Harold Bloom, whose critical system is itself a
garden of parricidal delights, gives us a clue to what would be at stake
for him in such an idea. In *A Map of Misreading* he writes:

> Nor are there Muses, nymphs who *know*, still available to tell us the
> secrets of continuity, for the nymphs certainly are now departing. I
> prophesy though that the first true break with literary continuity will
> be brought about in generations to come, if the burgeoning religion of
> Liberated Woman spreads from its clusters of enthusiasts to dominate
> the West. Homer will cease to be the inevitable precursor, and the
> rhetoric and forms of our literature then may break at last from
> tradition.[5]

In Bloom's prophetic vision of the breaking of tradition through the
liberation of woman, it is as though the Yale School were in danger of
becoming a Jael School.[6]

The dependence of Bloom's revisionary ratios upon a linear patriarchal filiation has been pointed out often enough—particularly in
the groundbreaking work of Sandra Gilbert and Susan Gubar—that
there is no need to belabor it here. I will therefore, instead, analyze the
opening lines of Bloom's essay "The Breaking of Form" as a strong
misreading of the question of sexual difference. The essay begins: "The
word *meaning* goes back to a root that signifies 'opinion' or 'intention,'
and is closely related to the word *moaning*. A poem's meaning is a
poem's complaint, its version of Keats' Belle Dame, who looked *as if* she
loved, and made sweet moan. Poems instruct us in how they break form
to bring about meaning, so as to utter a complaint, a moaning intended
to be all their own" (*DC*, p. 1). If the relation between the reader and the
poem is analogous to the relation between the knight-at-arms and the
Belle Dame, things are considerably more complicated than they ap-

pear. For the encounter between male and female in Keats' poem is a perfectly ambiguous disaster. Rather than a clear "as if," Keats writes: "She looked at me *as* she did love, / And made sweet moan." Suspicion of the woman is not planted quite so clearly, nor quite so early. In changing "as" to "as if," Bloom has removed from the poem the possibility of reading this first mention of the woman's feelings as straight description. Perhaps Bloom is here demonstrating what he says elsewhere about the study of poetry being "the study of what Stevens called 'the intricate evasions of as'." By the end of the poem, it becomes impossible to know whether one has read a story of a knight enthralled by a witch or of a woman seduced and abandoned by a male hysteric. And the fine balance of that undecidability depends on the "as."

If the poem, like the woman, "makes sweet moan," then there is considerable doubt about the reader's capacity to read it. This becomes all the more explicit in the knight's second interpretive assessment of the woman's feelings: "And sure in language strange she said— / 'I love thee true.'" The problem of understanding the woman is here a problem of translation. Even her name can only be expressed in another tongue. The sexes stand in relation to each other not as two distinct entities but as two foreign languages. The drama of male hysteria is a drama of premature assurance of understanding followed by premature panic at the intimation of otherness. Is she mine, asks the knight, or am I hers? If these are the only two possibilities, the foreignness of the languages cannot be respected. What Bloom demonstrates, perhaps without knowing it, is that if reading is the gendered activity he paints it as, the reading process is less a love story than a story of failed translation.

That the question of gender is a question of language becomes even more explicit in an essay by Paul de Man entitled "The Epistemology of Metaphor."[7] Translation is at issue in that essay as well, in the very derivation of the word *metaphor*. "It is no mere play of words," writes de Man, "that 'translate' is translated in German as '*übersetzen*' which itself translated the Greek '*meta phorein*' or metaphor" (p. 17) In all three words, what is described is a motion from one place to another. As we shall see, the question of the relation between gender and figure will have a great deal to do with this notion of *place*.

De Man's essay begins as follows:

> Metaphors, tropes, and figural language in general have been a perennial problem and, at times, a recognized source of embarrassment for philosophical discourse and, by extension, for all discursive uses of language including historiography and literary analysis. It appears that philosophy either has to give up its own constitutive claim to rigor in order to come to terms with the figurality of its language or

that it has to free itself from figuration altogether. And if the latter is considered impossible, philosophy could at least learn to control figuration by keeping it, so to speak, in its place, by delimiting the boundaries of its influence and thus restricting the epistemological damage that it may cause. (P. 13)

This opening paragraph echoes, in its own rhetoric, a passage which occurs later in the essay in which de Man is commenting on a long quotation from Locke. After detailing the reasons for avoiding rhetoric, Locke nevertheless concludes his discussion of the perils of figuration as follows: "Eloquence, like the fair sex, has too prevailing beauties in it to suffer itself ever to be spoken against. And it is in vain to find fault with those arts of deceiving wherein men find pleasure to be deceived" (p. 15). De Man glosses the Locke passage as follows:

> Nothing could be more eloquent than this denunciation of eloquence. It is clear that rhetoric is something one can decorously indulge in as long as one knows where it belongs. Like a woman, which it resembles ("like the fair sex"), it is a fine thing as long as it is kept in its proper place. Out of place, among the serious affairs of men ("if we would speak of things as they are"), it is a disruptive scandal—like the appearance of a real woman in a gentleman's club where it would only be tolerated as a picture, preferably naked (like the image of Truth), framed and hung on the wall. (Pp. 15–16)

Following this succinct tongue-in-cheek description of the philosophical tradition as a men's club, de Man goes on to claim that there is "little epistemological risk in a flowery, witty passage about wit like this one," that things begin to get serious only when the plumber must be called in, but the epistemological damage may already have been done. For the question of language in Locke quickly comes to be centered on the question, "What essence is the proper of man?" This is no idle question, in fact, because what is at stake in the answer is what sort of monstrous births it is permissible to kill. Even in the discussion of Condillac and Kant, the question of sexual difference lurks, as when de Man describes Condillac's discussion of abstractions as bearing a close resemblance to a novel by Ann Radcliffe or Mary Shelley, or when Kant is said to think that rhetoric can be rehabilitated by some "tidy critical housekeeping." De Man's conclusion can be read as applying to the epistemological damage caused as much by gender as by figure: "In each case, it turns out to be impossible to maintain a clear line of distinction between rhetoric, abstraction, symbol, and all other forms of language. In each case, the resulting undecidability is due to the asymmetry of the binary model that opposes the figural to the proper meaning of the figure" (p.

28). The philosopher's place is always within, not outside, the asymmetrical structures of language and of gender, but that place can never, in the final analysis, be proper. It may be impossible to know whether it is the gender question that is determined by rhetoric or rhetoric by gender difference, but it does seem as though these are the terms in which it might be fruitful to pursue the question.

In order to end with a meditation on a possible female version of the Yale School, I would like now to turn to the work of a Yale daughter. For this purpose I have chosen to focus on *The Critical Difference* by Barbara Johnson.[8] What happens when one raises Mary Jacobus's question: "Is there a woman in this text?" The answer is rather surprising. For no book produced by the Yale School seems to have excluded women as effectively as *The Critical Difference*. No women authors are studied. Almost no women critics are cited. And, what is even more surprising, there are almost no female characters in any of the stories analyzed. *Billy Budd*, however triangulated, is a tale of three *men* in a boat. Balzac's *Sarrasine* is the story of a woman who turns out to be a castrated man. And in Johnson's analysis of "The Purloined Letter," the story of oedipal triangularity is transformed into an endlessly repeated chain of fraternal rivalries. In a book that announces itself as a study of difference, the place of the woman is constantly being erased.

This does not mean, however, that the question of sexual difference does not haunt the book from the beginning. In place of a dedication, *The Critical Difference* opens with a quotation from Paul de Man in which difference is dramatized as a scene of exasperated instruction between Archie Bunker and his wife:

> Asked by his wife whether he wants to have his bowling shoes laced over or laced under, Archie Bunker answers with a question: "What's the difference?" Being a reader of sublime simplicity, his wife replies by patiently explaining the difference between lacing over and lacing under, whatever this may be, but provokes only ire. "What's the difference?" did not ask for difference but means instead "I don't give a damn what the difference is." The same grammatical pattern engenders two meanings that are mutually exclusive: the literal meaning asks for the concept (difference) whose existence is denied by the figurative meaning. As long as we are talking about bowling shoes, the consequences are relatively trivial; Archie Bunker, who is a great believer in the authority of origins (as long, of course, as they are the right origins) muddles along in a world where literal and figurative meanings get in each other's way, though not without discomforts. But suppose that it is a *de*-bunker rather than a "Bunker," and a de-bunker of the arche (or origin), an archie Debunker such as Nietzsche

or Jacques Derrida, for instance, who asks the question "What is the Difference?"—and we cannot even tell from his grammar whether he "really" wants to know "what" difference is or is just telling us that we shouldn't even try to find out. Confronted with the question of the difference between grammar and rhetoric, grammar allows us to ask the question, but the sentence by means of which we ask it may deny the very possibility of asking. For what is the use of asking, I ask, when we cannot even authoritatively decide whether a question asks or doesn't ask?

Whatever the rhetorical twists of this magnificent passage, the fact that it is framed as an intersexual dialogue is not irrelevant.

Another essay in *The Critical Difference*, a study of Mallarmé's prose poem "The White Waterlily," offers an even more promising depiction of the rhetoric of sexual difference. The essay begins:

If human beings were not divided into two biological sexes, there would probably be no need for literature. And if literature could truly say what the relations between the sexes are, we would doubtless not need much of it then, either. Somehow, however, it is not simply a question of literature's ability to say or not to say the truth of sexuality. For from the moment literature begins to try to set things straight on that score, literature itself becomes inextricable from the sexuality it seeks to comprehend. It is not the life of sexuality that literature cannot capture; it is literature that inhabits the very heart of what makes sexuality problematic for us speaking animals. Literature is not only a thwarted investigator but also an incorrigible perpetrator of the problem of sexuality. (P. 13)

But the prose poem in question ends up dramatizing an inability to know whether the woman one is expecting to encounter has ever truly been present or not. It is as though *The Critical Difference* could describe only the escape of the difference it attempts to analyze. This is even more true of the essay subtitled "What the Gypsy Knew." With such a title, one would expect to encounter at last something about female knowledge. But the point of the analysis is precisely that the poem does not tell us what the gypsy knew. Her prophecy is lost in the ambiguities of Apollinaire's syntax.

There may, however, be something accurate about this repeated dramatization of woman as simulacrum, erasure, or silence. For it would not be easy to assert that the existence and knowledge of the female subject could simply be produced, without difficulty or epistemological damage, within the existing patterns of culture and language. *The Critical Difference* may here be unwittingly pointing to "woman" as one of the things "we do not know we do not know." Johnson concludes her preface with some remarks about ignorance that apply ironically well to her book's own demonstration of an ignorance that pervades Western discourse as a whole: "What literature often seems to tell us is the consequences of the way in which what is not known is not *seen* as unknown. It is not, in the final analysis, what you don't know that can or cannot hurt you. It is what you don't *know* you don't know that spins out and entangles 'that perpetual error we call life' " (p. xii). It is not enough to be a woman writing in order to resist the naturalness of female effacement in the subtly male pseudogenderlessness of language. It would be no easy task, however, to undertake the effort of reinflection or translation required to retrieve the lost knowledge of the gypsy, or to learn to listen with retrained ears to Edith Bunker's patient elaboration of an answer to the question, "What *is* the difference?"

5

Deconstruction, Feminism, and Pedagogy

It is better to fail in teaching what should not be taught than to succeed in teaching what is not true.
—Paul de Man

The old folks say, "It's not how little we know that hurts so, but that so much of what we know ain't so."
—Toni Cade Bambara

The purpose of this chapter is to attempt to articulate deconstruction and feminism in terms of pedagogical theory and practice, to make a link, in a sense, between "what is not true" and "what ain't so." My remarks will be based on two texts: (1) an essay by Paul de Man (from which the first epigraph is taken) entitled "The Resistance to Theory," which first appeared in an issue of *Yale French Studies* called *The Pedagogical Imperative: Teaching as a Literary Genre,* and (2) a recent collection of essays on pedagogy edited by Margo Culley and Catherine Portuges entitled *Gendered Subjects: The Dynamics of Feminist Teaching.*[1]

I will begin by reinserting the first epigraph into its original context. Speaking about the question of whether theory and scholarship are compatible, de Man writes:

> A question arises only if a tension develops between methods of understanding and the knowledge which those methods allow one to reach. If there is indeed something about literature, as such, which allows for a discrepancy between truth and method, between *Wahrheit* and *Methode,* then scholarship and theory are no longer necessarily compatible; as a first casualty of this complication, the notion of "literature as such" as well as the clear distinction between history and interpretation can no longer be taken for granted. For a method that cannot be made to suit the "truth" of its object can only

teach delusion. . . . These uncertainties are manifest in the hostility directed at theory in the name of ethical and aesthetic values. . . . The most effective of these attacks will denounce theory as an obstacle to scholarship and, consequently, to teaching. It is worth examining whether, and why, this is the case. For if this is indeed so, then it is better to fail in teaching what should not be taught than to succeed in teaching what is not true. (*PI*, p. 4)

In order to make some headway with this assertion, we might examine the ways in which the essay itself functions pedagogically. What, if anything, does the essay teach? Interestingly, it opens by placing itself under the sign of failure. "This essay was not originally intended to address the question of teaching directly, although it was supposed to have a didactic and an educational function—which it failed to achieve" (*PI*, p. 3). The essay itself, in other words, can be read as an *enactment* of the failure to teach that it promotes. De Man explains that the essay was commissioned to provide a summary of recent work in literary theory for an MLA volume entitled *Introduction to Scholarship in Modern Languages and Literatures.* "I found it difficult to live up, in minimal good faith, to the requirements of this program, and could only try to explain, as concisely as possible, why the main theoretical interest of literary theory consists in the impossibility of its definition. The Committee rightly judged that this was an inauspicious way to achieve the pedagogical objectives of the volume and commissioned another article." It is not pedagogically auspicious, it seems, to be sent on a mission of scholarship and to come back with a tale of impossibility. Yet it is the value of such a failure to teach that de Man is asserting as the moral of his pedagogical tale. What is of pedagogical interest for him is precisely what resists pedagogical mastery.

Feminist theories of pedagogy, too, involve a critique of masterful meaning and an interest in the resistance to reductive appropriation. One of the most visible differences, however, lies in the status of the pedagogical subject. De Man makes a clear case for teaching as an impersonal rather than an interpersonal phenomenon: "Overfacile opinion notwithstanding, teaching is not primarily an intersubjective relationship between people but a cognitive process in which self and other are only tangentially and contiguously involved. The only teaching worthy of the name is scholarly, not personal" (*PI*, p. 3). When de Man ultimately concludes that the resistance to theory is ineradicable because theory is its own self-resistance, that self-resistance is also a form of resistance to the very notion of a self.

The title *Gendered Subjects,* on the other hand, indicates a move to reverse the impersonalization that de Man radicalizes and to reintroduce the personal, or at least the positional, as a way of disseminating authority and decomposing the false universality of patriarchally institutionalized meanings. Not only has female personal experience tended to be excluded from the discourse of knowledge, but the realm of the personal itself has been coded as female and devalued for that reason. In opposition, therefore, many of the essays of the volume consciously assume a first-person autobiographical stance toward the question of pedagogical theory: this is how it looks *to me* as the only black woman in an English department, or as a male feminist, or as a teacher of feminist theory. This is where I am positioned in the institutions of pedagogy. Explicitly speaking from *where one is* turns out to allow for an expansion rather than a contraction of the range of pedagogical experiences available. While de Man urges maximum abstraction, Michele Russell, for one, exhorts us to "use everything":

> The size and design of the desks, for example. They are wooden, with one-sided stationary writing arms attached. The embodiment of a poor school. Small. Unyielding. Thirty years old. Most of the black women [students] are ample-bodied. . . . Sitting there for one hour— not to mention trying to concentrate and work—is a contortionist's miracle, or a stoic's. It feels like getting left back.
>
> With desks as a starting-point for thinking about our youth in school, class members are prompted to recall the mental state such seats encouraged. They cite awkwardness, restlessness, and furtive embarrassment. When they took away our full-top desks with interior compartments, we remember how *exposed* we felt. . . . We talk about all the unnecessary, but deliberate, ways the educational process is made uncomfortable for the poor. . . . We remember that one reason many of us stopped going to school was that it became an invasion of privacy. (*GS*, p. 163)

The constraints of positionality here *literally* become the access route to a whole rethinking of the educational enterprise. This, too, is a story of the pedagogical recuperation of a failure of teaching, but in a very different sense from de Man's.

I find both these versions of the resistance to pedagogy equally compelling and equally difficult to put into genuine—as opposed to apparent—practice. Both versions involve an imperative not to lose, but rather to work through, that resistance. The question I want to ask here is whether there is a *simple* incompatibility between the depersonalization of deconstruction and the repersonalization of feminism, or whether each is not in reality haunted by the ghost of the other.

The personal in fact returns in de Man in two very different ways. On the one hand, he has always been and is increasingly being lionized as the embodiment of the great teacher: the recent issue of *Yale French Studies* entitled *The Lesson of Paul de Man* (1985) opens by saying, "He was never not teaching." Testimonials repeatedly assert that it was precisely his way of denying personal authority that engendered the unique power of his personal authority. What is not clear, of course, is whether his personal impact should be seen as a sign of the success or of the failure of his pedagogical project as he conceived it. Another sign of this paradox is the function of proper names in the present essay: the name of de Man occupies a focal position that no proper name assumes—and this is part of the point—in the feminist collective volume, however personal the narratives. (Is it by chance, moreover, that he should be named "the Man"?)

The other return of the personal in de Man's work takes a rhetorical form. Even a cursory perusal of his essays reveals that their insistant rhetorical mode—in the service of their irony, paradoxes, and chiasmuses—is personification. In the absence of a personal agent of signification, the rhetorical entities themselves are constantly said to "know," to "renounce," or to "resign themselves" in the place where the poet or critic as subject has disappeared. It is as though the operations of personhood could not be eliminated but only transferred—which does not necessarily imply that their rightful place is within the self. Rather, it implies that personification is a trope available for occupancy by either subjects or linguistic entities, the difference between them being ultimately indeterminable, if each is known only in and through a text. The teacher, in any event, becomes neither impersonal nor personal: the agent of pedagogy is a personification.

What the transfer of personhood to rhetorical entities does enable de Man to achieve, however, is an elimination of sexual difference. By making personhood the property of an "it," de Man is able to claim a form of universality which can be said to inhere in language itself, and which is not directly subject to ordinary feminist critique, however gender-inflected language can in fact be shown to be. The analysis of the rhetorical operations of self-resistance is, as de Man asserts, irrefutable in its own terms. But the question *can* be asked why de Man's discourse of self-resistance and uncertainty has achieved such authority and visibility, while the self-resistance and uncertainty of *women* has been part of what has insured their lack of authority and their invisibility. It would seem that one has to be positioned in the place of power in order for one's self-resistance to be valued. Self-resistance, indeed, may be one of the few viable postures remaining for the white male establishment.

But does this imply that the task of feminism would be the overcoming of self-resistance? In many of the essays in *Gendered Subjects*, this would seem to be the case. A typical essay (this one by Susan Stanford

Friedman) begins: "I choose to address the issue of feminist pedagogy in a personal narrative not only because the cornerstone of that pedagogy has been the validation of experience, but also because my own evolution as a teacher in a university setting over the last twelve years illuminates a pedagogical problem we all must face" (*GS*, p. 203). What is interesting about this attempt at personalization is how quickly it slides into an assumption of generalizability ("a problem we all must face"). The recourse to "experience" is always, in these essays, a double-edged sword. On the one hand, it would be impossible to deny that female experience has been undervalidated. On the other hand, the moment one assumes one knows what female experience is, one runs the risk of creating another reductive appropriation—an appropriation that consists in the reduction of experience *as* self-resistance. While deconstructive discourse may be in danger of overvaluing self-resistance, feminist discourse may be in danger of losing self-resistance as a source of insight and power rather than merely of powerlessness. While de Man's writing is haunted by the return of personification, feminist writing is haunted by the return of abstraction. The challenge facing both approaches is to recognize these ghosts not as external enemies but as the uncannily familiar strangers that make their own knowledge both possible and problematic.

Generalization

II

SIGNIFICANT GAPS

6

A Hound, a Bay Horse, and a Turtle Dove

Obscurity in *Walden*

The experience of reading Thoreau's *Walden* is often a disconcerting one. The very discrepancy between the laconic, concrete chapter titles and the long, convoluted sentences of the text alerts the reader to a process of level-shifting that delights and baffles—indeed, that delights because it baffles. Consider, for example, the following passage:

> I sometimes despair of getting anything quite simple and honest done in this world by the help of men. They would have to be passed through a powerful press first, to squeeze their old notions out of them, so that they would not soon get upon their legs again; and then there would be some one in the company with a maggot in his head, hatched from an egg deposited there nobody knows when, for not even fire kills these things, and you would have lost your labor. Nevertheless, we will not forget that some Egyptian wheat was handed down to us by a mummy.[1]

It is difficult to read this passage without doing a double take. The logical seriousness of the style of "Nevertheless, we will not forget. . ." in no way prepares the reader for the sudden appearance of wheat in a mummy. The passage shifts with unruffled rapidity from abstract generalization to dead figure ("squeeze their old notions out of them") to a soon-to-reawaken figure hidden in a cliché ("maggot in the head") to mininarrative ("deposited there nobody knows when") to folk wisdom ("Not even fire kills these things") to counterclaim ("Nevertheless, we will not forget. . ."). By the time one reaches the mummy, one no longer knows what the figure stands for, whether it, like the mummy, is dead or alive, or even where the boundaries of the analogy (if it *is* an analogy) lie.

It is paradoxical that a writer who constantly exhorts us to "Simplify, simplify" should also be the author of some of the most complex and difficult paragraphs in the English language. What is it about this seemingly simple account of life in the woods that so often bewilders the reader, making him, in Emerson's words, "nervous and wretched to read it"?

In an article entitled *"Walden's* False Bottoms," Walter Benn Michaels amply demonstrates the book's capacity to engender nervousness as he details the long history of readers' attempts to cope with *Walden's* obscurity, first by attributing it to Thoreau's alleged "want of continuity of mind" (James Russell Lowell), then by subsuming it under the larger patterns of *Walden's* literary unity (Matthiessen, Anderson), then by considering it as a challenge to the reader's ability to read figuratively (Cavell, Buell). Walter Benn Michaels ends his own account of the undecidability of *Walden's* contradictions by saying, "It's heads I win, tails you lose. No wonder the game makes us nervous."[2]

The passage through which I would like to gain access to one of the principal difficulties of *Walden's* game is precisely a passage about losing. It is one of the most often-discussed passages in the book, a fact that is in itself interesting and instructive. The passage stands as an isolated paragraph, seemingly unrelated to what precedes or follows:

> I long ago lost a hound, a bay horse, and a turtle dove, and am still on their trail. Many are the travellers I have spoken concerning them, describing their tracks and what calls they answered to. I have met one or two who had heard the hound, and the tramp of the horse, and even seen the dove disappear behind a cloud, and they seemed as anxious to recover them as if they had lost them themselves. (P. 16)

It should come as no surprise that the hound, the bay horse, and the turtle dove are almost universally seen as symbols by Thoreau's readers. The questions asked of this passage are generally, What do the three animals symbolize? and Where did the symbols come from? The answers to these questions are many and varied: for T. M. Raysor, the animals represent the "gentle boy" Edmund Sewall, Thoreau's dead brother John, and the woman to whom he unsuccessfully proposed marriage, Ellen Sewall; for Francis H. Allen, the symbols represent "the vague desires and aspirations of man's spiritual nature"; for John Burroughs, they stand for the "fine effluence" that for Thoreau constitutes "the ultimate expression of fruit of any created thing." Others have seen in the symbols "a mythical record of [Thoreau's] disappointments" (Emerson), a "quest . . . for an absolutely satisfactory condition of friendship" (Mark Van Doren), the "wildness that keeps man in touch with nature, intellectual stimulus, and purification of spirit" (Frank

Davidson), and a "lost Eden" (Alfred Kazin). Sources for Thoreau's symbols are said to be found in such diverse texts as Voltaire's *Zadig* (Edith Peairs), the "Chinese Four Books" that Thoreau edited for *The Dial,* an old English ballad, an Irish folk tale, and a poem by Emerson.[3]

The sense shared by all readers that the hound, the bay horse and the turtle dove *are* symbols, but that what they symbolize is unclear, is made explicit in the following remarks by Stanley Cavell:

> I have no new proposal to offer about the literary or biographical sources of those symbols. But the very obviousness of the fact that they are symbols, and function within a little myth, seems to me to tell us what we need to know. The writer comes to us from a sense of loss; the myth does not contain more than symbols because it is no set of desired things he has lost, but a connection with things, the track of desire itself.[4]

The notion that what is at stake here is not any set of lost *things* but rather the very fact of *loss* seems to find confirmation in the replies that Thoreau himself gave on two different occasions to the question of the passage's meaning. In a letter to B. B. Wiley, dated April 26, 1857, he writes:

> How shall we account for our pursuits if they are original? We get the language with which to describe our various lives out of a common mint. If others have their losses, which they are busy repairing, so have I *mine,* & their hound & horse may *perhaps* be the symbols of some of them. But also I have lost, or am in danger of losing, a far finer & more etherial treasure, which commonly no loss of which they are conscious will symbolize—this I answer hastily & with some hesitation, according as I now understand my own words. (*Annotated Walden,* pp. 157–58)

And on another occasion, as the *Variorum* tells it:

> Miss Ellen Watson, in "Thoreau Visits Plymouth" . . . , reports that when Thoreau visited Plymouth, Mass., a year or two after the publication of *Walden,* he met there "Uncle Ed" Watson who asked him what he meant when he said he lost "a hound, a horse, and a dove." Thoreau replied, "Well, Sir, I suppose we have all our losses." "That's a pretty way to answer a fellow," replied Uncle Ed. (P. 270)

Most readers have shared Uncle Ed's disappointment at this answer that seems no answer at all. The editors of the *Annotated* and *Variorum Waldens* both conclude their surveys of the literature on the subject in a similar way:

> In conclusion, however, it should be pointed out that there is no unanimity on interpretation of these symbols and the individual critic is left free to interpret as he wishes. (*Variorum*, p. 272)

> Since there is no clear explanation, each reader will have to supply his own. (*Annotated Walden*, p. 158)

In attempting to fill these enigmatic symbols with interpretive content, most readers have assumed that the hound, the bay horse, and the turtle dove were figurative containers or concrete vehicles into which some deeper, higher, or more abstract meanings could be made to fit. This is what the business of interpreting symbols is all about. In cases like the present, where there exists no unanimity or clarity about the symbols' meanings, readers tend to believe *not* that there is something inadequate about the way they are asking the question, but that each individual becomes "free" to settle on an answer for himself.

Before going back to attempt a different type of analysis of this passage, I would like first to quote in its entirety the paragraph that immediately precedes the hound-horse-dove passage in the text:

> In any weather, at any hour of the day or night, I have been anxious to improve the nick of time, and notch it on my stick too; to stand on the meeting of two eternities, the past and the future, which is precisely the present moment; to toe that line. You will pardon some obscurities, for there are more secrets in my trade than in most men's, and yet not voluntarily kept, but inseparable from its very nature. I would gladly tell all that I know about it, and never paint "No Admittance" on my gate.
>
> I long ago lost a hound, a bay horse, and a turtle dove, and am still on their trail. Many are the travellers I have spoken concerning them, describing their tracks and what calls they answered to. I have met one or two who had heard the hound, and the tramp of the horse, and even seen the dove disappear behind a cloud, and they seemed as anxious to recover them as if they had lost them themselves. (P. 16)

There appears at first sight to be no relation between these two paragraphs. Yet the very abruptness of the transition, the very discrepancy of rhetorical modes, may perhaps indicate that the first paragraph consists of a set of instructions about how to read the second. It is surely no accident that one of the most enigmatic passages in *Walden* should be placed immediately after the sentence "You will pardon some obscurities." If the secret identities of the hound, the horse, and the dove are never to be revealed, it is not, says Thoreau, that they are being *voluntarily* withheld. Such secrets are simply inseparable from the nature of my trade—that is, writing. "I would gladly tell all that I know about it, and never paint 'No Admittance' on my gate." But all I *know* about it is not all there *is* about it. You are not being forcibly or gently kept away from a knowledge I possess. The gate is wide open, and that is why the path is so obscure. The sign "obscurity" is pointing directly at the symbols, making the sentence read, "I long ago lost an X, a Y, and a Z," and you are supposed to recognize them not as obscure symbols, but as symbols standing for the obscure, the lost, the irretrievable.

But yet, we insist, your X, Y, and Z are so *particular*—so hound-like, so horselike, so birdlike. If they merely symbolize the lost object as such, why do we hear the baying of the hound and the tramp of the horse? Why do those fellow travellers give us such precise reports?

Ah, but you see, Thoreau might answer, the symbols *are* symbols, after all. What is lost is always intensely particular. Yet it is known only in that it is lost—lost in one of the two eternities between which we clumsily try to toe the line.

To follow the trail of what is lost is possible only, it seems, if the loss is maintained in a state of transference from traveller to traveller, so that each takes up the pursuit as if the loss were his own. Loss, then, ultimately belongs to an other; the losses we treat as our own are perhaps losses of which we never had conscious knowledge ourselves. "If others have their losses, which they are busy repairing, so have I *mine*, & their hound & horse may *perhaps* be the symbols of some of them. But also I have lost, or am in danger of losing, a far finer & more etherial treasure, which commonly no loss *of which they are conscious* will symbolize."

Walden's great achievement is to wake us up to our own lost losses, to make us participate in the transindividual movement of loss in its infinite particularity, urging us passionately to follow the tracks of we know not quite what, as if we had lost it, or were in danger of losing it, ourselves.

In order to communicate the irreducibly particular yet ultimately unreadable nature of loss, Thoreau has chosen to use three symbols that clearly *are* symbols but that do not really symbolize anything outside themselves. They are figures for which no literal, proper term can be substituted. They are, in other words, catachreses—"figures of abuse," figurative substitutes for a literal term that does not exist. Like the "legs" and "arms" of our favorite recliner, Thoreau's hound, horse, and dove belong to a world of homely figurative richness, yet the impersonal literality they seem to presuppose is nowhere to be found. The structure of catachretic symbolism is thus the very structure of transference and loss. Through it Thoreau makes us see that every lost object is always, in a sense, a catachresis, a figurative substitute for nothing that ever could be literal.

It could be said that Nature itself is for Thoreau a catachretic symbol that enables him to displace his discourse without filling in its symbolic tenor. But in order to analyze a more particular aspect of the way in which Thoreau's catachretic rhetoric creates obscurity in *Walden*, let us first look at a more traditional and semantically "full" use of nature imagery: the *analogies* drawn between natural objects and human predicaments.

I begin with a somewhat atypically explicit analogy:

> One day . . . I saw a striped snake run into the water, and he lay on the bottom, apparently without inconvenience, as long as I staid there, or more than a quarter of an hour; perhaps because he had not yet fairly come out of the torpid state. It appears to me that for a like reason men remain in their present low and primitive condition; but if they should feel the influence of the spring of springs arousing them, they would of necessity rise to a higher and more ethereal life. (P. 33)

No rhetorical strategy could be more classical than this weaving of analogy between the natural and the human worlds. It is the mark of the moralist, the evangelist, the satirist, and the lyric poet, all of which Thoreau indeed is. From the New Testament to Aesop and Swedenborg, the natural world has been a source of figures of the preoccupations and foibles of man. As Emerson puts it in his own essay on Nature:

> The memorable words of history and the proverbs of nations consist usually of a natural fact, selected as a picture or parable of a moral truth. Thus; A rolling stone gathers no moss; A bird in hand is worth two in the bush; A cripple in the right way will beat a racer in the wrong; Make hay while the sun shines; 'Tis hard to carry a full cup even; Vinegar is the son of wine; The last ounce broke the camel's back; Long-lived trees make roots first;—and the like. In their primary sense these are trivial facts, but we repeat them for the value of their analogical import. What is true of proverbs, is true of all fables, parables, and allegories.[5]

Yet although Thoreau draws on many centuries of analogical writing, there is a subtle difference in his rhetorical use of nature, and it is the specificity of that difference that I would like to attempt to identify in conclusion. The difference begins to become perceptible in the following examples:

> Why has man rooted himself thus firmly in the earth, but that he may rise in the same proportion into the heavens above?—for the nobler plants are valued for the fruit they bear at last in the air and light, far from the ground, and are not treated like the humbler esculents,

which, though they may be biennials, are cultivated only till they have perfected their root, and often cut down at top for this purpose, so that most would not know them in their flowering season. (P. 15)

We don garment after garment, as if we grew like exogenous plants by addition without. Our outside and often thin and fanciful clothes are our epidermis or false skin, which partakes not of our life, and may be stripped off here and there without fatal injury; our thicker garments, constantly worn, are our cellular integument, or cortex; but our shirts are our liber or true bark, which cannot be removed without girdling and so destroying the man. (P. 21)

In both these examples, what begins as a fairly routine analogy tends, in the course of its elaboration, to get wildly out of hand. The fascination with the vehicle as an object of attention in its own right totally eclipses the original anthropomorphic tenor. Words like "esculents," "biennials," "cortex," and "liber" pull away from their subordinate, figurative status and begin giving information about themselves, sidetracking the reader away from the original thrust of the analogy. In the first example, what begins as an opposition between nobler and humbler men and plants collapses as it is revealed that the humbler plants are humble only because they are never *allowed* to flower. In the second example, the hierarchy of integuments ends by privileging not the skin but the shirt as that part of a man that cannot be removed without destroying him. In an effort to show that man is confused about where his inside ends and his outside begins, Thoreau resorts to a logic of tree growth which entirely takes over as the exogenous striptease procedes.

It is perhaps in the "Bean-field" chapter that the rhetorical rivalries between the literal and the figurative, the tenor and the vehicle, become most explicit. On the one hand, Thoreau writes, "I was determined to know beans," and goes on to detail the hours of hoeing and harvesting, listing the names of weeds and predators, and accounting for outgo and income down to the last half penny. And on the other, he admits that "some must work in fields if only for the sake of tropes and expression, to serve a parable-maker one day." He speaks of sowing the seeds of sincerity, truth, simplicity, faith, and innocence, asking, "Why concern ourselves so much about our beans for seed, and not be concerned at all about a new generation of men?"

The perverse complexity of *Walden*'s rhetoric is intimately related to the fact that it is never possible to be sure what the rhetorical status of any given image is. And this is because what Thoreau has done in moving to Walden Pond is to move *himself*, literally, into the world of his own figurative language. The literal woods, pond, and bean field still assume the same classical rhetorical guises in which they have always appeared, but they are suddenly readable in addition as the non-figurative ground of a naturalist's account of life in the woods. The ground has shifted, but the figures are still figures. When is it that we decide that Thoreau never lost that hound, that horse, and that dove? It is because we can never be absolutely sure, that we find ourselves forever on their trail.

Walden is obscure, therefore, to the extent that Thoreau has *literally* crossed over into the very parable he is writing, where *reality itself* has become a catachresis, both ground and figure at once, and where, he tells us, "if you stand right fronting and face to face with a fact, you will see the sun glimmer on both its surfaces, as if it were a cimeter, and feel its sweet edge dividing you through the heart and marrow."

7

Erasing Panama

Mallarmé and the Text of History

In February 1893, Mallarmé published an article entitled "Faits-divers" in the *National Observer*, a British weekly journal of politics and literature edited by W. E. Henley (best known for his poem "Invictus," which includes the lines: "I am the master of my fate; / I am the captain of my soul"). Mallarmé's article was a comment upon the Panama Canal scandal then raging in France, in which the would-be builder of the canal, Ferdinand de Lesseps, had just been convicted of fraud. Mallarmé's article is quite explicitly concerned with the facts of the case, and its first-person narrator represents himself as a poet-reporter fascinated by the events of his day, but not for the same reasons as the general public.

Four years later, in 1897, Mallarmé published a book of his own prose entitled *Divagations*. Included in that volume is a piece composed of reworked sentences from the article "Faits-divers." The new text is much shorter, less expository, and more elliptical, and the chatty narrator has nearly disappeared. It is now called "Or" ("Gold") and is placed first in a sequence with the general title "Grands Faits Divers." In "Or," neither Panama nor Lesseps are mentioned explicitly, and the text develops not a reading of the Panama affair but a generalized theory of value. This process of textual revision, which so graphically refines diverse facts into gold, current events into a theory of currency, has always seemed a perfect paradigm for Mallarmé's brand of symbolism. The journalistic and the pure, the referentially historical and the symbolically absolute, are the two poles between which Mallarmé encourages his readers to suspend his practice of letters. These two texts are thus an appropriate place to analyze the contemporary theoretical oppositions between self-reflexivity and referentiality, textuality and historicism, the poetic and the political, and indeed the whole notion of the literarity of literature as such.[1]

Mallarmé has long been seen as the epitome of the "pure" poet. His critique of the referential claims of literature has indeed been fundamental to contemporary theories of textuality. The fact that he "revised" his own work repeatedly and scrupulously into ever less referential and more obscure mappings of linguistic self-reflection has led Mallarmé scholars to take the point toward which his writing strives as that which characterizes its essence. Mallarmé's revisions are read as tending toward a refinement of style through the gradual suppression of reference and historicity, a transposition of fact into idea, with idea the valorized term. As Norman Paxton puts it, "It would appear, then, that Mallarmé's personal style, which is only embryonically apparent in 1865, was forged around 1880 and thereafter developed unswervingly. . . . We may presume that Mallarmé wished to exclude from *Divagations* not only topical allusions but in fact anything which was not germane to his main aesthetic themes."[2] This privileging of the aesthetic and the stylistic, which is certainly present in Mallarmé, deserves a new look, to the extent that it takes for granted an opposition between history and poetry that Mallarmé was far from embracing. One has only to think of his report to the British public about the state of French poetry at the end of the nineteenth century to realize that Mallarmé was acutely concerned with what he often referred to as "ce siècle."

While Mallarmé's revisions do tend to reduce the role of historical anecdote, it seems to me that we have taken the revisionary vectors too seriously, that we have attempted to situate Mallarmé's notion of writing at the *limit* rather than along the asymptote of his teleology. Just as "verse would not exist" if there were a supreme language, so Mallarmé's writing would not exist if The Book were already at hand. At the base of nearly every late prose text there is a historical event or institution being commented upon, an otherness, accident, or chance without which the dice of writing would never have been thrown. As Mallarmé puts it in "Le Livre, instrument spirituel": "Un journal reste le point de départ; la littérature s'y décharge à souhait" ("A newspaper remains the starting point; literature unloads itself there as it wishes"). Even in *Divagations*, in which Mallarmé pushed his prose to the limits of purity, the journalistic impulse remains ineradicable, as he himself admits in his short preface:

> Un livre comme je ne les aime pas, ceux épars et privés d'architecture. Nul n'échappe décidément, au journalisme ou voudrait-il, en produit pour soi et tel autre espérons, sans qu'on jette par-dessus les têtes, certaines vérités, vers le jour. (P. 1538)
>
> [A book like those I don't like, those that are scattered and lacking in architecture. Decidedly, no one escapes journalism, or, willing it,

produces it for oneself and let us hope for some other, without tossing over many heads certain truths toward the light of day.]

What would it mean, then, to consider Mallarmé not as a timeless superpoet ensconced in his ivory tower, but as a mild-mannered reporter sending us delayed dispatches from nineteenth-century Paris? The first consequence of such a shift concerns the status of that most revered of academic literary objects, the Complete Works. Nowhere better than in the case of Mallarmé can one discern both the advantages and the problems of the Complete Works as a genre. On the one hand, Mallarmé's scattered, heterogeneous writings are united into a portable, commercially viable entity that enables his small, discontinous, and difficult poetic production to be organized and annotated as a developmental whole, with unfinished works such as *Igitur* assuming a form and an importance unthinkable apart from the editorial grounding of the Complete Works enterprise. Through the hierarchies established by type sizes, Mallarmé's nonpoetic works are seen to reflect—as counterparts or as supporting cast—the central poetic endeavor. The pathos of the unattainable is grounded in the sheer mass of seemingly subsidiary enterprises. And the potboilers are seen as crude furnaces out of which vapors of the Grand Oeuvre can dimly be perceived.

Such a presentation of a poet's production does a great deal to convey and support an art-for-art's-sake view of his work. Mallarmé's writings are centered on his verse, which is itself seen as an evolutionary sequence culminating in the late, the pure, and the obscure. And his writings are isolated from their context of production and publication so that they can relate only to each other. In this way the Complete Works *becomes* the ivory tower. But finally, and most importantly for the present discussion, the editorial rule that requires that the *last* published version of a text be privileged as definitive and that all other versions be relegated to the status of variants has profound consequences for the image we have of Mallarmé as a writer. The man who sends "Tennyson Viewed from Here" to a British journal is doing something different from the man who includes the same title in a series of portraits in a book of his own. Far from being oblivious to the contextual demands of his addressees, Mallarmé was acutely sensitive to a text's occasion and readership. This in itself explains some of the forms his revisions took. By reifying an author's writing into a series of discrete final products, the Complete Works erases any sense of their modes of production and interaction with contexts beyond themselves. By viewing Mallarmé's work through the hindsight of later "versions," one loses any sense of the earlier texts as different but equally vital speech acts in the world.

Before going on to a more detailed analysis of Mallarmé as a journalist and of the two texts that arise out of the Panama affair, I would like to digress a bit in order to bring into the discussion a few facts about the career of Ferdinand de Lesseps. While Mallarmé is being shifted from pure poet to man of action, I would like to suggest some ways in which Lesseps, the very image of the indefatigable doer, can in turn be seen as a Symbolist poet. It is true that Ferdinand de Lesseps is not numbered among the Symbolists in most manuals of literary history. Yet his enterprises epitomize nineteenth-century esthetics in a way that will, I hope, shed light on the historical specificity of what we know as the Symbolist movement.

Ferdinand de Lesseps was the driving force behind two great nineteenth-century enterprises. The first succeeded gloriously; the second failed scandalously. It was Lesseps who masterminded and oversaw the building of the Suez Canal between 1854 and 1869. And it was Lesseps who sought to repeat that exploit in the Isthmus of Panama between 1879 and 1888. The Suez enterprise ended in a triumphant inauguration ceremony attended by heads of state from every corner of the world. The Panama enterprise ended in the bankruptcy of the company; the ruin of thousands of small investors; the death of at least twenty thousand workers from yellow fever, malaria, and other diseases; a tremendous political and financial scandal in France during which 150 deputies were said to have taken bribes to assure the company's survival; a pre-Dreyfusian tide of anti-Semitism based on the alleged involvement of Jewish financiers; and the conviction of Lesseps and his son for fraud and abuse of confidence.[3] Yet Lesseps really did nothing diferent in Panama from what he had done in Suez. Indeed, that was his downfall: he tried to do the *same* thing.

While Mallarmé is said to be going from facts to ideas, Lesseps quite obviously attempts to go from ideas to facts—or to remake facts in the image of his fictions. His ambition was nothing less than to "couper la terre," "retoucher l'oeuvre de Dieu." To draw a line on a map and to cut a trench in the earth were essentially the same operation, only on staggeringly different scales. And it was the scale that excited the man Gambetta dubbed "le grand Français." Financial gain and worldly power seem never to have been motivating forces for Lesseps. He never derived great personal wealth from his enterprises and refused all but honorary titles. Instead, he wanted to stand, as Renan was to put it, as the embodiment of the ability of the human will to move mountains in the service of mankind—and for the greater glory of France. And for twenty years he did just that.

But why might Lesseps deserve the name of Symbolist? A first answer would obviously derive from his universalizing imagination, his tendency to view the world as a whole, as a system of relations—

commercial relations, one might add, viewed from an imperialistically European center. If it is desirable to join East and West, what could be simpler than to cut out a little piece of the East? To simplify the flow of goods is also to assure the permanence of certain trade patterns that might become dispersed and decentered if a circuitous route were to continue in effect. This view of the world as an object manipulated by technology and as a system of relations that must be grasped in their *ensemble* also underlies Mallarmé's description of art:

> La Nature a lieu, on n'y ajoutera pas; que des cités, les voies ferrées et plusieurs inventions formant notre matériel.
>
> Tout l'acte disponible, à jamais et seulement, reste de saisir les rapports, entre temps, rares ou multipliés; d'après quelque état intérieur et que l'on veuille à son gré étendre, simplifier le monde. (P. 647)

> [Nature takes place, it can't be added to; except for cities, railroads, and several inventions that form our material.
>
> The sole act at our disposal, forever and only, remains the grasping of relations, in the meantime, be they rare or multiplied; according to some internal state that one wishes to extend at will, to simplify the world.]

Lessep's imagination was Symbolist in another sense, too, as is attested by his account of the way in which he obtained permission to build the Suez Canal from the Egyptian viceroy, Mohammed Said. Lesseps had known Mohammed Said as a boy, when Lesseps, who was trained as a diplomat, not an engineer, had held a consular post in Egypt. When Said became the new ruler of Egypt, Lesseps went to congratulate him, carrying a detailed plan for a Suez canal in his pocket. He carried that plan around for several days, while Said regaled him with army maneuvers and banquets, waiting for a propitious moment to bring it up. Here is his description of that moment:

> At five o'clock in the morning, I was not yet dressed. The camp was beginning to stir; the cool air presaged the immanent sunrise. I changed from my dressing gown into warmer clothing and went back to my place at the door of my tent. Scattered rays of light began to gleam on the horizon; to my right lay the east in all its brightness; to my left, the dark and cloudy west.
>
> Suddenly, I saw a rainbow appear, glistening with the most vivid colors, spanning the sky from west to east. I must admit I felt my heart beat violently and I had to rein in my imagination, which saw in this sign of covenant, like that spoken of in Scripture, the portent of a true union between the Occident and the Orient, marking the day out for the success of my project. . . .

It is now ten o'clock; I am about to lunch with Zulfikar-Pasha. As I take my leave of the viceroy, I decide to show him that his horse, whose powerful legs I had already tested on the first day, is a top quality jumper; turning to wave to my host, I urge my steed over the tall stone parapet and gallop on up the hill toward my tent. You will soon see that this act of rashness may have been one of the causes for the approval the viceroy's entourage gave to my project, which was absolutely necessary for my success. The generals who came to lunch with me complimented me on it, and I saw that my boldness had considerably raised me in their esteem.[4]

Lesseps was thus a Symbolist not only in his reading of celestial signs, but in his skillful use of symbolic gestures as a persuasive device. This was to be his trademark and his genius: his equestrian exploits were as well known as his canals, and his ability to ride, eat, dance, lecture, and create ceremony day after day on his public-relations tours through the Continent and the United States until well into his eighties would be the envy of any fundraiser today. (Some sense of his physical presence can be obtained by picturing Colonel Sanders as Fitzcarraldo.) His sheer energy was legendary: among other exploits, he fathered twelve children after the age of sixty-four. When France was looking for the proper person to head the French delegation to the dedication ceremony of the Statue of Liberty, it chose Ferdinand de Lesseps, the most French of Frenchmen. When someone asked him what his line of work was, he answered, "isthmuses."

Celestial symbolism was of course not foreign to Mallarmé's system either. It is interesting to juxtapose to Lessep's journal the following description Valéry gives of his own state of mind after seeing the proofs of Mallarmé's *Coup de des:*

> Le soir du même jour, comme il m'accompagnait au chemin de fer, l'innombrable ciel de juillet enfermant toutes choses dans un groupe étincelant d'autres mondes, et que nous marchions, fumeurs obscurs, au milieu du Serpent, du Cygne, de l'Aigle, de la Lyre, il me semblait *maintenant* d'être pris dans le texte même de l'univers silencieux... Au creux d'une telle nuit, entre les propos que nous échangions, je songeais à la tentative merveilleuse: quel modèle, quel enseignement là-haut! Où Kant, assez naivement, peut-être, avait cru voir la Loi Morale, Mallarmé percevait sans doute l'Impératif d'une poésie, une Poét-ique... Il a essayé, pensai-je, *d'élever enfin une page à la puissance du ciel etoilé.* (Quoted in Mallarmé, p. 1582)

> [That evening, as he was accompanying me to the train, the numberless July skies enfolding everything in a sparkling cluster of other

worlds, and as we strode smoking in the dark among the Serpent, the Swan, the Eagle, and the Lyre, I felt that we *now* were caught up in the very text of the silent universe... In the dark of such a night, as we were talking, I thought about the marvelous experiment: what a model, what instruction up above us! Where Kant had perhaps na-ively felt he saw the Moral Imperative, Mallarmé doubtless perceived the imperative of poetry, or Poetics... What he has done, I thought, is to try *to raise a page to the power of a starry sky.*]

It is intriguing to note connections between the *Coup de dés* itself and the story of Lesseps' failure at Panama. The catastrophe at sea, the "vieil-lard," the "calculs," the uneasy relation between chance and human intentions, could all be read as a universalization of Lesseps' story. What is clear is that the Panama failure must have appealed to Mallarmé precisely as a referential version of the great nineteenth-century my-thology he was attempting to construct.

Reading man's fate in the heavens, however, is hardly a nine-teenth-century invention. To what extent does Lesseps belong with the specifically fin-de-siècle brand of Symbolism? It could be said that, at Suez, Lesseps was a Romantic; at Panama, he was definitely a Sym-bolist, to the extent that Symbolism can be seen as a self-consciously failed repetition of Romanticism. Although the ivory-tower estheticism that has been associated with Symbolism does not at first sight appear to characterize a literal mover of mountains, it is interesting to listen to the terms in which one historian has accounted for Lesseps' failure:

Lesseps, it should be remembered, was not a professional engineer, but, in the original sense of the word, an *entrepreneur.* One of his chief technical assistants at Panama, M. Bunau-Varilla, has described how politely and incredulously Lesseps listened to technical objections. "He saw in them obviously only another of those engineers' ideas that had hampered him so much at Suez, and which he had got over by letting Nature and common sense have their way." It was this bold empiricist who won over the Canal Congress to his pet idea, that the Panama, like the Suez Canal, was to be a sea-level canal, "A new Bosphorus." This inspiring idea was so magnificent that technical arguments for a canal with locks to get round the great difficulty that the canal had to be pushed through rain-soaked hills, not through a flat desert, were swept aside for what were largely *aesthetic reasons.* Faith would move mountains. Fundamentally, the Panama enterprise failed because faith was not enough; the back of the energy of the Company was broken in the unfinished Culebra Cut.[5]

At Panama, in other words, Lesseps pushed the universal analogy to the breaking point. His failure could thus in a sense be called "the revenge of the referent." For it is fin-de-siècle Symbolism that raises the question of the referent in its modern form. Much has been made of Mallarmé's supposed "elimination of the object." While Mallarmé makes an opposition between *to name* and *to suggest*, allude, or evoke, subsequent readers have located that opposition between referentiality and reflexivity, between texts about referents and texts about themselves. Lesseps' failure at Panama would suggest that the problem with the referent lies less in its inclusion or exclusion than in its *conception*. Lesseps did not simply disregard the referent; he saw it and touched it, but conceived of it as a mere *thing*, an inanimate object that could be infinitely transformed by a human subject. What Lesseps did not take into account was that the referent is itself a *process*, shaped by weather, disease, and social, economic, financial, and political institutions, just as the so-called human subject "mankind" is a conflictual field shaped by these same forces, and cannot be generalized as a unified agency. The question of whether Mallarmé's projects of finding the "explication orphique de la terre" and of achieving the "impersonality" of the poetic subject suffer from the same blindness as Lesseps' projects to "cut up the earth" and to personify civilization is too complicated and crucial a question to be dealt with adequately here, but common notions of Mallarmé's symbolism would lead one to believe that they do.

One last remark about Lesseps: my somewhat facetious characterization of him as a Symbolist seems, in a sense, to have been shared by that greatest of all French societies of letters: l'Académie française. Lesseps was elected to that august company of immortals in 1884. In 1896, following Lesseps' death, his eulogy was pronounced by his successor, none other than Anatole France. Mallarmé's 1893 article on the Panama affair in fact ends with the question of whether the academy, "gardienne si soucieuse de tout formalisme," will erase Lesseps' name from its rolls following his fraud conviction: "A doubt remains whether the French Academy, that scrupulous guardian of all formalism (it represents Letters), will vote the eradication [*la radiation*] of old Mr. de Lesseps, who was once rashly admitted through some extraliterary consideration." The fact that Lesseps was not ultimately excluded would indicate that his place was indeed among the formalists. For it was perhaps an excess of formalism that was his crime.

It is interesting that Mallarmé's article should end on a question of *radiation*. The ambiguities of this word, which can imply both "radiate" and "eradicate," pervade the article from start to finish. In the opening sentence, Mallarmé says that nothing about the Panama affair interests him merely through its "éclat"—its glitter. Indeed, it is gold's "defaut

d'éblouissement," "manque de splendeur," "effacement terne" that interests him. The more astronomical the numbers of francs involved, he
says, the less vivid they seem—as they tend to do in the case of Star
Wars technology or the national deficit. "The more a sum inreases or
backs up, as far as the simple man in the street is concerned, toward the
improbable, it includes, as it inscribes itself, more and more zeros; signifying that its total is equal to nothing, almost." The writer is called upon
to somehow make up for gold's vagueness and grayness by amassing
"radiant spots of clarity with the sole words that he proffers; such
as . . . Truth and Beauty." What Mallarmé is here suggesting is that
poetry exists because money has nothing but exchange value, that certain verbal structures have the capacity, which gold does not, of appear-
ing to contain radiance within themselves, whereas one can believe in
gold's brilliance only *while* it circulates, under the veil of its mystique.
But not all words have the effectiveness of "Truth" and "Beauty." The
word "fraud," for example, pronounced by Justice, only serves to show
Justice up as a fiction, the mouthpiece of too many people. The word
"fraud" has nowhere to inscribe itself, especially since the man that is to
be branded by it, Ferdinand de Lesseps, has himself been erased, as a
subject capable of understanding, by his own senility. Indeed, the pathos of his life is summed up in the question of wondering when,
exactly, his light went out. The *éclat* and the *effacement*, the "glitter" and
the "erasure"—that is, both halves of the word *radiation*—are thus summed up in the fallen athlete, Ferdinand de Lesseps.

What, then, do we make of the fact that his very *name* has itself
been erased from Mallarmé's subsequent version of the text, "Or?" In
that text, only the word *Banque* and the vague mention of a trial remain
of the Panama affair. Not that the problematics of brilliance and effacement have disappeared from that text. Quite the contrary. But it is
interesting to note that Mallarmé's writing *itself*, in its revisonary process, by erasing the proper names and concentrating on gold, has substituted a *textual* "radiation" for a thematic and historical one. Both sides
of the coin are in fact summed up in the new text's title: the word *or* can
mean both "gold"—the very image of semantic richness—and "then,"
"now," a conjunction that in French is so empty of meaning that it
stands simply to mark the fact that a transition is being made. That is the
word that, in "Faits-divers," marks the impossibility of understanding:
"Custom indeed has it that one cannot apprehend a man condemned in
his absence, as here, until one has signified to him the nature of the
sentence: now [*or*], since he would never understand, it will be forever
deferred."

Does this mean that Mallarmé has thereby erased History? A close
look at the two texts reveals not that history has disappeared from the

second text but that it is differently inscribed. While "Faits-divers" refers to a historical event that it points to as lying outside itself, in a cultural moment shared by Mallarmé and his readers, "Or" situates its historical reference in the ellipses of its own exposition. The first version speaks of "*this* collapse of Panama," "*the* trial," while the second speaks of "*a* Bank," "*a* trial." The elimination of many verbs and of most uses of the first person from "Or" suspends all that might situate it in specificity. And Lesseps disappears as a figure: history is no longer centered on a human agent, and Greek tragedy gives way to pure textuality. The reader of "Faits-divers" knows that she must do some historical research to recover the story Mallarmé shared with his contemporaries. The reader of "Or" knows that the blanks in the text—which is *about* blanks—are placeholders for historical structures, relatable but not reducible to anecdotal fact. It can thus be seen that Mallarmé, far from simply erasing history, is here putting history under erasure. The first text alludes to Panama, while the second inscribes Panama as a blank, a "zero" that, while being "equal to nothing, *almost*," holds the place and the attention of history in the text.

By using erasure and inscription, shadows and light, as a thematic preoccupation, and then going on to erase the specificity of events while retaining the way in which those events insist as a compellingly available paradigm for signifying structuration, Mallarmé is in a sense showing that history itself is involved in processes of inscription and erasure—that attitudes remain long after the reasons for them are forgotten, or that history can revolve around erasures as well as acts: think of Lesseps' senility, the eradication of the otherness of Panama, or even Nixon's eighteen-minute gap. Rather than choose between politics and stylistics, between historical reference and self-reflection, Mallarmé is showing the radical inseparability of these aspects of the functioning of writing in the world.

When a young poet comes to Mallarmé asking whether he should write poems or engage in political action, Mallarmé represents himself as answering:

> To act . . . signified . . . to produce on others a movement that gives you back the feeling that *you* originated it, and therefore exist, something no one is sure of. This praxis can be understood in two ways: either, by will, unbeknownst to others, to spend a whole life toward a multiple outburst—which would be *thinking*: or else, using the means available now—journals and their whirlwind—to send a force in some direction, any direction, which, when countered, gives you immunity from having no result.
>
> Your act is always applied to paper; for meditating without a

trace is evanescent, nor is the exalting of an instinct in some vehement, lost gesture what you were seeking. (P. 369)

"Your act is always applied to paper": writing is an integral part of action. In order for something to function as an act, it must be inscribed somewhere, whether it be on paper, in memory, on a tombstone, or on videotape, celluloid, or floppy discs. The historian's job is to discover those inscriptions that have been erased or overshadowed by the myths through which we have learned to see. The poet's job is to remind us of the interlocking relations *between* inscription and erasure, decision and undecidability, identity and difference, and the seductions and betrayals inherent in language itself.

8

Teaching Ignorance

L'Ecole des femmes

The teaching of ignorance is probably not what the majority of ped-
agogues have in mind. It may, indeed, be a structurally impossible task.
For how can a teacher teach a student not to know, without at the same
time informing her of what it is she is supposed to be ignorant of? This,
at any rate, is the problem faced by the would-be professor, Arnolphe,
in Molière's play *L'Ecoles des femmes*.

Negative Pedagogy

In the opening lines of the play, Arnolphe is explaining to his friend
Chrysalde his pedagogical method for turning an innocent young girl
into a faithful wife. He has picked out a docile four-year-old, paid off her
mother, and kept her locked up and ignorant ever since.

> I'm rich enough, I think, to have felt free
> To have my wife owe everything to me.
> From her dependency has come submission;
> She cannot flaunt her wealth or her position. . . .
> In a small convent, undisturbed by man,
> I had her raised according to my plan,
> Which was to have them try as best they could
> To keep her ignorant and therefore good.
> Thank God, the outcome answered my intent,
> And now she has grown up so innocent
> That I bless Heaven for having been so kind
> As to give me just the wife I had in mind.[1]

Young Agnes, in other words, has sprung fully disarmed from the brow of Arnolphe. But the middle-aged protector's belief that his charge's total ignorance of the world will ensure her fidelity to him is soon undercut by the arrival on the scene of young Horace, the son of an old friend of Arnolphe's. Horace gaily recounts to the older man the tale of his encounter with a young girl whom he has spotted on the balcony of a house in which some jealous old tyrant has tried to imprison her. Not realizing that his confidant is his foe, Horace keeps Arnolphe informed of the progress of his love, and for the rest of the play Arnolphe is condemned to hear from the mouth of his young rival the detailed account of the failure of his own desperate attempts to forestall the completion of his ward's education. In the seemingly gratuitous ending, the long-absent fathers of the two young people return to the city with the intention of joining their children in marriage, only to learn, much to their satisfaction, that this is the very plan their children have already conceived. Arnolphe, his dreams of domestic bliss thus dashed, leaves the stage in speechless frustration.

This *School for Wives* could thus be aptly renamed "the portrait of an antiteacher." Not only does Arnolphe intend that this student learn nothing, but even in this negative pedagogy, he fails. His methods are unsound, his lessons backfire, and his classroom is, at the end of the play, silent and empty. The pedagogical model presented to us by the play is apparently designed to be roundly disavowed. Indeed, perhaps the delight with which we literature teachers view the play arises out of the ease with which we can dissociate ourselves from Professor Arnolphe. Yet our delight is perhaps not without discomfort: this image of the ridiculousness of age, power, and authority is painted upon a figure whose role is after all similar to our own. For Molière, too, it seems that Arnolphe was mainly designed as an object of disavowal—precisely because the middle-aged suitor was also, secretly, an object of repressed identification. In 1662, at the age of forty, Molière himself had married the charming but spoiled twenty-year-old sister or daughter of his life-long companion or mistress, having doted on the girl since birth. In the context of what would seem to be a hyperbolic representation of denial, our concentration on the ridiculousness of the desire to possess and repress may therefore perhaps be blinding us to the ways in which Arnolphe's aims and strategies may not be so different from our own.

What, then, are Arnolphe's pedagogical imperatives? In the first scene of the play, Arnolphe is presented to us not as a teacher but as a critic. The object of his criticism is the rampant spread of cuckoldry in the city. It is when his friend Chrysalde warns him that the very out-spokenness of his widely published criticism may turn against him that

Arnolphe details the pedagogical strategies he has designed to keep his forehead free of decoration.

> *Chrysalde:* My fear for you springs from your mocking scorn,
> Which countless hapless husbands now have borne;
> No lord or rustic past his honeymoon
> Has to your criticism been immune;
> And everywhere you go, your chief delight
> Is in the secrets that you bring to light.
>
> .   .   .   .
>
> *Arnolphe:* In sum, when all around lies comedy
> May I not laugh, as spectator, at what I see?
> When fools. . .
> *Chrysalde:*   But he who laughs as loud as you
> Must fear that he'll in turn be laughed at, too.
>
> .   .   .   .
>
> *Arnolphe:* Lord, my friend, please don't be so upset:
> The one who catches *me* is not born yet.
> I know each cunning trick that women use
> Upon their docile men, each subtle ruse,
> And how they exercise their sleight-of-hand.
> And so against this mishap I have planned.
> My plighted wife will, through her innocence,
> Preserve my brow from noisome influence.

(1.1; TM)

Universal cuckoldry, in pedagogical terms, can be seen as the tendency of students to seek to learn from more than one teacher. The anxiety of influence Arnolphe expresses here involves the fear that *his* will not be the only school his future wife will attend. In Arnolphe's view of education, then, the sole measure of pedagogical success is to be the only teacher the student listens to.

At the same time, as critic, Arnolphe can maintain his smug spectator status only so long as he *is* his pupil's only teacher. As soon as she begins taking lessons from someone else, Arnolphe's critical detachment from the spectacle of cuckoldry will collapse. It would seem, then, that as soon as there is more than one effective source of authority in a pedagogical system, it is impossible for the teacher-critic to remain masterful, objective, and external to the object of his criticism.

The question of criticism and its exteriority to spectacle is in fact an extremely complex one in the context of Molière's *School for Wives*, not only because the play casts Arnolphe in the role of critic of cuckolds that make a spectacle of themselves but also because the play itself was the object of criticism in no fewer than nine subsequent theatrical productions, two of them by Molière himself. Hardly had the play proven itself to be a success when rival troupes and roving journalists began to attack it both in print and on the stage. Through the existence of these critical comedies, we begin to suspect that not only can *teaching* serve as a source of humor, but there appears to be something funny about criticism as well.

An Obscene Article

The first of Molière's comic defenses of *L'Ecole des femmes*, entitled *Critique de l'Ecole des femmes*, is a mocking representation of his critics. It opens, as do many of today's critical polemics, with a discussion of the fashionable tendency to resort to obscure jargon and far-fetched puns. It soon turns out that among these pretentious neologisms is the strange word "obscénité," which is used by the *précieuse* Climène to denounce the scandalous suggestiveness of some of Agnes's seemingly innocent remarks. The example chosen by Climène takes place in the course of an oral examination administered by Arnolphe to Agnes on the subject of the unauthorized visit of young Horace, about which Arnolphe has just learned.

Arnolphe:	Now, besides all this talk, these tendernesses,
	Didn't he also give you some caresses?
Agnes:	Indeed he did! He took my hands and arms
	And kissed and kissed them with unending charms.
Arnolphe:	Agnes, was there anything else he took?
	(*Seeing her taken aback*)
	Ouf!
Agnes:	Well, he . . .
Arnolphe:	What?
Agnes:	Took . . .
Arnolphe:	Augh!
Agnes:	My . . .[2]
Arnolphe:	Well?
Agnes:	Now look.
	I'm sure you will be angry. I don't dare.
Arnolphe:	No.
Agnes:	Yes.
Arnolphe:	Good lord, no.
Agnes:	Promise me, then, swear.
Arnolphe:	I swear.
Agnes:	He took . . . You'll be mad, I know you.
Arnolphe:	No.

Agnes: Yes.
Arnolphe: No, no. Damn it, what an ado!
                What did he take?
Agnes: He . . .
Arnolphe (aside):   I'm in agony.
Agnes: He took my ribbon that you'd given me.
                I couldn't help it, he insisted so.
Arnolphe (sigh of relief): All right, the ribbon. But I want to know
                If kiss your arms is all he ever did.
Agnes: What? Are there other things?

                                              (2.5; TM)

The teacher, here, is testing his pupil to make sure that she has not learned anything in his absence. The hesitations of the pupil all seem to the examiner to be signs that she has learned what he does not want her to know. While she only knows *that* she is being censured, he interprets her embarrassment to mean that she knows *what* she is being censured *for*. The farther the examination procedes, the closer the examiner comes to telling her what he does not want her to know—telling her, at least, that there are things he is not telling her.

In the discussion of this passage in the *Critique*, Climène views the ellipses after "he took my . . . " (*il m'a pris le . . .*) as a scandalous allusion, while Uranie defends its innocent literality.

> Climène: What! isn't modesty obviously wounded by what Agnes
>   says in the passage we are speaking of?
> Uranie: Not at all. She doesn't pronounce a single word that is not in
>   itself perfectly decent; and, if you want to hear something
>   else behind it, it's you who are making things dirty, not
>   Agnes; since all she's talking about is a ribbon taken from
>   her.
> Climène: Oh! ribbon all you want! but that *le* on which she pauses
>   wasn't put there for peanuts. Strange thoughts attach them-
>   selves to that *le*. That *le* is a furious scandal, and whatever
>   you may say, the insolence of that *le* is indefensible. (Scene
>   3;TM)

The discussants are thus divided between those with the apparent na-iveté of an Agnes and those with the overactive imagination of an Ar-nolphe. While there is something comical about the desire to censor something that is perceived only by those who wish to censor it, the Agnesian reading is clearly just as inadequate as the Arnolphian. Be-cause the play presents us not only with the suspended *le* but with Arnolphe's alarmed reaction to it, it is not possible for us not to know that strange thoughts can attach themselves to that *le*. Yet what is it of Agnes's, in fact, that Arnolphe is afraid Horace might have seized? No one obvious word offers itself to complete the thought in Arnolphe's horrified mind as he hears "Il m'a pris le . . . " He took my *what*? Perhaps the truly scandalous effect of this ellipsis lies neither in what it says nor in what it conceals but in the fact that while searching for something with which to fill the blank, the reader or spectator is forced to run mentally up and down the entire female anatomy. Represented both as an absence, a blank, and as a succession of dots, a plurality of small discrete points, female sexuality is both expressed and repressed through this impossibility of summing it up under a single article.

Arnolphe is here up against the problem faced by every parent: it is always either too soon or too late to teach children about sexuality. When the play begins, Arnolphe has been handling Agnes's sex education simply by attempting to insure that no learning will take place. Agnes is seen as a *tabula rasa*—a blank on which nothing is written unless some outside agency comes to write upon it. With the unexpected arrival of a more active tutor, Arnolphe is forced to change his pedagogical strategy. He now attempts to manipulate Agnes's dawning awareness of her own ignorance in such a way as to play up his superior knowledge and to cast doubt on his rival's good faith and on the value of what she has learned.

> *Arnolphe:* All this, Agnes, comes of your *innocence*.
> What's done is done. I've spoken. No offense.
> I *know* your lover wants but to deceive,
> To win your favor and then laugh and leave.
> *Agnes:* Oh, no! He told me twenty times and more.
> *Arnolphe:* You *do not know* what empty oaths he swore.
> But *learn this:* to accept caskets—or candies—
> And listen to the sweet talk of these dandies,
> Languidly acquiesce in their demands,
> And let them stir your heart and kiss your hands,
> This is a mortal sin, one of the worst.
>
> .   .   .   .
>
> *Agnes:* It's all, alas, so pleasant and so sweet!
> I marvel at the joy that all this brings
> And *I had never known* about such things.
> *Arnolphe:* Yes, there's great pleasure in this tenderness,
> In each nice word and in each sweet caress;
> But these have need of honor's discipline,
> And only marriage can remove the sin.
>
> (2.5; emphasis mine)

Arnolphe's challenge here is to give Agnes the impression that for every new thing she learns there is a danger of which she is still ignorant and from which his superior wisdom must save her. Yet it is impossible for Arnolphe to cast doubt on the meaning of Horace's pleasurable lessons without at the same time instructing Agnes in the possibility of deception and the manipulation of appearances. Agnes indeed soon proves herself to be a gifted student of the techniques of duplicity.

The Institutionalization of Ignorance

Satisfied that he has convinced Agnes that he has saved her from the road to perdition, Arnolphe decides to give his bride-to-be a full-fledged lesson in the virtue of wifely ignorance. And at this point where the paradoxes of teaching ignorance become most explicit, the tyrannical schoolmaster has recourse to the *book* as a pedagogical aid.

The book Arnolphe assigns to Agnes is entitled *The Maxims of Marriage; or, The Duties of the Married Woman*. In typical teacherly fashion, he asks the student to read the book through carefully and promises to explain it to her when she has finished. The book contains a list not of duties but of interdictions: a wife belongs to no one but her husband; she should dress up only for him, receive no visitors but his, accept presents from no man, and never seek to do any writing, to join any feminine social circles, to visit the gambling table, or to go on walks or picnics. In short, the book for the first time replaces the absence of teaching with the active teaching of the content of ignorance. In place of her former lack of knowledge, the pupil now possesses a knowledge of what she is not supposed to know.

It might perhaps be interesting to ask whether the pedagogical function of the book *in* the play is in any way parallel to the functioning of the play *as* book in its pedagogically oriented editions. For *The School for Wives*, like the rest of Molière's plays, is published in France in pocket editions copiously annotated for use in the high school classroom. Molière, indeed, is one of the central devices used by the French school system to teach children to become French. Through these schoolbook editions of French classics, the student absorbs along with the text a certain conception of what his cultural heritage is and what the study of classical texts involves. According to the Bordas edition of *L'Ecole de femmes*, however, this play is a relatively recent addition to the high school curriculum. The first two paragraphs of the discussion of the play are entitled respectively "Une pièce ignorée dans nos classes" ("A play that is unknown in our classrooms") and "Un chef d'oeuvre pourtant" ("A masterpiece nevertheless"). The editors explain the play's ostracism as follows: "The very theme of this comedy (the fear of cuckoldry), the boldness of the opinions and problems it raises, the salty Gallic vocabulary that comes up in the conversations between Arnolphe and Chrysalde, were all cause for alarm. But isn't this a form of narrow-mindedness that no longer corresponds to our time?"[3] The liberated attitudes of modern editors have thus made it possible to remedy French schoolchildren's ignorance of a play about teaching ignorance. But have all forms of ignorance been thereby dispelled?

What is striking about this particular play is precisely the fact that the female pupil in the play is of the same age as her high school readers. That this is a play about adult authority and adolescent sexuality seems to be completely glossed over by the editors. It is interesting to follow the techniques of avoidance manifested by the footnotes and commentaries that run the length of the play, sometimes taking up more room on the page than the play itself. Faced with that suggestive little *le* in "il m'a pris le . . . ," for example, the editor of the Larousse edition (whose professional title, I note, is "Censeur au lycée de Strasbourg") writes: "A slightly off-color double-entendre, which many contemporaries reproached Molière for, and which he made the mistake of denying in *The Critique of the School for Wives*."[4] The editor of the Bordas edition, on the other hand, doesn't see what all the fuss is about. "Much ink has been shed over these lines. They have been called scandalous. But all this is just a farcical device. Agnes's words are but a theatrical necessity designed to make us laugh at Arnolphe's stupidity. It is he who, through his questions and frowns, terrifies Agnes, prevents her from answering, and prolongs the suspense. Arnolphe is the one responsible for the ambiguity, which is well suited to his character. The whole scene, about which no one today would think of taking offense, is simply and openly funny, and the whole audience thinks of nothing but laughing" (Bordas, p. 71). Thus, either the ellipsis "il m'a pris le. . ." is an obscenity, or it is a mere joke, a "theatrical necessity." The idea that laughter and obscenity can go together is scrupulously avoided by those who are serving the text up to high school minds.

Yet behind the controversy of Agnes's *le* lies the whole question of female sexuality, which the controversy is in fact designed to occult. The editors' more direct reactions to Agnes's dawning sexuality are of two kinds: they drown it with erudition or they surround it with danger signs. When Agnes first describes her awakening desire, she says to Arnolphe:

He swore he loved me with a matchless passion
And said to me, in the most charming fashion,
Things which I found incomparably sweet
And every time I hear his voice repeat

Those things, I tingle deep inside me and I feel
I don't know what it is from head to heel.

(2.5; TM)

The last two lines render the French "Là-dedans remue / Certain je ne sais quoi dont je suis toute émue." In the Bordas edition, we find the following note on "je ne sais quoi": "Concerning the frequent use of 'je ne sais quoi' in the language of classicism, there is a very interesting study by Pierre-Henri Simon in his book, *The Garden and the Town*, 1962. This indeterminate expression expresses the irrational and mysterious sides of love, and this is why, according to Mr. Simon, it is the poets and novelists who deal with love that use the expression most frequently" (Bordas, p. 67). What this note does is to use knowledge provided by Mr. Simon to say "je ne sais quoi" about Agnes's "je ne sais quoi." The sexual component of Agnes's *non-savoir* is being occulted and defused through the asexual notions of irrationality and mystery.

But it is toward Agnes's so-called "pleasure principle" that the editors are most severe. When Agnes asks Arnolphe, "How can one chase away what gives such pleasure?" the editors ask, "Is this purely instinctive morality without its dangers?" (Bordas, p. 111). "Can Agnes understand that something pleasant might be morally forbidden?" (Larousse, p. 62). Both editors express relief that Agnes has not fallen into the hands of a lover whose intentions are less honorable than Horace's. "Judge Agnes's imprudence," exhorts the Larousse editor. "Show that Molière is also pointing out—for the benefit of the spectator—the danger Agnes would have been in if Horace had not been an honest man" (p. 104). Clearly, an honest man is required to protect unsuspecting girls against the dangers of their own liberation. In warning the young readers against learning too well the sexual lessons that Agnes seems to have learned, the editors of the school editions of *The School for Wives* thus unwittingly but inevitably find themselves playing a role similar to that of Arnolphe with respect to their students' sexual education. In repressing the nature of the lesson learned in the play, they, too, are in the business of teaching ignorance.

This similarity between the teachers *of* the text and the teacher *in* the text should give us pause. Could it be that the pedagogical enterprise as such is always constitutively a project of teaching ignorance? Are our ways of teaching students to ask *some* questions always correlative with our ways of teaching them *not to ask*—indeed, to be unconscious of—others? Does the educational system exist in order to promulgate knowledge, or is its main function rather to universalize a society's tacit agreement about what it has decided it does not and

cannot know? And is there some fundamental correlation between the
teaching of ignorance and the question of femininity?

Molière's "Feminism"

The question of education and the question of femininity are surprising-
ly interconnected in the seventeenth century. The burning feminist issue was not yet voting or working, but getting an education equal to a
man's. Treatises explaining at length the futility and even the danger of
educating women were long the order of the day. As Fénelon wrote in
his treatise on the education of women:

> Let us now take a look at what a woman needs to know. What are her
> jobs? She is in charge of her children's upbringing—the boys' up to a
> certain age and the girls' until they either marry or enter a convent.
> She must also oversee the conduct, morals, and service of the ser-
> vants, see to the household expenditures, and make sure all is done
> economically and honorably. . . .
>
> Women's knowledge, like men's, should be limited to what is
> useful for their functions; the difference in their tasks should lead to
> the difference in their studies. It is therefore necessary to restrict
> women's education to the things we have just mentioned.[5]

Because a woman was always under the protection of her father, her
husband, or the church, her education was confined to preparing her
for tasks in harmony with these forms of dependency.

Similarly, the governing purpose behind Arnolphe's pedagogical
enterprise was the fear that a learned wife would make him a cuckold.
Ignorance, it seemed, was the only way to ensure fidelity. What this
implies, paradoxically enough, is that education is an apprenticeship in
unfaithfulness. The fear of giving women an education equal to that of
men is clearly a fear that educated women will no longer remain faithful
to the needs of patriarchal society. Citing the case of Agrippa d'Au-
bigné, Gustave Fagnier writes in his study of women in the early seventeenth century:

> Even though he admired the women who in his time had achieved a
> scholarly reputation, Agrippa d'Aubigné declared to his daughters,
> who had consulted him on the question, that a more than ordinary
> education was, for middle-class girls like themselves, more of a disad-
> vantage than an advantage: the duties of married life and moth-
> erhood would take away its profit, for, as he graciously put it, "when
> the nightingale has her young, she sings no longer"; then, too, educa-

tion makes one vain, makes one neglect the household and disdain one's husband, blush at one's poverty, and it introduces discord into the home.[6]

The purpose of all education, then, was to foster the harmony of the patriarchal home.

So strong are the mechanisms for preserving the existing hierarchies of sex roles and social classes that the serious struggles of seventeenth-century women to cross the barriers of class and rank and achieve greater power and independence have come down to us through the distorting mirrors of the ridiculousness of *préciosité*. Yet behind the prudes, the coquettes, and the learned ladies, one can discern an attempt to avoid the bonds of the patriarchal marriage system, to free female sexuality from the constraints of annual childbirth and the double standard, to seek a female identity not exclusively defined in terms of men, and, in a gesture that seems almost post-Saussurian, to free language from its slavishly referential relation to a reality that might somehow thereby itself be escaped. The very extent to which these precious ladies are today not so much forgotten as they are *remembered as ridiculous* is a proof both of their power and of their impotence.[7] While Molière, in other plays, chooses to mock the *Précieuses* for their linguistic excesses and their self-delusions, this play in which no *précieuse* actually appears puts its finger on a much more serious cause for concern. It is precisely when Agnes argues with Arnolphe—clearly and without periphrasis—as *a subject who knows what she wants* that Arnolphe compares her to a *Précieuse*: "Just hear how this bitch argues and replies. Damn it! Would a *précieuse* say any more?" (5.4; TM)

It is interesting to note that in the updated Larousse edition of *L'Ecole des femmes,* one of the questions proposed as a discussion topic to the students is "Was Molière a feminist?" (p. 142). It is even more interesting to note that the answer is already tucked away in the presentational material that precedes the play: "We should recognize that Molière, who, in this play, shows himself to be a feminist, has sided for the education of women and for the liberalization of morals and religion" (p. 18). The assertion of Molière's feminism has indeed become almost a commonplace of academic criticism. As one of the pillars of seventeenth-century studies, Georges Mongrédien, puts it, "It is clear that *L'Ecole des femmes* is a feminist play—as indeed is *Les Précieuses ridicules* in a certain way—that [Molière] is militating for a girl's freedom to choose on the basis of love (Brunetière called it 'nature')."[8]

These notions of freedom of choice, love, and nature are all, of course, names for the granting of greater happiness to women without their acquiring greater power or independence and without any changes being made in the structure of society. By saying that Molière has written a feminist play, the schoolbook editors are not only saving him from the charge of misogyny; they are also offering their students a nonsubversive conception of what feminism is: something designed to make women happier with society as it is.

It can easily be seen that although Molière in *L'Ecole des femmes* is taking women's side in advocating their right to marry the man of their choice, he is not really suggesting that anything in the social *structure* be changed. Agnes's newly discovered sense of her own desire is quickly reintegrated into structures that are in no way disturbed by it. When Agnes takes the independent step of fleeing from Arnolphe to Horace, Horace can think of nothing better to do with her than to entrust her to the father-surrogate Arnolphe, unaware that he is the very rival from whom she has just escaped. Agnes's final liberation from Arnolphe, indeed, occurs only through the fortuitous fact that her long-lost father has arranged with Horace's father that the two young people should marry. The happy ending is decreed by the same kind of paternal authority as that represented by Arnolphe. The liberation of the woman here occurs merely as a change of fathers. Agnes will "belong" to Horace no less surely, although more willingly, than she would have "belonged" to Arnolphe. What has been seen as Molière's feminism is actually a form of benevolent paternalism and not in any sense a plea for the reorganization of the relations between the sexes. Like all forms of liberalism, it is an attempt to change attitudes rather than structures.

And yet surely a play that so lucidly personifies and ridicules the excesses of patriarchal power cannot simply be located within phallocentric discourse. Molière's irony would seem to baffle any clear-cut inside/outside categorization. The play consistently undercuts the ideology to which it nevertheless still adheres. Can literature somehow escape or transform power structures by simultaneously espousing and subverting them? The question must be asked of all great literary demystifications: to what structure of authority does the critique of authority belong? This is perhaps *the* feminist question par excellence. For some help in dealing with it, we will now return to the more specifically pedagogical level of our inquiry.

How Agnes Learns

What, then, does Agnes learn in this School for Wives, and what do we learn from her about teaching? Of all the things that Arnolphe wants Agnes *not* to learn, it seems that writing is the object of his most violent suspicions. Not only is writing included in the book of don'ts for the married woman, but from the very beginning it is clear that in Arnolphe's mind feminine writing constitutes the husband's royal road to cuckoldry. "A woman who's a writer knows too much," he tells Chrysalde; "I mean that mine shall not be so sublime, and shall not even know what's meant by rhyme" (1.1). In the game of "corbillon," in which each contestant must answer the question "Qu'y met-on?" ("What goes into it?") with something that rhymes with *on*, Arnolphe hopes his wife will answer "une tarte à la crème." Her virginal innocence thus depends on her having absolutely no sense of an ending that rhymes with *on*. What Arnolphe wishes to exclude from Agnes's knowledge is play—here, the play of language for its own sake, the possibility that language could function otherwise than in strict obedience to the authority of proper meaning. Agnes indeed demonstrates her ignorance of wordplay when she answers the go-between's report that she has wounded the heart of young Horace by saying, "Did I drop something on him?" Yet when Arnolphe attempts to stop all commerce between the two young people, Agnes is able to come up with the idea of attaching a secret love letter to the stone she has been instructed by Arnolphe to toss at Horace. How has this naive literal reader so quickly learned the art of sending a double message? What teacher has made her into so skilled a wielder of ambiguity?

According to Horace, fatuously enough, that teacher is "love."

> Love is a great teacher, you must agree,
> Making us what we never thought to be
> And in a moment, under his direction,
> Our character can change its whole complexion.
> He breaks down even natural obstacles
> And seems to manage sudden miracles. . . .
> He makes the dullest soul agile and fit
> And gives the most naive its share of wit.
> That miracle has happened to Agnes. (3.4)

As an explanation of Agnes's ingenuity in hitting upon the paper and stone device, Horace personifies love as a master teacher. Yet it is not love alone that has made Agnes clever. It is the necessity of complying with the contradictory demands of *two* ardent teachers. As long as the first teacher's power remained absolute and unquestioned, Agnes remained ignorant and unimaginative. Her first acquaintance with her second teacher was not very promising, either. As Agnes describes it:

> Out on the balcony to get the air
> I saw, under those trees right over there
> A most attractive young man passing by
> Who bowed most humbly when he caught my eye.

And I, not wishing to be impolite,
Returned a deep bow, as was only right.
Promptly he makes another bow, and then,
I naturally bow to him again;
And since he then goes on to number three,
Without delay he gets a third from me.
He passes by, comes back . . . well, anyhow,
Each time he does he makes another bow,
And I, observing this most carefully,
Returned him every bow he made to me.
The fact is, if the light had not grown dim,
I would have gone on trading bows with him
Because I did not want to yield, and be
Inferior to him in courtesy.   (2.5)

If Arnolphe is a teacher of the "do as I say" school, Horace clearly
belongs to the school of "do as I do." This opposition between the
didactic and the mimetic is in fact the classical polarity into which teaching methods can be divided. From the moment there are two teachers at
work, however, they both resort to the method of telling Agnes that she
is somehow in the wrong. From Horace she learns of the wound her
eyes have inflicted, which she must cure by applying more of the evil as
its own remedy. From Arnolphe she learns that she must cleanse the sin
of Horace's caresses by marrying. When Arnolphe clarifies the point by
indicating that *he* is the one she must marry, she suddenly, for the first
time, learns to turn to rhetoric, to find a linguistic substitute, however
minimal, for the thought she realizes she must not say.

 Agnes: How happy I will be with him!
 Arnolphe: With whom?
 Agnes: With . . . h'm.
 Arnolphe: H'm? h'm is not my taste.
   In choosing a husband you're showing undue haste.
              (2.5; TM)

At the end of the scene, Agnes is still protesting the necessity of renouncing such a good-looking man, and Arnolphe, to end the discussion, says, "Enough, I am master. I speak, you obey." This, in its
simplest terms, is Arnolphe's conception of teaching. His pedagogical
aim is to apply and guarantee his own mastery: mastery over language,
over knowledge and ignorance, and over the types of outside influence
he will or will not permit. In Arnolphe's system, everything is divided
between mastery and cuckoldry, between univocal instructions and
treacherous ambiguity.

While Arnolphe says "I am your master," Horace says "I am your victim." The position of pseudo-weakness seems to work better than the position of absolute power, but it nevertheless takes the powerful pull of two contradictory systems of demands to shape Agnes into a fully intelligent subject—a writing subject. In learning to manipulate both writing and ambiguity, Agnes marks the destruction of *any* position of absolute mastery. Indeed, when Arnolphe learns of Agnes's letter, he exclaims: "Her writing has just about killed me" (3.5; TM). Let us now look at that letter in order to analyze the way it manifests its discovery of intelligence at the intersection of contradictory lessons.

> I want to write you, and I am at a loss how to set about it. I have thoughts that I would like you to know [J'ai des pensées que je désirerais que vous sussiez]; but I don't know how to go about telling them to you, and I mistrust my own words. As I am beginning to realize that I have always been kept in ignorance, I am afraid of putting down something that may not be right and saying more than I ought. Truly, I don't know what you've done to me; but I feel that I am mortally unhappy over what they're making me do to you, that it will be terribly hard for me to get along without you, and that I would be very glad to be yours. Perhaps it's a bad thing to say that; but anyway I can't help saying it, and I wish it could be done without its being wrong [Peut-être qu'il y a du mal à dire cela; mais enfin je ne puis m'empêcher de le dire, et je voudrais que cela se pût faire sans qu'il y en eût]. They keep telling me that all young men are deceivers, that I mustn't listen to them, and that everything you say to me is only to take advantage of me; but I assure you that I have not yet been able to imagine that of you, and I am so touched by your words that I cannot possibly believe they are lies. Tell me frankly what the truth is in all this; for after all, since there is no malice in me, you would be doing a terrible wrong if you deceive me, and I think I would die of sorrow. (3.4)

In many ways, this letter shows the simultaneity of liberation and repression. It is the only passage in the play written in prose. This stylistic change is felt as a liberation from the artifice of verse, but at the same time the letter is not given any line numbers, thus making it impossible to refer to the letter as one refers to the rest of the play. Editorial tradition treats the letter as if it does not count, while by that very exclusion giving the letter a special privilege. The letter is primarily an expression of Agnes's fear of being somehow in the wrong. The desire not to transgress any rule, even a grammatical one, leads to acrobatics of subordination on every level. Agnes's crucial discovery that she might not know what she is still ignorant of is accompanied by a generalized distrust of saying what she means. This love letter is less an expression of love than an inquiry into the conditions under which an expression of love might be possible.

Yet time and again this heavily self-censored letter has been viewed as the very voice of innocent nature. Horace rhapsodizes:

> All that was in her heart, her hand has penned,
> But that in touching terms of kindliness,
> Of simple innocence and tenderness.
> In short, just the way I'm speaking of,
> Nature expresses the first pangs of love. (3.4)

And the editor of Larousse edition instructs his students to "analyze the freshness and spontaneity of the feelings expressed in this letter" (p. 80). This tendency to view Agnes's self-censorship as spontaneous and natural would indicate that, for Horace and for the Censor from Strasbourg, the desire not to displease is an innate component of women's nature.

Contradiction; or, The Subject of Teaching

We have thus come to a paradoxical set of conclusions about the nature of the pedagogical process. Learning seems to take place most rapidly when the student must respond to the contradiction between *two* teachers. And what the student learns in the process is both the power of ambiguity and the non-innocence of ignorance. It could be objected, however, that while the efficacy of contradiction-as-teacher may be demonstrable in the burlesque world of tyrannical cuckolds and ingenious ingenues, not every pedagogue is as repressive as an Arnolphe. What if the schema were reversed, for example, and the teacher, instead of saying "I am master," should choose to say "I am ignorant"?

If, as Neil Hertz would have it, the allusion to Socrates is characteristic of "the earnest moment in teachers' imaginings of themselves,"[9] it would seem that we have now begun speaking in earnest. It is therefore all the more astonishing to discover the very same conjunction of love, writing, and pedagogical rivalry as the mainspring of the Socratic dialogue itself, as we find it exemplified in Plato's *Phaedrus*, which can indeed be read as one of the most fundamental of Western treatises on teaching.

The dialogue begins on a street in Athens, where Socrates runs into the handsome Phaedrus, fresh from a lesson with his master, Lysias. It seems that Lysias has written a speech demonstrating that one should yield rather to a nonlover than to a lover (isn't this precisely what Arnolphe is trying to convince Agnes of?), and that Phaedrus is now heading for the fields in order to practice reciting it. Socrates, contrary to his usual habits, is lured out of the city by the promise of hearing the words of this rival teacher. Inspired by the subject and by the fair interlocutor, Socrates, after hearing Lysias' discourse, launches into two contradictory speeches of his own on love, then goes on to try to teach Phaedrus what effective teaching ought to be. A crux of the Socratic view of teaching is his apparent preference for direct speech over writing. The man who has real knowledge to impart "will not, when he's in earnest, resort to a written form . . . , using words which are unable either to argue in their own defense when attacked or to fulfill the role of a teacher in presenting the truth. . . . Far more noble and splendid is the serious pursuit of the dialectician, who finds a congenial soul and then proceeds with true knowledge to plant and sow in it words which are able to help themselves and help him who planted them; words which will not be unproductive, for they can transmit their seed to other natures and cause the growth of fresh words in them."[10] What is odd about this law of living dialectical teaching is that Socrates refuses to abide by it in the opening lines of the dialogue. When Phaedrus offers to recite Lysias' speech from memory, Socrates replies, "Good, good, dear boy, if you will start out by showing me what you have under your cloak in your left hand. As a matter of fact, I'd guess that you're clutching the very speech. If that's the case, please realize that though I'm very fond of you, *when we have Lysias right here,* I have no intention of lending you my ears to practice on" (p. 5; emphasis mine). While Socrates is profiting from the fact that Lysias' written words cannot defend themselves aloud, he nevertheless grants them greater authority than he does to Lysias' supposedly more legitimate seed-carrier, Phaedrus himself. The proponent of spoken dialectic has thus been prompted to deny the power of the written word only after he has first been seduced out of himself precisely by the power of the written word. The devaluation of writing that has, according to Jacques Derrida, structured the whole of Western thought can thus be seen as a mere tactical move in a game of pedagogical rivalry.

Before Socrates and Lysias come to look too much like Horace and Arnolphe, it might be well to analyze the two texts with respect to the project—expressly undertaken by both Arnolphe and Socrates—of teaching nothing but ignorance. Up to now we have been viewing the teaching of ignorance in a purely negative light, as a repressive method of instructing the student *not to know.* What Socrates seeks, on the other hand, is to teach the student *that he does not know.* To teach ignorance is, for Socrates, to teach to *un*-know, to become conscious of the fact that what one thinks is knowledge is really an array of received ideas, prejudices, and opinions—a way of *not* knowing that one does not know.

"Most people are unaware that they do not know" (p. 16.) "I am not teaching . . . anything, but all I do is question."[11] "I know only that I am ignorant."

Plato's challenge as a writer and a student was to cast an igno-ramus in the role of *sujet supposé savoir*. The philosophical debate over "how far Socrates was serious about his ignorance," as Kierkegaard puts it,[12] arises out of the contradiction between Plato's transferential fantasy of the teacher as subject presumed to know and the content and method of that teacher's teaching, namely, the constant profession of ignorance. Because we see Socrates only through the eyes of Plato's transference, we will never really know whether or not he was "se-rious" about his ignorance. But the dynamism of the Socratic dialogue in a sense makes the question irrelevant. For if the ideal pedagogical cli-mate, in the *Phaedrus* as well as in the *School for Wives*, is one in which the conflicts and contradictions *between* teachers serve as the springboard for learning, then learning does not result from a personifiable cause. Whether the teacher professes to be in possession of knowledge or of ignorance, the student in effect learns from what the teacher is not in possession of.

To retain the plurality of forces and desires within a structure that would displace the One-ness of individual mastery could perhaps be labeled a feminization of authority. For just as Agnes's *le* cannot desig-nate any single organ as the graspable center of female sexuality, and just as the existence of more than one sex problematizes the universality of any human subject of knowledge, so contradiction suspends and questions the centering of Western pedagogical paradigms around the single authoritative teacher. In this sense, paradoxically enough, it could be said that Plato's belief in Socrates' pedagogical mastery is an attempt to repress the inherent "feminism" of Socrates' ignorance. And it is out of this repression of Socrates' feminism that Western pedagogy springs. The question of education, in both Molière and Plato, is the question not of how to transmit but of how to *suspend* knowledge. That question can be understood in both a positive and a negative sense. In a negative sense, not knowing results from repression, whether con-scious or unconscious. Such negative ignorance may be the necessary by-product—or even the precondition—of any education whatsoever. But positive ignorance, the pursuit of what is forever in the act of escap-ing, the inhabiting of that space where knowledge becomes the obstacle to knowing—*that* is the pedagogical imperative we can neither fulfill nor disobey.

III

POETIC DIFFERENCES

9

Strange Fits

Poe and Wordsworth on the Nature of Poetic Language

No two discussions of poetry could at first sight appear more different than Wordsworth's "Preface to the *Lyrical Ballads*" and Poe's "Philosophy of Composition."[1] The first has been read as an important Romantic manifesto, sometimes inconsistent, sometimes dated, but always to be taken seriously. The second has been read as a theoretical spoof which, because it cannot be taken at face value, cannot be taken seriously at all. Both, however, can be read as complex texts in their own right—as texts whose very complexities tell us a great deal about the nature of poetic language. I would like to suggest here some directions for such a reading, first by examining the rhetorical slipperiness of each theoretical text, then by invoking for each a poem—Wordsworth's "Strange Fits of Passion" and Poe's "The Raven"—that both exemplifies and undermines the neatness of the explicit theory.

Despite their differences, Poe and Wordsworth do in fact agree on one thing: that the object of poetry is to produce pleasure:

Wordsworth:
The first Volume of these Poems has already been submitted to general perusal. It was published, as an experiment, which, I hoped, might be of some use to ascertain, how far, by fitting to metrical arrangement a selection of the real language of men in a state of vivid sensation, that sort of pleasure and that quantity of pleasure may be imparted, which a Poet may rationally endeavor to impart. (P. 69)

Poe:
Beauty is the sole legitimate province of the poem. . . . That pleasure which is at once the most intense, the most elevating, and the most

pure, is, I believe, found in the contemplation of the beautiful. (P. 1082)

The nature of the pleasure in question, however, is, in both cases, pushed to the edge of trauma: dead women, mad mothers, idiot boys, lugubrious birds—the poems are populated with images that are clearly situated beyond any simple notion of a pleasure principle. Poe indeed goes so far as to make his poem aim for the utmost "luxury of sorrow" to be obtained by "the human thirst for self-torture" (p. 1088). What is at stake in both cases would seem to have something to do with the beyond of pleasure, which for Freud was associated with two highly problematic and highly interesting notions: the repetition compulsion and the death instinct. Questions of repetition and death will indeed be central to our discussion both of Wordsworth and of Poe.

I will begin by outlining, somewhat reductively, the broadest possible differences between the two theoretical texts. Many of the differences are, of course, historical, and can be derived from the type of fashionable poetry each poet is writing *against*. Poe designs his poetics in opposition to the American tradition of long, sentimental, or didactic poetry associated with such figures as Longfellow or Bryant. Wordsworth is writing against the eighteenth-century British tradition of witty, polished, mock-heroic or rhetorically ornate verse associated with such names as Johnson, Pope, and Gray. But the poetic boundary lines each poet attempts to draw are perhaps of broader applicability, and their attempts can be read as exemplary versions of tensions inherent in the modern Western poetic project as such.

What, then, are the salient differences between these two theories of poetic language? In a well-known passage from the Preface, Wordsworth states that "Poetry is the spontaneous overflow of powerful feelings: it takes its origin from emotion recollected in tranquillity" (p. 85). Poe, on the other hand, writes of his method of composing "The Raven" that it was written backwards, beginning with a consideration of the desired *effect*. "It is my design to render it manifest that no one point in its composition is referrible either to accident or intuition—that the work proceeded, step by step, to its completion with the precise and rigid consequence of a mathematical problem" (p. 1081). Poe's poetic calculus leads him to choose an optimal length of about one hundred lines; then, after consideration of the desired effect and tone (beauty and sadness), he decides that the poem should be structured around a refrain ending in the most sonorous of letters, *o* and *r*. The syllable *-or* is thus the first element of the text of the poem to be written. "The sound of the refrain being thus determined," Poe goes on, "it became necessary to select a word embodying this sound, and at the same time in the fullest possible keeping with that melancholy which I had predetermined as the tone of the poem. In such a search it would have been absolutely impossible to overlook the word 'Nevermore.' In fact it was the very first which presented itself" (pp. 1083–84).

Spontaneous overflow versus calculation, emotion versus rigid consequence, feelings versus letters of the alphabet: a first comparison would lead us to see Wordsworth's poetry as granting primacy to the *signified* while Poe's grants primacy to the *signifier*. This distinction is borne out by the fact that while Wordsworth claims that the language of poetry should be indistinguishable from that of good prose, Poe aims to maximize the difference between prose and poetry, excluding for that reason the long poem from the canon of true poetry. But neither text presents its case as simply as it might appear.

For all his emphasis on emotion, Wordsworth is of course acutely conscious of the centrality of form to the poetic project. He describes the use of verse as a kind of contract made between form and expectation. Form itself constitutes a promise which Wordsworth then claims to have broken:

> It is supposed, that by the act of writing in verse an Author makes a formal engagement that he will gratify certain known habits of association; that he not only apprizes the Reader that certain classes of ideas and expressions will be found in his book, but that others will be carefully excluded. I will not take upon me to determine the exact import of the promise which by the act of writing in verse an Author, in the present day, makes to his reader; but I am certain, it will appear to many persons that I have not fulfilled the terms of an engagement thus voluntarily contracted. (P. 70)

Verse, then, is a contract made by form, a formal promise to include and to exclude certain classes of ideas. Wordsworth's violation of that contract comprises both inclusions and exclusions. He warns the reader that these shifts in boundary lines may produce "feelings of strangeness and awkwardness." Feelings of strangeness are, of course, often the subjects of the poems, as is the case with the poem to which we will later turn, "Strange Fits of Passion." That poem may well tell us something about the nature of strangeness of Wordsworth's poetics, but strangeness is not the only metapoetic expression glossed by the poem. For Wordsworth's first description of his experiment, in the opening paragraph of the Preface, speaks of the poems as *"fitting* to metrical arrangement a selection of the real language of men in a state of vivid sensation." The word "fit," which occurs several times in the preface,[2] thus in the poem takes on the double meaning of both uncontrolled overflow and formal containment. Interestingly, the word "fytt" is also a term for a medieval stanza form. As I will try to show, Wordsworth's entire preface can be read as an attempt to fit all the senses of the word "fit" together.

What does Wordsworth mean by "the real language of men"? In the 1798 "Advertisement to the *Lyrical Ballads*," Wordsworth had spoken of "the language of conversation in the middle and lower classes of society." These, then, are the "classes of ideas" that poetry had previously excluded. But Wordsworth includes them only to again exclude them; the substitution of the expression "the real language of men" for "the conversation of the middle and lower classes" acts out an erasure of "class," a gesture of dehistoricization and universalization. Poetic inclusions and exclusions clearly operate on more than one level at a time. Others are more qualified than I am to comment on Wordsworth's tendency to pastoralize away the historical reality of the rural along with the urban and the industrial, grounding "*human* nature" instead in a state of congruence with "the beautiful and permanent forms" of *external* Nature. Let it suffice here to suggest that, in the discussion that follows, the complex fate of the word "mechanical" may not be unconnected to a set of attitudes toward the industrial revolution.

There is one type of exclusion about which Wordsworth's preface is very clear—or at least it tries to be. The crucial exclusion for Wordsworth would seem to be the exclusion of personification.

> The reader will find that personifications of abstract ideas rarely occur in these volumes; and, I hope, are utterly rejected as an ordinary device to elevate the style, and raise it above prose. I have proposed to myself to imitate, and, as far as possible, to adopt the very language of men; and assuredly such personifications do not make any natural or regular part of that language. They are, indeed, a figure of speech occasionally prompted by passion, and I have made use of them as such; but I have endeavored utterly to reject them as a mechanical device of style. (P. 74)

The operative opposition here is the opposition between the "natural" and the "mechanical." Personifications, says Wordsworth, are not "natural," but rather "a mechanical device of style." But already there is an exception: they are sometimes naturally prompted by passion. If poetry is located at a point of vivid sensation, if it is defined as always being in some sense a strange fit of passion, then where does Wordsworth draw the line? Are personifications natural or mechanical? How natural is the natural language of passion?

Let us look further at Wordsworth's attempts to distinguish between the natural and the mechanical. Since his whole sense of value and originality seems to depend on his making that distinction clear, we would expect him to clarify it in the essay. One of the ways in which Wordsworth works the distinction over is by telling it as a story. He tells it twice, once as a story of degradation, and once as a story of recollection. The first is a history of abuse; the second, a history of recovery. What we will do is look closely at the rhetorical terms in which the two stories are told. They are both, of course, stories *of* rhetoric, but what we will analyze will be the rhetoric of the stories.

First, from the "Appendix on Poetic Diction," the history of abuse:

The earliest Poets of all nations generally wrote from passion excited by real events; they wrote *naturally*, and as men: feeling powerfully as they did, their language was daring, and figurative. In succeeding times, Poets, and men ambitious of the fame of Poets, perceiving the influence of such language, and desirous of producing the same effect, without having the same animating passion, set themselves to a *mechanical* adoption of those figures of speech, and made use of them, sometimes with propriety, but much more frequently applied them to feelings and ideas with which they had *no natural connection* whatsoever. A language was thus insensibly produced, differing materially from the real language of men in *any situation* [original emphasis]. The Reader or Hearer of this *distorted language* found himself in a perturbed and unusual state of mind: when affected by the genuine language of passion he had been in a perturbed and unusual state of mind also: in both cases he was willing that his common judgment and understanding should be laid asleep, and he had no instinctive and infallible perception of the true to make him reject the false. . . . This *distorted language* was received with admiration; and Poets, it is probable, who had before contented themselves for the most part with *misapplying* only expressions which at first had been dictated by real passion, *carried the abuse still further*, and introduced phrases composed apparently in the spirit of the original figurative language of passion, yet altogether of their own invention, and distinguished by various degrees of *wanton deviation* from good sense and *nature*. . . . In process of time metre became a symbol or promise of this unusual language, and whoever took upon him to write in metre, according as he possessed more or less of true poetic genius, introduced less or more of this *adulterated phraseology* into his compositions, and the true and false became so inseparably interwoven that the taste of men was gradually *perverted*; and this language was received as a *natural* language; and at length, by the influence of books upon men, did to a certain degree really become so. (Pp. 90–91; emphasis mine unless otherwise indicated)

In this history of abuse, the natural and the mechanical, the true and the false, become utterly indistinguishable. It becomes all the more necessary—but all the more difficult—to restore the boundary line. Each time Wordsworth attempts to do so, however, the distinction breaks down. The natural becomes unnatural, life imitates art, and mechanical inventions are mistaken for the natural language of passion.

Wordsworth's other developmental narrative is one that leads not to degradation but to amelioration. This time the story takes place in a temporality of the self, the temporality expressed by the juxtaposition of the two clauses: "Poetry is the spontaneous overflow of powerful feelings," and "it takes its origin from emotion recollected in tranquillity." For Wordsworth, in other words, the poet is a man who attempts to write in obedience to the classic example of the double bind: "be spontaneous." In an early paragraph in the preface, Wordsworth makes the double bind into a developmental narrative, in which the acrobatics of grammar—the sustained avoidance of any grammatical break—mimes the desire for seamless continuity. If the whole story can be told in one breath, Wordsworth implies, then nothing will be lost, the recuperation of the spontaneous will be complete.

> For all good poetry is the spontaneous overflow of powerful feelings: but though this be true, Poems to which any value can be attached, were never produced on any variety of subjects but by a man, who being possessed of more than usual organic sensibility, had also thought long and deeply. For our continued influxes of feeling are modified and directed by our thoughts, which are indeed the representatives of all our past feelings; and, as by contemplating the relation of these general representatives to each other we discover what is really important to men, so, by the repetition and continuance of this act, our feelings will be connected with important subjects, till at length, if we be originally possessed of much sensibility, such habits of mind will be produced, that, by obeying blindly and mechanically the impulses of those habits, we shall describe objects, and utter sentiments, of such a nature and in such connection with each other, that the understanding of the being to whom we address ourselves, if he be in a healthful state of association, must necessarily be in some degree enlightened, and his affections ameliorated. (P. 72)

The astonishing thing about this story is that it uses the word "mechanical"—which has been the name of a negative value everywhere else in the preface—as the height of poeticity. "Obeying blindly and mechanically the impulses of habits" was exactly what produced abuse and corruption in the other story, but here it produces health, enlightenment, and amelioration. What can be said about the relation between the two stories?

Both stories are designed to define and judge the relation between an original moment of feeling and utterance and its later repetition. Wordsworth's task is to distinguish between good repetition and degraded, hollow repetition. In describing his own creative process, he speaks of the art of developing habits that will lead to a "blind, mechanical" reproduction of the original emotion. In describing the poetic degradations he wants to condemn, he again speaks of a "mechanical" adoption of figures of speech. For Wordsworth's theory to stand, it is urgent for him to be able to distinguish between good and bad repetition. Yet the good and the bad are narrated in almost the same terms. Wordsworth again and again repeats the story of repetition, but is never able to draw a reliable dividing line. He can *affirm* good repetition, but he can't tell a story that will sufficiently distinguish it from bad. What Wordsworth's essay shows is that talking about poetry involves one in an urgent and impossible search for that distinction, for a recipe for reliable blindness. This is not an inability to get it right, but rather the acting out of an insight into the nature of poetry and the poetic process. For what, indeed, is the problem in any modern theory of poetic language, if not the problem of articulating authenticity with conventionality, originality and continuity, freshness with what is recognizably "fit" to be called poetic?

While Wordsworth is thus attempting to instate the naturalness of "genuine" repetition, Poe would seem to be doing just the opposite: mechanical repetition is clearly in some sense what "The Raven" is all about. In turning to Poe, we can therefore expect some sort of inversely symmetrical plea for the poeticity of the mechanical, the empty, and the hollow. It is as though a talking bird were the perfect figure for the poetic parroting of personification that Wordsworth would like to leave behind. But before moving on to Poe, let us look at Wordsworth's "Strange Fits of Passion" as another inscription of the theories expounded by the preface.

It has already become clear in our discussion that the phrase "Strange Fit of Passion" can be read in at least two ways as a summary of Wordsworth's poetic project: poetry is a fit, an outburst, an overflow, of feeling;[3] and poetry is an attempt to fit, to arrange, feeling into form. The poem would seem to be about an example of an experience fit to be made into poetry:

Strange fits of passion have I known:
And I will dare to tell,

> But in the Lover's ear alone,
> What once to me befell.
>
> When she I loved looked every day
> Fresh as a rose in June,
> I to her cottage bent my way,
> Beneath an evening-moon.
>
> Upon the moon I fixed my eye,
> All over the wide lea;
> With quickening pace my horse drew nigh
> Those paths so dear to me.
>
> And now we reached the orchard-plot;
> And, as we climbed the hill,
> The sinking moon to Lucy's cot
> Came near, and nearer still.
>
> In one of those sweet dreams I slept,
> Kind Nature's gentlest boon!
> And all the while my eyes I kept
> On the descending moon.
>
> My horse moved on; hoof after hoof
> He raised, and never stopped:
> When down behind the cottage roof,
> At once, the bright moon dropped.
>
> What fond and wayward thoughts will slide
> Into a lover's head!
> 'O mercy!' to myself I cried,
> 'If Lucy should be dead!'

The lover's alarm at his wayward thought indicates that he does not know what put it into his head, that he sees no connection between that thought and any part of his waking or dreaming life. The obvious connection the poem invites us to make is between the moon dropping and Lucy dying. But in the poem, that connection is elided, replaced by a mere discontinuity. That connection can in fact be made only in a world that admits the possibility of personification. The moon must be seeable as a correlative, a personification of Lucy.[4] And the hiatus marks the spot where that possibility is denied. The strange fit depicted in the poem can in some sense be read, therefore, as the revenge of personification, the return of a poetic principle that Wordsworth had attempted to exclude. The strangeness of the passion arises from the poem's uncanny encounter with what the theory that produced it had repressed.[5] Indeed, this is perhaps why the *Lyrical Ballads* are so full of ghosts and haunting presences. It is as though poetry could not do without the figures of half-aliveness that the use of personification provides. Or perhaps it is the other way around: that personification gives us conventionalized access to the boundary between life and death which Wordsworth, by repressing explicit personification, uncovers in a more disquieting way.[6]

It is doubtless no accident that a by-product of this fit is the death of a woman. In speaking to the lover's ear alone, Wordsworth is profoundly, as he says in the preface, "a man speaking to men." Even when Wordsworth speaks of or as a woman, the woman tends to be abused, mad, or dead. If Wordsworth's aim in these poems is to undo the abuse of dead poetic figures and recover a more natural language, he seems to have transferred the abuse from personifications to persons.

Poe makes the connection between poetry and dead women even more explicit when he writes, "The death of a beautiful woman is, unquestionably, the most poetic topic in the world—and equally is it beyond doubt that the lips best suited for such topic are those of a bereaved lover" (p. 1084). The work of poetry may well be the work of mourning, or of murder—the mourning and murder necessitated by language's hovering on the threshold between life and death, between pleasure and its beyond, between restorative and abusive repetition. But why, in Poe's case, does the male mourner require a talking bird to make his grief into a poem?

The raven, as Poe explains it in "The Philosophy of Composition," is chosen as a plausible vehicle for the repetition of the refrain—the word "nevermore." The bird is thus a figure for mechanical poetic repetition. The purveyor of the burden has to be a bird: the intentional relation to a signified is denied through the nonhuman repetition of a pure signifier. The word "nevermore," offered here as the most poetical of words, in fact crops up uncannily in Wordsworth's essay too as a distinguishing poetic mark. In differentiating between admirable and contemptible uses of "real language," Wordsworth juxtaposes two short stanzas, one by Dr. Johnson, the other from "Babes in the Wood." Johnson's contemptible stanza goes:

> I put my hat upon my head,
> And walked into the Strand,
> And there I met another man
> Whose hat was in his hand.

The admirable stanza reads:

These pretty Babes with hand in hand
Went wandering up and down;
But never more they saw the Man
Approaching from the Town.

It is hard to see what Wordsworth considers the key distinction between the two if it is *not* the expression "never more." In choosing to have the raven repeat the single word "nevermore," Poe may well have put his finger on something fundamental about the poetic function as a correlative, precisely, of loss.

If the word "nevermore" stands in Poe as a figure for poetic language as such, a number of theoretical implications can be drawn. Since the bird is not human, the word is proffered as a pure signifier, empty of human intentionality, a pure poetic cliché. The empty repetition of the word therefore dramatizes the theoretical priority of the signifier over the signified which Poe claimed when he said that he began the text of the poem with the letters *o* and *r*. The plot of "The Raven" can be read as the story of what happens when the signifier encounters a reader. For the narrator of the poem first introduces himself as a reader, not a lover—a reader of "quaint and curious forgotten lore." Poe's claim, in "The Philosophy of Composition," that the poem was written backwards (commencing with its *effect*) applies both to the poem and to the essay about it: both are depictions not of the writing but of the *reading* of "The Raven."

The poem's status as mechanical repetition is signified in another way as well. It would be hard to find a poem (except perhaps "Strange Fits of Passion") which is packed with more clichés than "The Raven": ember, remember, December, midnight, darkness, marble busts—all the bric-a-brac of poetic language is set out in jangling, alliterative trochees to hammer out a kind of ur-background of the gothic encounter. And the conversation begins in pure politeness: "Tell me what thy lordly name is," asks the speaker of the bird, and the bird says, "Nevermore."

The poem within the poem—the single word "nevermore"—has at this point finally been spoken and the reader sets out to interpret it. He begins by finding it obscure:

Much I marveled this ungainly fowl to hear discourse so plainly,
Though its answer little meaning—little relevancy bore.

Then he tries a little biographical criticism:

"Doubtless," said I, "what it utters is its only stock and store
Caught from some unhappy master whom unmerciful Disaster
Followed fast and followed faster. . . .

Sinking onto a velvet couch, the reader then turns to free association—"linking fancy unto fancy"—until the air grows denser and the reader sees the bird as a messenger of forgetfulness (psychoanalytic criticism), to which the Raven's "nevermore" comes as a contradiction. It is at this point that the reader begins to ask questions to which the expected "nevermore" comes as a ferociously desired and feared answer. The reader cannot leave the signifier alone. Reader-response criticism has set in. In this way, he writes his *own* story around the signifier, letting it seal the letter of his fate until, finally, it utterly incorporates him:

> And my soul from out that shadow that lies floating on the floor
> Shall be lifted—nevermore.

Sense has been made through the absorption of the subject by the signifier. The poem has sealed, without healing, the trauma of loss. What began as a signifier empty of subjectivity has become a container for the whole of the reader's soul. A poetry of the pure signifier is just as impossible to maintain as a poetry of the pure signified. Repetition engenders its own compulsion-to-sense. Poetry works *because* the signifier cannot remain empty—because, not in spite, of the mechanical nature of its artifice.

Paradoxically, then, Poe is writing a highly artificial poem that describes the signifier as an artifice that somehow captures the genuine. Yet generations of American readers have responded to it backwards: rejecting it for the artifice its own genuineness is demystifying. It cannot communicate its insight about how poems work if it does not work as a poem. Yet if the poem worked better, it would not carry the insight it carries.

Wordsworth and Poe are thus telling symmetrically inverse stories about the nature of poetic language. Wordsworth attempts to prevent the poetic figure from losing its natural passion, from repeating itself as an empty, mechanical device of style. But the formula for recollection in tranquillity involves just such a blind, mechanical repetition of the lost language. Poe writes a poem packed with clichés in order to show that those clichés cannot succeed in remaining empty, that there is also a natural passion involved in repetition, that the mechanical is of a piece with the profoundest pain. Yet the poem's very success in embodying its message entails its failure to make it true. If it were possible to differentiate clearly between the mechanical and the passionate, between the empty and the full, between the fit and the fit, between "real" language and "adulterated phraseology," there would probably be no need for extensive treatises on the nature of poetic language. But there would also, no doubt, be no need for poetry.

10

Disfiguring Poetic Language

Baudelaire's prose poems can often be read as ironic reflections on the nature of poetic language as such.[1] Yet their way of repeating and transforming traditional *topoi* is sometimes unaccountably violent. Why are Baudelaire's rewritings of poetic figures so frequently poems of disfigurement? Is this a mere symptom of Baudelaire's disturbed psyche, or is there perhaps some fundamental link between figure and violence?

While the cutting force of rhetoric as persuasion has long been recognized, the conception of rhetoric as a system of tropes has always appeared much more static and benign. What I intend to analyze here is the way in which two of Baudelaire's prose poems not only displace certain traditional poetic figures but also dramatize, in their very plot and framework, the structure and functioning of figure as such.

Let Them Eat Cake

The first of the two poems, "Le Gâteau," begins with a self-consciously stereotypical lyric description of alpine felicity, which is soon subverted by the intrusion of the "real" world of human ferocity. The poem is worth quoting in its entirety.

Le Gâteau

Je voyageais. Le paysage au milieu duquel j'étais placé était d'une grandeur et d'une noblesse irrésistibles. Il en passa sans doute en ce moment quelque chose dans mon âme. Mes pensées voltigeaient avec une légèreté égale à celle de l'atmosphère; les passions vulgaires, telles que la haine et l'amour profane, m'apparaissaient maintenant aussi éloignées que les nuées qui défilaient au fond des abîmes sous mes pieds; mon âme me semblait aussi vaste et aussi pure que la coupole du ciel dont j'étais enveloppé; le souvenir des choses terrestres n'arrivait à mon coeur qu'affaibli et dimimué, comme le son de la clochette des bestiaux imperceptibles qui paissaient loin, bien loin, sur le versant d'une autre montagne. Sur le petit lac immobile, noir de son immense profondeur, passait quelquefois l'ombre d'un nuage, comme le reflet du manteau d'un géant aérien volant à travers le ciel. Et je me souviens que cette sensation solennelle et rare, causée par un grand mouvement parfaitement silencieux, me remplissait d'une joie mêlée de peur. Bref, je me sentais, grâce à l'enthousiasmante beauté dont j'étais environné, en parfaite paix avec moi-même et avec l'univers; je crois même que, dans ma parfaite béatitude et dans mon total oubli de tout le mal terrestre, j'en étais venu à ne plus trouver si ridicules les journaux qui prétendent que l'homme est né bon; — quand, la matière incurable renouvelant ses exigences, je songeai à réparer la fatigue et à soulager l'appétit causés par une si longue ascension. Je tirai de ma poche un gros morceau de pain, une tasse de cuir et un flacon d'un certain élixir que les pharmaciens vendaient dans ce temps-là aux touristes pour le mêler à l'occasion avec de l'eau de neige.

Je découpais tranquillement mon pain, quand un bruit très léger me fit lever les yeux. Devant moi se tenait un petit être déguenillé, noir, ébouriffé, dont les yeux creux, farouches et comme suppliants, dévoraient le morceau de pain. Et je l'entendis soupirer, d'une voix basse et rauque, le mot: *gâteau!* Je ne pus m'empêcher de rire en entendant l'appellation dont il voulait bien honorer mon pain presque blanc, et j'en coupai pour lui une belle tranche que je lui offris. Lentement il se rapprocha, ne quittant pas des yeux l'objet de sa convoitise; puis, happant le morceau avec sa main, se recula vivement, comme s'il eût craint que mon offre ne fût pas sincère ou que je m'en repentisse déjà.

Mais au même instant il fut culbuté par un autre petit sauvage, sorti je ne sais d'où, et si parfaitement semblable au premier qu'on aurait pu le prendre pour son frère jumeau. Ensemble ils roulèrent sur le sol, se disputant la précieuse proie, aucun n'en voulant sans doute sacrifier la moitié pour son frère. Le premier, exaspéré, empoigna le second par les cheveux; celui-ci lui saisit l'oreille avec les dents, et en cracha un petit morceau sanglant avec un superbe juron patois. Le légitime propriétaire du gâteau essaya d'enfoncer ses petites griffes dans les yeux de l'usurpateur; à son tour celui-ci appliqua toutes ses forces à étrangler son adversaire d'une main, pendant que de l'autre, il tâchait de glisser dans sa poche le prix du combat. Mais, ravivé par le désespoir, le vaincu se redressa et fit rouler le vainqueur par terre d'un coup de tête dans l'estomac. A quoi bon décrire une lutte hideuse qui dura en vérité plus longtemps que leurs forces enfantines ne semblaient le promettre? Le gâteau voyageait de main en main et changeait de poche à chaque instant; mais, hélas! il changeait aussi de volume, et lorsque enfin, exténués, haletants, sanglants, ils s'arrêtèrent par impossibilité de continuer, il n'y avait plus, à vrai dire, aucun sujet de bataille; le morceau de pain avait disparu, et il était éparpillé en miettes semblables aux grains de sable auxquels il était mêlé.

Ce spectacle m'avait embrumé le paysage, et la joie calme où s'ébaudissait mon âme avant d'avoir vu ces petits hommes avait totalement disparu; j'en restai triste assez longtemps, me répétant sans cesse: "Il y a donc un pays superbe où le pain s'appelle du *gâteau*, friandise si rare qu'elle suffit pour engendrer une guerre parfaitement fratricide!"[2]

The Cake

I was traveling. The landscape in which I stood possessed an irresistible grandeur and nobility, some of which no doubt at that moment passed into my soul. My thoughts flitted about with a lightness equal to that of the atmosphere; vulgar passions like hate and profane love seemed to me now as far away as the clouds that filed across the abysses beneath my feet; my soul seemed to me as vast and pure as the cupola of the sky that enveloped me; the memory of terrestrial matters reached my heart greatly diminished and muffled, like the sound of the bells of the imperceptible flocks grazing far, far away, on the slope of another mountain. On the small still lake, black with its immense depth, there passed now and then the shadow of a cloud, like the reflection of the cloak of an aerial giant flying through the sky. And I remember that the solemn, rare sensation caused by this vast, perfectly silent motion filled me with a joy mixed with fear. In short, thus enthused by the beauty that surrounded me, I felt at perfect peace with myself and the universe; I even think that, in my perfect beatitude and total obliviousness to all earthly evil, I had come to the point where I no longer found so ridiculous those tracts that claim that man is born good—when, incurable matter renewing its demands, I gave thought to repairing the fatigue and appeasing the appetite caused by such a long ascent. I drew out of my pocket a thick slice of bread, a leather cup, and a flask of a certain elixir that pharmacists used to sell to tourists, to be mixed with water from melted snow whenever the need arose.

I was calmly cutting up my bread when a very faint sound made me raise my eyes. Before me stood a small, dark, tattered, disheveled creature whose hollow, wild, and seemingly beseeching eyes were devouring the piece of bread. And I heard him sigh, in a hoarse low voice, the word *cake*. I couldn't help laughing when I heard the appellation with which he deigned to honor my nearly white bread, and I sliced off a nice piece and offered it to him. Slowly he approached, never taking his eyes off the object he coveted; then, snatching the slice with his hand, he leaped back as though he feared that my offer had not been sincere or that I already regretted it.

But at that very instant he was jumped by another little savage, who had appeared out of nowhere, and who was so exactly like the first that one could have taken them for twins. Together they rolled on the ground, fighting over their precious prey, neither one willing to sacrifice half for his brother. The first, exasperated, grabbed the second by the hair; the latter sank his teeth into the former's ear, and spit out a bloody piece of it with a superb provincial expletive. The legitimate proprietor of the cake tried to dig his little claws into the eyes of the usurper; the latter in turn used all his strength to strangle his opponent with one hand while he tried to slip the prize of the fight into his pocket with the other. But, revived by despair, the loser got up and knocked the winner to the ground by smashing him in the stomach with his head. What good would it do to describe a hideous struggle that lasted in truth much longer than one would have expected from their childish powers? The cake traveled from hand to hand and changed pockets once a minute; but alas! it also changed size; and when at last, exhausted, panting, and bleeding, they stopped out of an inability to continue, there no longer existed, to tell the truth, any object of battle; the piece of bread had disappeared, and the crumbs strewn about resembled the grains of sand with which they were mixed.

This spectacle had clouded the landscape for me, and the calm joy in which my soul had delighted before I saw these little men had totally disappeared. I remained saddened for quite a while, repeating over and over: "There is thus a superb country where bread is called *cake*, a delicacy so rare that it suffices to start a perfectly fratricidal war!"

In the first part of the poem, a state of sublime exaltation is expressed in terms of the perfect correspondence or equivalence between the narrator's inner nature ("my soul") and the surrounding outer nature ("the landscape"). His thoughts and the atmosphere have an "equal" lightness; his soul is as vast and pure as the sky. The first metaphor, then, is an equation between the soul and the scene:

soul = landscape

This equivalence between soul and landscape has as its desired meaning the hyperbolic state of sublime peace felt by the narrator:

(soul = landscape) = perfect peace

In the second part of the poem, an equation is set up between the two little savages who are "exactly alike":

$$savage_1 = savage_2$$

But in this case, instead of a sublime peace, the metaphor engenders a fratricidal war between the two terms, the "legitimate proprietor" or *proper* meaning and the "usurper" or *figurative* meaning. Here, it is the *cake*, a hyperbole for "bread," that functions as the metaphor's meaning—the "object of battle," the "prize of the fight":

$$(savage_1 = savage_2) = perfectly\ fraticidal\ war$$

The equations established in the two parts of the poem appear in themselves to be flawless, yet the state of perfect equivalence contains in both cases the principle of its own destruction. In the case of lyric beatitude, the sublime equivalence between soul and scenery through which terrestrial considerations are forgotten is attained by an act of ascension which brings about the fatigue and appetite that will dissipate the ecstasy. The act of eating is then the literalization of the ingestion of the sublime ("The landscape . . . possessed an irresistible grandeur and nobility, some of which . . . passed into my soul"), indicating that the state of sublime beatitude rests on the possibility of living on air, of becoming truly equal to the inanimate:

$$(soul = landscape) = perfect\ peace \rightarrow sublimation\ of\ the\ subject$$

In the second part, the two equivalent terms, distinguished only by the moment of their appearance, can go on fighting over their hyperbolic object only until it becomes equal to the grains of sand among which it is scattered:

$$(savage_1 = savage_2) = perfect\ war \rightarrow disappearance\ of\ the\ object$$

It can easily be seen that the "I" in the first part of the poem plays exactly the same role as the "cake" in the second part—the role of the meaning or value-object around which the metaphor is built. The similarity is reinforced by the repetition of the verb *to travel*: the poem begins, "I was traveling," and later, "the cake traveled from hand to hand." Through this isomorphic relation between the "I" and the "cake," between the structure of jubilant resemblance (soul = landscape) and the structure of fratricidal resemblance (proprietor = usurper), the two antithetical parts of the poem have thus become metaphors of each other:

[(soul = landscape) = peace → sublimation] = [(savage$_1$ = savage$_2$) = war → disappearance]

Lyric beatitude, in other words, is the very image of realist ferocity. Both are engendered by the same metaphorical structure, which thus possesses the capacity both to exalt and to annihilate. Fraternal peace is structured like fratricidal war, and the sublime subjective internalization of inanimate nature becomes the mirror image of the erasing of all differences between bread and sand.

This is not to say that death is the final meaning of all metaphorical structures. For it is precisely out of the flaw or excess in an equation that meaning springs. Without hyperbole, the metaphorical energy in the poem would collapse. The meaning of the equivalence between the two savages depends on the maintaining of their *inequality* (the difference between the one that has the cake and the one that doesn't). The moment the cake disappears, the metaphor has no meaning. And yet it is precisely through the way in which the cake vanishes as the meaning of the struggle that the struggle emerges as the mirror image of the lyrical peace that prevailed in the beginning of the poem.

The equivalence between the "I" and the "cake," between fraternal exhilaration and fratricidal obliteration, between the sublime and the inanimate, between the first and the second parts of the poem, thus constitutes a deconstruction of the lyric illusions evoked in the first part. But since this deconstruction takes place precisely through the creation of equivalences, it can only demystify metaphor by participating in it. What Baudelaire's prose poem thus engenders as a problem for the understanding of metaphor is precisely the impossibility of finding a critical metalanguage that would not be enmeshed in the very metaphorical structures it attempts to comprehend. And if meaningful metaphor requires that its equations be flawed, then the metaphorical act of understanding metaphor can never even truly be in possession of the meaningfulness of its own hyperbolic aberrations.

A second poem, "Le Galant Tireur," goes even further in its unmasking of the mechanisms of figurative language. By italicizing the sentence "*je me figure que c'est vous,*" Baudelaire explicitly underlines this poem's status as a metafigural allegory.

Le Galant Tireur

Comme la voiture traversait le bois, il la fit arrêter dans le voisinage d'un tir, disant qu'il lui serait agréable de tirer quelques balles pour *tuer* le Temps. Tuer ce monstre-là, n'est-ce pas l'occupation la plus ordinaire et la plus légitime de chacun? —Et il offrit galamment la main à sa chère, délicieuse et exécrable femme, à cette mystérieuse femme à laquelle il doit tant de plaisirs, tant de douleurs, et peut-être aussi une grande partie de son génie.

Plusieurs balles frappèrent loin du but proposé; l'une d'elles s'enfonça même dans le plafond; et comme la charmante créature riait follement, se moquant de la maladresse de son époux, celui-ci se tourna brusquement vers elle, et lui dit: "Observez cette poupée, là-bas, à droite, qui porte le nez en l'air et qui a la mine si hautaine. Eh bien! cher ange, *je me figure que c'est vous.*" Et il ferma les yeux et il lâcha la détente. La poupée fut nettement décapitée.

Alors s'inclinant vers sa chère, sa délicieuse, son exécrable femme, son inévitable et impitoyable Muse, et lui baisant respectueusement la main, il ajouta: "Ah! mon cher ange, combien je vous remercie de mon adresse!"[3]

The Gallant Marksman

As the carriage was driving through the woods, he stopped it in the neighborhood of a shooting gallery, saying that he would enjoy firing off a couple of rounds in order to *kill* Time. Isn't the killing of that monster indeed the most ordinary and legitimate occupation of every man? And he gallantly offered his arm to his dear, delightful, execrable wife, to that mysterious woman to whom he owes so many pleasures, so many pains, and perhaps also a large part of his genius.

Several bullets landed far from the proposed target; one of them even lodged in the ceiling; and as the charming creature was laughing wildly, mocking her husband's bad aim [*maladresse*], the latter turned abruptly toward her and said, "Take a good look at that doll down there on the right with her nose in the air, looking so stuck up. Well, angel face, *I figure that that's you.*" And he closed his eyes and pulled the trigger. The doll was neatly decapitated.

Then, bowing toward his dear, delightful, execrable wife, his inevitable and pitiless Muse, he respectfully kissed her hand and added, "Ah! dear angel, how can I thank you for my aim [*adresse*]!"

Killing Time

As of the very first sentence, the question of figure—or the figure of the question—is raised typographically. In writing "to *kill* Time" instead of "to kill time," Baudelaire restores to a dead figure the original impact that has been lost through linguistic habit. The italics give back to the verb *to kill* all its literality, especially in this shooting-gallery context. Thus, paradoxically, it is through the verb *to kill* that the "dead" figure is resuscitated. But the figurality of the figure is also restored by the capital *T* of "Time," which increases the word's personification. On the one hand, then, there is an increase in literality; on the other, an increase in figurality. Some would call this a widening of the gap between figure and letter. But *where*, in fact, is the figure in this phrase? Is the figural space located between the literal and the figurative, or between a dead figure and a resuscitated one?

In the first case, the figure's effectiveness would result from what Jean Cohen has called "predicative impertinence":[4] the verb *to kill*, which can apply only to an animate being, is here associated with an abstraction, Time, whose meaning is, by association, modified. This, however, brings us to a paradox: the figure endows Time with life only in order to take it away again; Time is personified only to be killed. This paradox is even more subtle than it appears. For in making Time alternate between life and death, the figure "forgets" that there is no other name for such an alternation than, precisely, Time. The text's figural logic can thus be read as follows:

The figurative meaning of "Time"	1. The figure tries to kill time.
	2. In order to kill time, the figure grants it life by personifying it; but time is given life only so as to be killed.
The inscription of the figure	3. The figure thus turns on an alternation between life and death.
The literal meaning of "Time"	4. The name of such an alternation between life and death is *time*.
The figural paradox	5. Therefore, if the figure succeeded in eliminating time, it would eliminate the very alternation that alone makes it capable of eliminating time: the figure would eliminate the law that makes it function.
The figure's self-erasure	6. The figure must therefore "forget" the literal meaning of the word *time* in its attempt to kill time figuratively. And by the same token, it is the very *gap* between the literal and the figurative that is thus eliminated through this foreclosure of the literal meaning. In order to function, the figure *erases* the literal meaning with respect to which it is supposed to constitute itself as a *deviation*.

The gap between the literal and the figurative meanings of the word *time* is then but a mask for the figural work of forgetting, of erasing the gap, an operation that is carried out throught the foreclosure of the existence of the literal meaning. Figural space is not located *between* one meaning and another but *within* the very possibility of meaning.

Let us now turn to the second reading, according to which the figure is located not between the literal and the figurative but between a dead figure and a resuscitated figure, between "to kill time" and "to *kill* Time." If the figure of "killing time" is indeed dead, what can have killed it? The answer, of course, is time. The resuscitated figure, in which the effects of time *on* the figure are erased, thus effectively kills the time through which the figure had lost its freshness and "died": this figural resurrection is the very acting out of the sense of the resurrected figure, "to kill time." But the canceling out of the action of time *upon* the figure can only be achieved through the increased personification of the word *Time within* the figure. In other words, the time that acts *on* the figure can be killed only if the time to be killed *in* the figure is still alive.

But is this resuscitated figure the same as the one that died? Isn't it, rather, a parody of it? A parody created not only by the hyperbolic setting in which a man literally shoots in order to kill time, but also by the fact that the figure can resuscitate itself only by *playing with* its own death?

Whether one locates the figural operation in the relation between the literal and the figurative senses of the word *time* or between the dead figure and its reanimation, the figural functioning revealed is essentially the same. In the first case, we have shown that the gap between the literal and the figurative could be founded only upon its own erasure. In the second case, we have seen that the resuscitated figure could live only upon its own corpse. In both cases, fundamental presuppositions are dismantled in the process of arriving at the same paradoxical conclusion: the figure lives only through its own death. In each case the figure's effectiveness depends on the forgetting, erasing, or killing of its component parts. The figure carries its own death within it, not because it contains the seeds of its destruction, but because it is through the destruction of what founds it that it constitutes itself.

Decapitation

While Baudelaire's marksman begins by aiming his gun at Time, it is nevertheless not Time that he ends up shooting, but a doll—a doll whose figurative status is literally underlined by the text. "Take a good look at that doll down there on the right with her nose in the air, looking so stuck up. Well, angel face, *I figure that that's you*." The doll becomes the woman by means of a trope, a substitutive turn which is also drama-tized in the text ("the latter *turned* abruptly toward her"). The text would thus seem to illustrate the traditional conception of metaphor as the substitution of one term for another by means of resemblance (we as-sume that the doll with her nose in the air is being seen by the marks-man as similar to his wife).

But this resemblance between the doll and the woman, however vivid, is in fact but a visual screen over the more fundamental change of places that constitutes the figure. The doll becomes the woman not because she looks like the woman but because she takes her place—the place of her decapitation. The meaning of the figure, its signified, is not "woman" but "woman's decapitation." Yet this is precisely the signified the figure will never reach, since in order to *be* a figure it can decapitate but an effigy.[5] While the figure is *aimed* at the woman, it can *mean* only by missing its target. It is thus the figure itself that is decapitated, can never come to a head; it can only continue to aim toward a beheading that will never take place, since the beheading it points to is its own.

Let us now examine the relation between the two figures we have just analyzed: the figure "to *kill* Time" and the figure of the doll/wom-an's decapitation. There are, clearly, certain analogies between them. Like Time in the first figure, the doll, an inanimate object, takes on the status of an animate being in the act of standing for the woman. But the doll, like Time, is given life only in order to be shot, decapitated. In both cases, the figure goes from the axis animate/inanimate to the axis liv-ing/dead. And in both cases, the figure functions only through its own contradiction: Time, in order to be killed, must remain alive; the absence of the woman from the locus of her decapitation cuts the figure off from the meaning it is heading toward.

The two figures, then, like the two parts of the poem "The Cake," turn out to be metaphors of each other. But they are linked by something more than analogy: they are also spatially *contiguous* to each other, since they intersect on the spot where the bullet hits the doll. This spatial relation makes them stand as metonymies, not just as metaphors, of each other. For while the marksman is aiming first at Time and then at his wife, he nevertheless points his gun only at a doll: "to shoot the doll" thus metonymically means both "to kill time" and "to blow the wom-an's head off."

This apparent symmetry is nevertheless grounded in a fundamen-tal asymmetry: although the doll does stand as the place where the two figures substitute for each other, the second figure arises only because the goal of the first has been missed. "Several bullets landed far from the proposed target; one of them even lodged in the ceiling." In trying to kill time, the marksman was clearly aiming too high. But it is precisely because his wife makes fun of his *bad* aim that she becomes the aim, the goal, of the second figure. That is, the woman becomes the target of the second figure only because she stands as the *figure of the failure of the first figure*. The success of the figure of decapitation is inscribed upon the failure of the figure of killing time.

But if the doll signifies at once "Time" and "woman," isn't her decapitation a sign that the first figure, too, reaches its goal? The answer to this question remains suspended, since the correction of the marksman's aim requires the assistance of the figure of his impotence. The success of the figure "to kill Time" can be achieved only by means of the figure of its own failure.

In a sense, it could perhaps be said that *all* figures are figures of the failure of the figure "to kill Time." For what is time but a figure for our own deaths, that unfigurable source of all figure? As Michel Deguy has put it, "Death, whose reality is entirely metaphorical, sets life at a distance from itself; death is the very epitome of metaphor."[6]

Contradiction in Abeyance

Can it be said, then, that it is the essence of figure to be founded on its own contradiction? In his "Théorie de la figure," Jean Cohen indeed states that since "the principle of contradiction" is "the fundamental principle of logic and the norm that governs both language and metalanguage . . . the semantic rhetorical figures constitute so many violations of that fundamental principle."[7] Cohen's theory, however, goes on to assert that a figure, while it does violate the norm of noncontradiction, can become readable only through a process of decoding whose object is to correct that violation:

> Every figure entails a two-step process of decoding: the first is the perception of the anomaly, and the second is its *correction*, through an exploration of the paradigmatic field in which relations of resemblance, contiguity, etc., are created, in which one can find a signified capable of providing the expression with an *acceptable* semantic interpretation. . . . The figure is thus . . . articulated according to two perpendicular axes, the syntagmatic axis where the gap or deviation is established, and the paradigmatic axis where it is eliminated through a change in meaning. ("Théorie," p. 22; italics mine)

The figure Cohen chooses to illustrate this decoding is precisely a variant of our figure of "killing Time." It is a verse from *Athalie:* "pour réparer des ans l'irréparable outrage" ("to repair the irreparable insult of the years"). Cohen describes the "two-step mechanism" of his decoding as follows: (1) contradiction between "repair" and "irreparable"; (2) substitution of "seemingly repair" for "repair," which removes the contradiction (p. 21). It could be objected that the substitution of "seemingly repair" for "repair" is not the only *logical* possibility. Why not "seemingly irreparable" instead of "irreparable"? But that is beside the point. For can it not be said that in this play of substitutions it is contradiction itself that has been "seemingly repaired"? How can one maintain that the correct, or rather corrected, reading of this figure is "to seemingly repair the irreparable insult of the years"? And if the criterion for this substitution is its greater "acceptability," why should "seemingly repair" be more "acceptable" than "repair," when the figure is telling us that it is precisely the *irreparable* that is unacceptable? What is judged "false" by the laws of logic may indeed lie at the very heart of the laws of desire, according to which it is perhaps precisely the law of noncontradiction itself that is unacceptable.

If the figure does violate the logic of contradiction, it is not in order to call for a "corrective" reading that would bring it back to that logic, but rather to lead us into the domain of a different logic. The logic of figure is such that it makes the logic of contradiction dysfunction. It suspends the system of binary oppositions on which contradiction is based (presence vs. absence, animate vs. inanimate, life vs. death, reparable vs. irreparable), but without reducing these oppositions to the same. The gap described by such polarities remains as irreducible as it is undecidable, for while each pole can cross over to the other, it is not thereby totally erased. Time remains at once animate and inanimate, reparable and irreparable; the head remains at once severed and attached; the woman is both here and there, present and absent. The figure cannot be fixed on any one of its movements.

Just as the child in Freud's *Beyond the Pleasure Principle* enters into what Lacan calls the "symbolic order" by playing a game that consists of tossing a spool away and pulling it back again while pronouncing the syllables *fort-da* ("away-here"), so, too, the figure, through the detour of its doll, can only "play at jumping" over the contradiction by which it is constituted. As Lacan puts it:

> For the game of the cotton reel is the subject's answer to what the mother's absence has created on the frontier of his domain—the edge of his cradle—namely, a *ditch*, around which one can only play at jumping.
>
> This reel is not the mother reduced to a little ball by some magical game worthy of the Jivaros—it is a small part of the subject that detaches itself from him while still remaining his, still retained. This is the place to say, in imitation of Aristotle, that man thinks with his

object. It is with his object that the child leaps the frontiers of his domain.[8]

It is by leaping back and forth over contradiction, and not by substituting one thing for another, that the figure deploys the nets of the subject's desire.

But to return to the figure "to *kill* Time," *where*, exactly, are the "frontiers of its domain"? Doesn't the binary dysfunction that constitutes the figure amount to a shattering of the very boundaries of the figure, a disturbance of the opposition between inside and outside that would alone enable us to isolate the figural phenomenon? Is the word *time*, whose literal meaning is equivalent to the law that makes the figure function, inside or outside the figure it governs? Is the typographical resurrection of the figure ("to *kill* Time") being carried out *on* the figure or *in* the figure? What logic is the figure obeying if it thus constitutes itself through the principle of the uncertainty of its own frontiers?

The problem is clearly one of isolating the set of elements constitutive of the figure, which, forming a closed system, might be analyzed with nothing left over. Yet modern set theory would suggest that in this case no such set can exist. Just as "the set of all possible sets in a universe is not a set," the set of all signifiers in a signifying system can never be closed.

> One cannot put all the signifiers belonging to the same "family" in the same bag, and . . . when one tries to group them together, there is a split, an exclusion, through which *one* of the signifiers, which has become other, is carried outside, in such a way that the others can function as such. . . .
>
> The effect of what is thus excluded and detached is to "hold together" the set it is excluded from . . . and, in so doing, to give it a name; or at least to occupy the place from which the law of the name can function.[9]

In the set of elements that constitutes the figure "to *kill* Time," it is, as we have seen, the word *time* itself that finds itself excluded, crossed out, "forgotten," in order for the figure to function. The word *time* is thus at once inside and outside: inside, it stands as the figure's target; outside, it is the name of the alternation (life/death) that makes the figure function as such. In the second figure in the text, it is the woman who is both inside and out: inside as the target of decapitation, and outside as the Muse that guides the shot aright. In both cases, one of the elements in the figural set is at once outside, governing the figural operation, and inside, serving as the target of that operation. And hence, it is the very difference between inside and outside that the figural violence undoes.

To split so that what holds it together can leap out—such is the very law of figure. But if the frontiers of each particular figure are thus blown up by the law that installs them, what about the entire set of figures as such? Can "figurative language" ever constitute a closed object of analysis? If, as Fontanier would have it, the term *figure* first signified "the contours, traits, or external form of a man, animal, or palpable object";[10] if it is *figuratively* that the term comes to designate a rhetorical space—"a surface," as Genette defines it, "marked out by two lines: that of the present signifier and that of the absent signifier";[11] if the term *figure* is thus itself a figure, is it inside or outside the phenomenon it names? And if the set of all figures can be literally named only by a figure, where is the boundary line between figurative language and its other? This detachment of the figure "figure" from what is supposed to be the set of all figures, a detachment which allows it to fill the role of the name of the set so that the other elements can function as such, is precisely what prevents that set from constituting itself as a finite, definite, circumscribed object. By moving to the outside of the set, the word *figure* destroys the boundaries of the figural domain. Hence, if the law of figure dictates that the polarities constitutive of contradiction dysfunction, we can now see that such a law would end up dismantling and erasing *itself*, since it would in fact suspend the very difference between literal and figurative on which it is based.

The Other's Address

Figure, therefore, has always already begun: whenever we seek to isolate it, it has already invaded the ground we stand on. But if figure has always already begun, how can one be the originator of one's own rhetoric, the possessor of one's own figurative *adresse?* This is the question dramatized in the text's final paragraph.

In suspending itself between the failure of one figure and the success of the figure of that failure, "The Gallant Marksman" ultimately opens up *between* its two figures (*between* its first two paragraphs) the paradoxical space of a third figure, a figure to the second power, a figure of the figural operation itself. This figure of the functioning of figure is given an allegorical name in the third paragraph's "inevitable and pitiless Muse."

What, indeed, is a muse? According to the poem, she is that to which the marksman owes both his *"adresse"* and "a large part of his genius." And what is genius other than a gift for manipulating figure?

As the founder of Western poetics puts it: "The greatest thing by far is to have a command of metaphor. This alone cannot be imparted by another; it is the mark of genius" (Aristotle, *Poetics* 1459a). Yet here, it is precisely such genius that *does* seem to be imparted by another. It is not the marksman himself but the "inevitable and pitiless Muse"—both target and governing spirit, both sender and receiver of the bullet—that serves as the source of the marksman's *adresse*. And she does so because, by laughing, she had stood as the figure of his *maladresse*. While the marksman is thus aiming at his own bad aim, his success is a proof of his figural dispossession. The straighter he shoots, the more he gets his address *from* the very Muse his bullet is addressed to. It is thus from the Other that his genius must come, an Other that designates not a person but a place: the place of decapitation. For the woman becomes a Muse, the figure of the poet's *adresse*, only when she stands as the address—the destination—of the poet's bullet. She is a figure of figurative power only insofar as she is disfigured; she acquires her capital letter through her own decapitation. The Muse's capital letter, which allegorically severs her from herself, is also a sign that the severing has yet to occur, that her head remains potently on her shoulders. And yet that head, always already cut off by a cut that has not yet taken place, springs up out of the figure, never to return to a state prior to the cut, even if the cut, in the end, will never really reach it. An effective Muse is a Muse that is killed, not once, but over and over again; her power is to be both powerful and dead, present and absent, a severed and yet unsevered head. At the same time the woman becomes a Muse only by remaining absent from the place of her disfigurement, so that, in the final analysis, the marksman's address consists of *missing* the address he aims at.

The very notion of transitive action, of cause and effect, of acts and agents, is skewed by the two-way lines of figural force in which the Other, at once sender and receiver, is potent as sender only insofar as s/he is missed as receiver. Indeed, the decapitation which the marksman both succeeds and fails at turns out, unsettlingly enough, to be his own. For what has he done to correct his aim? "He closed his eyes and pulled the trigger. The doll was neatly decapitated." The lack of connection between the two sentences, the passive description of decapitation as an effect without an agent or cause, inscribes the marksman's *adresse* in a textual blank. At the moment of decapitation, it is the marksman's own head that is out of the game, and his blindness that somehow insures his good aim. Far from being the origin of his address, his head is rather the address the bullet is sent to. At the heart of the text and of the figure, the decapitated doll is thus literally a *blind spot*, not only because it constitutes the empty space in which the figures of time and woman exchange places, but because it designates the place of rhetorical substitution as a place of darkness, a focus of blindness: the mark is hit only because one remains blind to the law of one's own address. It is thus at the very moment the marksman appears to master figure that he is mastered *by* it. It is always the Other—Time or the Muse—that possesses the Capital.

In reading Baudelaire's two prose poems as allegories of figure, it has not been my intention to reduce all marital ambivalence or fratricidal rivalry to a matter of metaphor and metonymy, but rather to point out the co-implication of human violence and human figuration. If violence is structured like figure, and figure like violence, then the study of rhetoric can hardly remain a subsidiary, trivial matter. But, like violence, it will always be a matter that involves its analyst in greater and greater tangles of its own proliferation. In our search for a language capable of understanding figure, we have indeed not been immune to the law of the Other that robs the marksman of any possession of his marks. For when we speak of dead and resuscitated figures, of decapitated meanings and battle prizes, is it not always *from the figures themselves* that we derive our language? Whenever we try to comprehend figure, we find that we are already comprehended *by* it. We thus find ourselves in a position similar to that of the prospective hashish smoker who is told by Baudelaire: "Through a singular equivocation, . . . you will feel as though you are evaporating, and you will endow your pipe (in which you can feel yourself squatting, tamped down like tobacco) with a strange faculty for *smoking you*."[12] Is it not, indeed, precisely the law of figure to erase even the difference between subject and object, Same and Other, and to confer upon each text that strange faculty for *figuring us?*

11

Les Fleurs du Mal Armé

Some Reflections on Intertextuality

> Oui, le suspens de la Danse, crainte contradictoire ou souhait de voir
> trop et pas assez, exige un prolongement transparent.
> —Mallarmé

Contemporary discussions of intertextuality can be distinguished from
"source" studies in that the latter speak in terms of a transfer of property
("borrowing") while the former tend to speak in terms of misreading or
infiltration, that is, of violations of property. Whether such violations
occur in the oedipal rivalry between a specific text and its precursor
(Bloom's anxieties of influence) or whether they inhere in the immer-
sion of any text in the history of its language and literature (Kristeva's
paragrams, Riffaterre's hypograms), "intertextuality" designates the
multitude of ways a text has of not being self-contained, of being traversed by otherness. Such a conception of textuality arises out of two
main theoretical currents: (a) Freud's discovery of the unconscious as an
"other scene" that intrudes on conscious life in the form of dreams, slips
of the tongue, parapraxes, and the like; and (b) Saussure's discovery of
the haunting presence of proper names anagrammatically dispersed in
the writing of certain late Latin poets. These two discoveries have been
combined by Jacques Lacan into a conception of the "signifying chain"
that "insists" within the human subject in such a way that "the unconscious is structured like a language." One might say by analogy that for
modern theorists of intertextuality, the language of poetry is structured
like an unconscious. The integrity and intentional self-identity of the
individual text are put in question in ways that have nothing to do with
the concepts of originality and derivativeness, since the very notion of a
self-contained literary "property" is shown to be an illusion. When read

in its dynamic intertextuality, the text becomes differently energized, traversed by forces and desires that are invisible or unreadable to those who see it as an independent, homogeneous message unit, a totalizable collection of signifieds.

What happens, though, when a poet decides to transform the seemingly unconscious "anxiety of influence" into an explicit theme in his writing? Can the seepage and rivalry between texts somehow thereby be mastered and reappropriated? In an early piece of poetic prose entitled "Symphonie littéraire," Mallarmé prefaces his homage to his three "masters" (Gautier, Baudelaire, and Banville) with the following invocation:

> Muse moderne de l'Impuissance, qui m'interdis depuis longtemps le trésor familier des Rythmes, et me condamnes (aimable supplice) à ne faire plus que relire, —jusqu'au jour où tu m'auras enveloppé dans ton irrémédiable filet, l'ennui, et tout sera fini alors, —les maîtres inaccessibles dont la beauté me désespère; mon ennemie, et cependant mon enchanteresse aux breuvages perfides et aux melancoliques ivresses, je te dédie, comme une raillerie ou, —le sais-je? —comme un gage d'amour, ces quelques lignes de ma vie où tu ne m'inspiras pas la haine de la création et le stérile amour du néant. Tu y découvriras les jouissances d'une âme purement passive qui n'est que femme encore, et qui demain peut-être sera bête.[1]

> [O modern Muse of Impotence, you who have long forbidden me the familiar treasury of Rhythms, and who condemn me (pleasurable torture) to do nothing but reread—until the day you will envelop me in your irremediable net, ennui, and all will then be over—those inaccessible masters whose beauty drives me to despair; my enemy, yet my enchantress, with your perfidious potions and your melancholy intoxications, I dedicate to you, in jest or—can I know?—as a token of love, these few lines of my life written in the clement hours when you did not inspire in me a hatred of creation and a sterile love of nothingness. You will discover in them the pleasures of a purely passive soul who is yet but a woman and who tomorrow perhaps will be a dumb animal.]

It would seem that this text is quite explicitly describing the castrating effect of poetic fathers upon poetic sons. The precursors' beauty drives the ephebe to despair: he is impotent, passive, feminized, *mal armé*. Yet this state of castration is being invoked as a Muse: the lack of inspiration has become the source of inspiration. Mallarmé, as has often been noted, has transformed the incapacity to write into the very subject of his writing. In the act of thematizing an oedipal defeat, Mallarmé's

writing thus maps out the terms of an escape from simple oedipal polarities: it is no longer possible to distinguish easily between defeat and
success, impotence and potency, reading and writing, passivity and
activity.

Before pursuing further the Mallarméan relation between impotence and writing, let us glance for a moment at the father's side of the
story. At a time when Baudelaire would have had ample occasion to read
Mallarmé's "Literary Symphony" along with the prose poems Mallarmé
had dedicated to him, the older poet wrote the following remarks in a
letter to his mother in which he had enclosed an article about himself
written by Verlaine:

> Il y a du talent chez ces jeunes gens; mais que de folies! quelles exag-
> érations et quelle infatuation de jeunesse! Depuis quelques années je
> surprenais, ça et là, des imitations et des tendances qui m'alarmaient.
> Je ne connais rien de plus compromettant que les imitateurs et je
> n'aime rien tant que d'être seul. Mais ce n'est pas possible; et il paraît
> que l'*école Baudelaire* existe.[2]

> [These young people do have talent, but there is such madness! such
> exaggeration and such youthful infatuation! For several years now I
> have here and there come across imitations and tendencies that
> alarmed me. I know of nothing more compromising than imitators,
> and I like nothing so well as being alone. But it is not possible; and it
> seems that the *Baudelaire school* exists.]

The "father" here is "alarmed" not by the hostility but by the
imitative devotion of his "sons," whose writing lacks the measure and
maturity that he, Baudelaire, by implication attributes to his own. To be
imitated is to be repeated, multiplied, distorted, "compromised." To be
alone is at least to be unique, to be secure in the boundaries of one's self.
And to have the luxury of rejecting one's imitators is both to profit from
the compliment and to remain uncontaminated by the distortions. Yet
even in Baudelaire's expression of alarm and self-containment, otherness surreptitiously intrudes. For while Baudelaire is ambivalently but
emphatically imprinting his own name on the writing of his admirers,
another proper name is manifesting itself in the very writing of his
letter: in speaking of "des tendances qui *m'alarmaient*," Baudelaire has
unwittingly inscribed the name of one of the sources of his alarm. The
almost perfect homophony between "m'alarmaient" and "Mallarmé"
reveals a play of intertextuality in which the text, while seeming to decry
the dangers of imitation, is actually *acting out*, against the express purposes of its author, the far graver dangers of usurpation. And what is
usurped is not only Baudelaire's claims to authority over the work of his

disciples, but also and more significantly the claims of his conscious intentions to authority over the workings of his own writing. The suppressed name of Mallarmé shows through.

Both of these thematizations of the oedipal dynamics of intertextuality are thus more complex than they at first appear. In both cases, the ongoingness of literary history is acted out by the text despite an apparent attempt to arrest it. Mallarmé carves new territory for poetry out of what looks like a writing block; Baudelaire's writing, in the act of blocking out the successors, inscribes the inevitability of their usurpation.

But what are the effects of this Muse of Impotence not on Mallarmé's critical prose but on his poetry itself? In a poem entitled "L'Azur," written the same year as the "Symphonie littéraire," Mallarmé dramatizes the predicament of the poet who seeks forgetfulness as a cure for impotence (thus implying that what the impotent poet is suffering from is too much memory). The poem begins:

De l'éternel azur la sereine ironie
Accable, belle indolemment comme les fleurs,
Le poëte impuissant qui maudit son génie
A travers un désert stérile de Douleurs.

[The eternal azure's serene irony
Burdens, with the indolent grace of flowers,
The impotent poet who damns his genius
Across a sterile desert of sorrows.]

The poet tries to flee this oppressive azure, throwing night, smoke, and fog across it, until he reaches a moment of illusory victory, followed by a recognition of defeat:

— Le Ciel est mort. — Vers toi, j'accours! donne, ô matière,
L'oubli de l'Idéal cruel et du Péché
A ce martyr qui vient partager la litière
Où le bétail heureux des hommes est couché,

Car j'y veux, puisque enfin ma cervelle, vidée
Comme le pot de fard gisant au pied du mur,
N'a plus l'art d'attifer la sanglotante idée,
Lugubrement bâiller vers un trépas obscur...

En vain! l'Azur triomphe, et je l'entends qui chante
Dans les cloches. Mon âme, il se fait voix pour plus
Nous faire peur avec sa victoire méchante,
Et du métal vivant sort en bleus angélus!

Il roule par la brume, ancien et traverse
Ta native agonie ainsi qu'un glaive sûr;
Où fuir dans la révolte inutile et perverse?
Je suis hanté. L'Azur! l'Azur! l'Azur! l'Azur! (Pp. 37–38)

[—The sky is dead. —To you I run! give, O matter,
Forgetfulness of the cruel Ideal and Sin
To this martyr who comes to share the straw
Where the happy herd of men is stabled,

For I wish—since my brain no longer, emptied
Like the grease-paint pot that lies against the wall,
Has the art to prettify the sobbing idea—
To yawn lugubriously toward an obscure death...

In vain! The Azure triumphs, I can hear it sing
In the bells. My soul, it becomes voice,
The better to scare us with its mean success,
And from the living metal bluely rings the angelus.

It rolls through the mist, of old and pierces
Like a skillful sword your native agony;
Where is there to flee, in useless and perverse revolt?
I am haunted. Azure! Azure! Azure! Azure!]

This text has always been read—even by Mallarmé himself—as a description of the struggle between the desire to reach a poetic or metaphysical ideal and the attempt to escape that desire for fear of failing. As Guy Michaud puts it, "Even if the poet is freed neither of his dream nor of his impotence, he has at least affirmed the originality of his poetry. He has achieved the *general effect* he was seeking: the obsessive concern with the eternal, which the azure symbolizes."[3] But should this "azure" be understood only in a symbolic sense? The fact that the word is repeated four times at the end of the poem would seem to indicate that what haunts Mallarmé is not simply some ideal symbolized by azure but the very word *azure* itself. Even a casual glance at nineteenth-century French poetry reveals that the word is par excellence a "poetic" word—a sign that what one is reading is a poem. The repetition of this word can thus be read as the return of stereotyped poetic language as a reflex, a moment when initiative is being taken by the words *of others,* which is one of the things Mallarmé will later call "chance." Azure, says Mallarmé, "becomes voice." The text ends: "I am haunted: cliché! cliché! cliché! cliché!"[4]

Impotence is thus not a simple inability to write, but an inability to write *differently.* The agony experienced before the blank page arises out of the fact that the page is in fact never quite blank enough.

To write thus becomes for Mallarmé a constant effort to silence the automatisms of poetry, to "conquer chance word by word" (p. 387), to perceive words "independent of their ordinary sequence" (p. 386). But if the blankness of the page is in a sense the place from which literary history speaks, Mallarmé ends up writing not by covering the white page with the blackness of his own originality but rather by including within his writing the very spaces where poetic echoes and reflexes have been suppressed. "Leaving the initiative to words" (p. 366) is a complex operation in which the linguistic work of poetic calculation must substitute for the banalities of poetic inspiration. And the blanks figure as a major ingredient in that calculation. As Mallarmé puts it in a note on the *Coup de dés,* his symphony in white: "The 'blanks' indeed take on importance. . . . The paper intervenes each time an image, of its own accord, ceases or dies back, accepting the succession of others" (p. 455). And as for prose, Mallarmé explains that his blanks take the place of empty transitions: "The reason for these intervals, or blanks. . . . —why not confine the subject to those fragments in which it shines and then replace, by the ingenuousness of the paper, those ordinary, nondescript transitions?" (p. 1576). The act of reading Mallarmé, of sounding that "transparency of allusions" (p. 317), becomes—in his own words—a "desperate practice" (p. 647) precisely because "to read" means "to rely, depending on the page, on the blank" (p. 387), to take cognizance of the text as a "stilled poem, in the blanks" (p. 367). Through the breaks and the blanks in his text, Mallarmé internalizes intertextual heterogeneity and puts it to work not as a relation *between* texts but as a play of intervals and interruptions *within* texts. Mallarmé's intertextuality then becomes an explicit version of the ways in which a text is never its own contemporary, cannot constitute a self-contained whole, conveys only its noncoincidence with itself. While the desire to escape banality seemed to situate the challenge of poetry in the impossibility of saying something *different,* Mallarmé here reveals through the text's own self-difference an equal impossibility inherent in the attempt to say something s̲a̲me̲. Indeed, his notion of the Book the world is to end up becomīng is a correlative to this: if for Mallarmé all poets have unwittingly yet unsuccessfully attempted to write *the* Book, and if at the same time "all books contain the fusion of a small number of repeated sayings" (p. 367), then d̲i̲f̲f̲e̲r̲e̲n̲c̲e̲ can arise only out of repetition, and the "d̲e̲f̲e̲c̲t̲ o̲f̲ l̲a̲n̲g̲u̲a̲g̲e̲s̲" that verse is supposed to make up for resides in the fact that it is just as impossible to say the same thing as to say something different.

It is perhaps this paradox of intertextual relations, this "unan-

imous blank conflict between one garland and the same" (p. 74), that is
staged by the famous "Swan" sonnet:

Le vierge, le vivace et le bel aujourd'hui
Va-t-il nous déchirer avec un coup d'aile ivre
Ce lac dur oublié que hante sous le givre
Le transparent glacier des vols qui n'ont pas fui!

Un cygne d'autrefois se souvient que c'est lui
Magnifique mais qui sans espoir se délivre
Pour n'avoir pas chanté la région où vivre
Quand du stérile hiver a resplendi l'ennui.

Tout son col secouera cette blanche agonie
Par l'espace infligé à l'oiseau qui le nie,
Mais non l'horreur du sol où le plumage est pris.

Fantôme qu'à ce lieu son pur éclat assigne,
Il s'immobilise au songe froid de mépris
Que vêt parmi l'exil inutile le Cygne.

[The virgin, vivacious, and lovely today—
Will it rend with a blow of its dizzying wing
This hard lake, forgotten yet haunted beneath
By the transparent glacier of unreleased flights!

A bygone day's swan now remembers it is he
Who, magnificent yet in despair struggles free
For not having sung of the regions of life
When the ennui of winter's sterility gleamed.

All his neck will shake off this white agony space
Has inficted upon the white bird who denied it,
But not the ground's horror, his plumage inside it.

A phantom assigned by his gloss to this place,
Immobile he stands, in the cold dream of scorn
That surrounds, in his profitless exile, the Swan.]

The poetry of "today" would thus constitute the rending of something
that is both forgotten and haunted—haunted by the way in which a
"bygone day's swan" *did not sing*. The choice of a swan as a figure for the
precursor is both appropriate and paradoxical. On the one hand, if the
swan sings only at the moment of death, then the poet who says he is
haunted by the precursor swan's song would in reality be marking the
death of the father. But on the other hand, to seek to silence the father,
to speak of his *not* having sung, is to run the risk of bringing the father

back to life, since, if he does not sing, there is no proof that he is dead. In other words, the survival of the father is in a sense guaranteed by the way in which the son does *not* hear him.

It is interesting to note that this sonnet about a bygone day's swan actually itself refers to the swan of a bygone day—a poem entitled "The Swan," written by Baudelaire and dedicated to *his* poetic precursor, Victor Hugo. It would seem that the swan comes to designate the precursor as such, and it is doubtless no accident that the predecessor figure in Proust's *Remembrance of Things Past* should also be called by the name of Swann.

But in each of these cases, what is striking about the precursor figure, what in a sense seals his paternity, is the way in which he himself is already divided, rent, different from himself. In Proust's novel, Swann is the model of a man who is never the contemporary of his own desires. Baudelaire's "Swan" poem tells of being divided between the loss of what can never be recovered and the memory of what can never be forgotten, so that irreparable loss becomes the incapacity to let anything go. To return to Mallarmé's sonnet, we can see that the very division between "aujourd'hui" ("today") and "autrefois" ("bygone day") names the temporality of intertextuality as such. And this division in itself constitutes a textual allusion—to the division of Hugo's *Contemplations* into two volumes entitled "Autrefois" and "Aujourd'hui." "They are separated by an abyss," writes Hugo: "the tomb."[5]

In his preface to *Contemplations*, Hugo suggests that his book should be read "as one reads the work of the dead." In reflecting on this quotation, one can begin to see a supplementary twist to the traditional oedipal situation. For if the father survives precisely through his way of affirming himself dead, then the son will always arrive too late to kill him. What the son suffers from, then, is not the simple desire to kill the father, but the impotence to kill him whose potency resides in his ability to recount his own death.

It is perhaps for this reason that the so-called "fathers of modern thought"—Mallarmé, Freud, Marx, Nietzsche—maintain such a tremendous authority for contemporary theory. In writing of the subversion of the author, the father, God, privilege, knowledge, property, and consciousness, these thinkers have subverted in advance any grounds on which one might undertake to kill off an authority that theorizes the death of all authority. This is perhaps the way in which contemporary theory in its turn has *lived* the problematics of intertextuality.

From the foregoing it would appear that intertextuality is a struggle between fathers and sons, and that literary history is exclusively a male affair. This has certainly been the presumption of literary historians in the past, for whom gender becomes an issue only when the writer is female. In the remainder of this essay, I would like to glance briefly at the ways in which questions of gender might enrich, complicate, and even subvert the underlying paradigms of intertextual theory. What, for example, does one make of Mallarmé's experience of the "pleasures of a purely passive soul who is yet but a woman"? Is Mallarmé's femininity a mere figure for castration? Or is the Muse of Impotence also a means of access to the experience of femininity? Or, to approach it another way, how might we factor into these intertextual relations the fact that Baudelaire's protestations of solitude and paternity are written to his *mother*, and that the tomb that separates "autrefois" and "aujourd'hui" for Hugo is that of his *daughter?* What, in other words, are the poetic uses to which women—both inside and outside the text—have been put by these male poets?

It is interesting that the only text by Mallarmé on which Baudelaire is known to have commented is a prose poem in which a beautiful, naked woman stands as a figure for the poetry of the past. Mallarmé's poem, "Le Phénomène futur," describes a degenerating world in which a "Displayer of Things Past" is touting the beauties of a "Woman of Bygone Days." Drooping poets-to-be are suddenly revived, "haunted by rhythm and forgetting that theirs is an era that has outlived beauty" (p. 270). Baudelaire, in his notes on Belgium, has this to say about Mallarmé's vision of the future: "A young writer has recently come up with an ingenious but not entirely accurate conception. The world is about to end. Humanity is decrepit. A future Barnam is showing the degraded men of his day a beautiful woman artificially preserved from ancient times. 'What?' they exclaim, 'could humanity once have been as beautiful as that?' I say that this is not true. Degenerate man would admire himself and call beauty ugliness."[6] This encounter between the two poets is a perfect figuration of the progress of literary history from one generation to another. But the disagreement on which Baudelaire insists is less profound than it appears. While the elder poet fears that people will admire something he no longer recognizes as beautiful and the younger poet fears that beauty may no longer be recognizable in his work, Baudelaire and Mallarmé actually agree on two things: beauty is a function of the past, and beauty is a woman.

Nothing could be more traditional than this conception of Beauty as a female body: naked, immobile, and mute. Indeed, the beauty of female muteness and reification reaches its highest pitch when the woman in question is dead (cf. Poe's statement that the most poetic subject is the death of a beautiful woman) or at least—as here—artifically preserved and statufied. The flawless whiteness of the female body is the very image of the blank page, to be shaped and appropriated by the male creative pen. As Susan Gubar remarks in an article entitled " 'The Blank Page' and Female Creativity": "When the metaphors of literary creativity are filtered through a sexual lens, female sexuality is often identified with textuality. . . . This model of the pen-penis writing on the virgin page participates in a long tradition identifying the author as a male who is primary and the female as his passive creation—a secondary object lacking autonomy, endowed with often contradictory meaning but denied intentionality."[7] In Mallarmé's work, the correlation between Poetry and Femininity is pervasive from the very beginning. The great unfinished poem "Hérodiade," begun in 1864 and still lying uncompleted on Mallarmé's desk at the time of his death in 1898, provides a telling record of the shifting importance and complexity of his attempt to make poetry speak as a female Narcissus, self-reflexive and self-contained. The failure of Mallarmé's attempt to dramatize his poetics under the guise of female psychology is certainly as instructive as the centrality of that project, and deserves more extensive treatment than is possible here. But in Mallarmé's later writing, the identification of femininity with textuality, which becomes both more explicit and more complex, becomes as well completely depsychologized:

> A déduire le point philosophique auquel est située l'impersonnalité de la danseuse, entre sa féminine apparence et un objet mimé, pour quel hymen: elle le pique d'une sûre pointe, le pose; puis déroule notre conviction en le chiffre de pirouettes prolongé vers un autre motif, attendu que tout, dans l'évolution par où elle illustre le sens de nos extases et triomphes entonnés à l'orchestre, est, comme le veut l'art même, au théatre, *fictif ou momentané.* . . .
>
> A savoir que la danseuse *n'est pas une femme qui danse,* pour ces motifs juxtaposés qu'elle *n'est pas une femme,* mais une métaphore résumant un des aspects élémentaires de notre forme, glaive, coupe, fleur, etc., et *qu'elle ne danse pas,* suggérant, par le prodige de raccourcis ou d'élans, avec une écriture corporelle ce qu'il faudrait des paragraphes en prose dialoguée autant que descriptive, pour exprimer, dans la rédaction: poëme dégagé de tout appareil du scribe. (Pp. 296, 304)
>
> [To deduce the philosophical point at which the dancer's impersonality is located, between her feminine appearance and a mimed object, for what Hymen: she pricks it with a confident point and poses it; then unrolls our conviction in the cipher of pirouettes prolonged toward another motif, presuming that everything, in the evolution

through which she illustrates the sense of our ecstasies and triumphs intoned in the orchestra, is, as art itself requires it, in theatre, *fictive or momentary.* . . .]

[That is, that the dancer *is not a woman dancing*, for the juxtaposed motives that she *is not a woman*, but a metaphor epitomizing one of the elementary aspects of our form, sword, goblet, flower, etc., and that *she is not dancing*, suggesting, through the prodigy of short cuts and leaps, with a corporal writing what it would take paragraphs of dialogue and descriptive prose to express, if written out: a poem freed from all scribal apparatus.]

This would certainly seem to be an example of the denial of female interiority and subjectivity and the transformation of the woman's body into an art object. Textuality becomes woman, but woman becomes poet only unconsciously and corporally. But is it different for a man? The question of autonomy and intentionality becomes sticky indeed when one recalls that for Mallarmé it is precisely the intentionality of the poet as such that must disappear in order for initiative to be left to words: "L'oeuvre pure implique la disparition élocutoire du poëte, qui cède l'initiative aux mots" (p. 366). Therefore, the fact that the dancer here is objectified and denied interiority is not in itself a function of her gender. That state of "scribelessness," of "impersonality," is, rather, the ideal Mallarmé sets up for poetry. But the fact remains that the poet is consistently male and the poem female:

L'unique entraînement imaginatif consiste, aux heures ordinaires de fréquentation dans les lieux de Danse sans visée quelconque préalable, patiemment et passivement à se demander devant tout pas, chaque attitude si étranges, ces pointes et taquetés, allongés ou ballons, "Que peut signifier ceci" ou mieux, d'inspiration, le lire. A coup sûr on opérera en pleine rêverie, mais adéquate: vaporeuse, nette et ample, ou restreinte, telle seulement que l'enferme en ses circuits ou la transporte par une fugue la ballerine illettrée se livrant aux jeux de sa profession. Oui, celle-là (serais-tu perdu en une salle, spectateur très étranger, Ami) pour peu que tu déposes avec soumission à ses pieds d'inconsciente révélatrice ainsi que les roses qu'enlève et jette en la visibilité de régions supérieures un jeu de ses chaussons de satin pâle vertigineux, la Fleur d'abord *de ton poétique instinct*, n'attendant de rien autre la mise en évidence et sous le vrai jour des mille imaginations latentes: alors, par un commerce dont paraît son sourire verser le secret, sans tarder elle te livre à travers le voile dernier qui toujours reste, la nudité de tes concepts et silencieusement écrira ta vision à la façon d'un Signe, qu'elle est. (P. 307)

[The sole imaginative training consists, in the ordinary hours of frequenting Dance with no preconceived aim, patiently and passively, of wondering at every step, each attitude, so strange, those points and *taquetés, allongés* or *ballons,* "What can this signify?" or, better, by inspiration, of reading it. One will definitely operate in full reverie, but adequate: vaporous, crisp, and ample, or restrained, such only as it is enclosed in circlings or transported in a fugue by the illiterate ballerina engaging in the play of her profession. Yes, that one (be you lost in the hall, most foreign spectator, Friend) if you but set at the feet of this unconscious revealer, submissively—like the roses lifted and tossed into the visibility of the upper regions by a flounce of her dizzying pale satin slippers—the Flower at first *of your poetic instinct,* expecting nothing but the evidencing and in the true light of a thousand latent imaginations: then, through a commerce whose secret her smile appears to pour out, without delay she delivers up to you through the ultimate veil that always remains, the nudity of your concepts and silently begins to write your vision in the manner of a Sign, which she is.]

What the woman is a sign of, what she *unconsciously* reveals, is the nudity of "your" concepts and the flower of "your" poetic instinct. The woman, dancing, is the necessary but unintentional medium through which something fundamental to the male poetic self can be manifested. But this state of unconsciousness, which would seemingly establish the possibility of a female poet, turns out to be valuable only when reappropriated by the male poet. This becomes clear in Mallarmé's discussion of women and jewels.

Precious stones figure often in Mallarmé's descriptions of poetry:

L'oeuvre pure implique la disparition élocutoire du poëte, qui cède l'initiative aux mots, par le heurt de leur inégalité mobilisés; *ils s'allument de reflets réciproques comme une virtuelle traînée de feux sur des pierreries,* remplaçant la respiration perceptible en l'ancien souffle lyrique ou la direction personnelle enthousiaste de la phrase. (P. 366; italics mine)

[The pure work implies the elocutionary disappearance of the poet, who leaves the initiative to words, through the shock of their inequality, mobilized; *they light up with reciprocal reflections like a virtual trail of fire over precious stones,* replacing the breath perceptible in the old lyric inspiration or the passionate personal direction of the sentence.]

In an interview with Jules Huret, Mallarmé expands upon the image of jewelry in the following terms:

— *Que pensez-vous de la fin du naturalisme?*

   — L'enfantillage de la littérature jusqu'ici a été de croire, par exemple, que de choisir un certain nombre de pierres précieuses et en mettre les noms sur le papier, même très bien, c'était *faire* des pierres précieuses. Eh bien! non! La poésie consistant à *créer*, il faut prendre dans l'âme humaine des états, des lueurs d'une pureté si absolue que, bien chantés et bien mis en lumière, cela constitue en effet les joyaux de l'homme: là, il y a symbole, il y a création, et le mot poésie a ici son sens: c'est, en somme, la seule création humaine possible. Et si, véritablement, les pierres précieuses dont on se pare ne manifestent pas un état d'âme, c'est indûment qu'on s'en pare... La femme, par exemple, cette éternelle voleuse...

   Et tenez, *ajoute mon interlocuteur en riant à moitié,* ce qu'il y a d'admirable dans les magasins de nouveautés, c'est, quelquefois, de nous avoir révélé, par le commissaire de police, que la femme se parait indûment de ce dont elle ne savait pas le sens caché, et qui ne lui appartient par conséquent pas... (Pp. 870–71)

[— *What do you think of the end of naturalism?*

   — The childishness of literature up to now has been to think, for example, that to choose a certain number of precious stones and to put their names down on paper, even superbly well, was to *make* precious stones. Not at all! Since poetry consists of creating, one must take from the human soul certain states, certain glimmerings of such absolute purity that, skillfully sung and brought to light, they indeed constitute the jewels of man: there, there is symbol, there is creation, and the word poetry takes on its meaning: that, in sum, is the only human creation possible. And if, truly, the precious stones one dresses in do not manifest a state of mind or mood, then one has no right to wear them... Woman, for example, that eternal thief...

   And think, *adds my interlocutor half laughing:* what is admirable about those high-fashion stores is that they have sometimes revealed to us, through the chief of police, that women have been illegitimately wearing what they didn't know the hidden meaning of, and which consequently does not belong to them...]

Women's unconsciousness of meaning—that which makes them capable of *standing for* the male poetic instinct—is what denies the legitimacy of their ever occupying the role of poetic subject. Men know what they are doing when they leave initiative to words or jewels; women don't. It is interesting to recall that Mallarmé almost single-handedly produced a fashion journal, *La Dernière Mode,* which dealt in great detail with jewelry, clothing, and other items of female decoration, and which he often signed with a feminine pseudonym. It is as though Mallarmé's interest in writing like a woman about fashion was to steal back for consciousness what women had stolen by unconsciousness, to write *consciously* from out of the female unconscious, which is somehow more intimately but illegitimately connected to the stuff of poetry. Intertextuality here becomes intersexuality.

Mallarmé's instatement of the impersonal or unconscious poetic subject thus somehow exposes rather than conceals a question that haunts him from the very beginning: is writing a gendered act? It is this question that informs a poem entitled "Don du poème," which serves as a dedicatory poem to "Hérodiade." The fact that Hérodiade and Mallarmé's daughter Genevieve were "born" at the same time serves as the background for Mallarmé's reflection on gender differences:

> Je t'apporte l'enfant d'une nuit d'Idumée!
> Noire, à l'aile saignante et pâle, déplumée,
> Par le verre brûlé d'aromates et d'or,
> Par les carreaux glacés, hélas! mornes encor,
> L'aurore se jeta sur la lampe angélique.
> Palmes! et quand elle a montré cette relique
> A ce père essayant un sourire ennemi,
> La solitude bleue et stérile a frémi.
> O la berceuse, avec ta fille et l'innocence
> De vos pieds froids, accueille une horrible naissance:
> Et ta voix rappelant viole et clavecin,
> Avec le doigt fané presseras-tu le sein
> Par qui coule en blancheur sibylline la femme
> Pour les lèvres que l'air du vierge azur affame? (P. 40)

> [I bring you the child of a night spent in Edom!
> Black, with pale and bleeding wing, quill-less,
> Through the glass burned with spices and gold,
> Through the icy panes, alas! mournful still,
> The dawn flew down on the angelic lamp.
> Palmes! and when it had shown this relic
> To this father attempting an enemy smile,
> The blue and sterile solitude was stirred.
> O cradler, with your daughter and the innocence
> Of your cold feet, welcome a horrible birth:
> And your voice recalling viol and harpsichord,
> With faded finger will you press the breast
> Through which in sibylline whiteness woman flows
> For lips half starved by virgin azure air?]

The question of gender is raised immediately in two very different ways in the first line. The word "enfant" is one of the few words in French that can be either masculine or feminine without modification. And the name "Idumée" refers to ancient Edom, the land of the outcast Esau, or, according to the Kabbalah, the land of pre-Adamic man, where sexless beings reproduced without women, or where sexual difference did not exist. The poem thus begins on a note of denial of sexual difference only to end with a plea that the woman agree to nurture the fruit of such a denial. The means of such nourishment is "blancheur sibylline": white textuality, the blankness that challenges interpretation. The woman, then, is to provide the nourishing blanks without which the newborn poem might die of "azure," which, as we have seen, represents the weight of poetic history. "Idumée" too refers to a glut of poetic clichés: the same strange juxtaposition of "Idumée" and "Palmes" can be found in Boileau's satire 9 in a passage in which he lists a string of Malherbian poetic commonplaces.[8]

It would seem at first sight that Mallarmé in this poem draws a contrast between the fecundity of natural reproduction and the sterility of poetic creation, and that this poem stands as a typical example of the male pen expressing its womb envy. Yet the masculine here is equated with sexlessness, while the woman functions not as a womb but as a source of music and sibylline whiteness. The opposition between male and female is an opposition between half-dead language and nourishing nonlanguage. But while many writers have valued the woman as something extratextual, such nonlanguage is valued in Mallarmé's system not because it is outside, but because it is *within*, the poetic text. Both music and whiteness are extraordinarily privileged in Mallarmé's poetics precisely because they function as articulations *without content*. Mallarmé's insistence that what the word *flower* evokes is what is *absent* from any bouquet, that the text is a structure of relations and not a collection of signifieds, that there is no given commensurability between language and reality, functions polemically in the late-nineteenth-century debates over realism and naturalism. His emphasis on music as a "system of relations" and on blankness as a structured but "stilled" poem functions precisely as a *critique* of the pretensions to representationalism and realism in the literary text. By thus opposing naive referentiality and privileging blankness and silence, Mallarmé also, however, implicitly shifts the gender values traditionally assigned to such questions. If the figure of woman has been repressed and objectified by being equated with the blank page, then Mallarmé, by *activating* those blanks, comes close to writing from the place of the silenced female voice.[9] In his ways of throwing his voice as a woman, of figuring textuality as a dancing ballerina, and of questioning simplistic pretensions to expressivity, potency, and (masculine) authority, Mallarmé's critique of logocentrism opens up a space for a critique of phallocentrism as well. Intertextuality can no longer be seen simply as a relation between fathers and sons. But although Mallarmé's many feminine incarnations make it impossible to read him as "simply" masculine, the revaluation of the *figure* of the woman by a male author cannot substitute for the actual participation of women in the literary conversation. Mallarmé may be able to speak from the place of the silenced woman, but as long as *he* is occupying it, the silence that is broken in theory is maintained in reality. And while there is no guarantee that when a "real" woman speaks, she is truly breaking that silence, at least she makes it difficult to avoid facing the fact that literal "women" and figurative "woman" do not meet on the same rhetorical level of discourse.

In conclusion, I would like to look briefly at two poems that carry out, in very different ways, a female revision of the Western male poetic tradition of poems about the female body and, in particular, the breast. As we have seen, two aspects of the woman's breast have long been celebrated by male poets: its static, objectlike perfection and its pure, inviting whiteness. Two further examples—the first from Clément Marot and the second from Edmund Spenser—will suffice to establish the lineaments of this male vision:

> Tétin refaict plus blanc qu'un oeuf,
> Tétin de satin blanc tout neuf,
> Tétin qui fait honte à la Rose,
> Tétin plus beau que nulle chose,
> Tétin dur non pas Tétin, voire,
> Mais petite boule d'Ivoire.[10]

> [Plump breast, whiter than an egg,
> Breast of brand new white satin,
> Breast that puts the Rose to shame,
> Breast more beautiful than anything,
> Firm breast, not a breast but
> A little round ball of Ivory.]

> Her forehead yvory white
> Her cheekes lyke apples which the sun hath rudded,
> Her lips lyke cherryes charming men to byte,
> Her brest like to a bowle of creame uncrudded,
> Her paps lyke lyllies budded
> Her snowie necke lyke to a marble towre.[11]

As ivory, marble, satin, eggs, or cream, the breast is at once edible and marmorial, homey and luxurious. In any case, it has no history, no story, no interior of its own. In Anne Sexton's poem "The Breast," on the other hand, we get the inside story of the ivory ball that is never quite round enough:

> A xylophone maybe with skin
> stretched over it awkwardly.
> Only later did it become something real.
>
> Later I measured my size against movie stars.
> I didn't measure up. Something between
> my shoulders was there. But never enough.[12]

The breast here is no longer a mere trope, a figure for the unchanging object of male desire; it becomes a narrative—of change, development, and disappointment. The poetic voice speaks from between the shoulders, from the place where there is never enough. The breast is not even called a breast here, but only a "something." Recounted from the inside, the breast fails to measure up to the idealized image inherited from male fantasies. The newness of Sexton's poetry lies in its way of bringing to light the discomforts and discoveries of this failure, the other stories hidden behind the bowl of cream.

A second revision of the image of the white breast occurs in the following poem by Lucille Clifton:

> If I stand in my window
> naked in my own house
> and press my breasts
> against my windowpane
> like black birds pushing against glass
> because I am somebody
> in a New Thing
>
> and if the man come to stop me
> in my own house
> naked in my own window
> saying I have offended him
> I have offended his
>
> Gods
>
> let him watch my black body
> push against my own glass
> let him discover self
> let him run naked through the streets

crying
praying in tongues[13]

The black breasts pressed against the windows of a house owned by the speaker constitute the bold self-assertion of a voice formerly denied artistic authority. Their blackness is all the more affirmative for being the "negative" of the traditional European image. The windowpane, which, in such poems as Mallarmé's "Les Fenêtres," comes to symbolize the poetic process itself, here delimits a spectacle that is not static but pushes against its own frame. Breasts under glass, framed by an objectifying male gaze, have been the stock-in-trade of male poetry, but here the male gaze is returned and judged by the female speaker, the object turned subject. But Clifton's revision is not a simple symmetrical reversal: while white doves have been replaced by black birds and the female has become the possessor rather than the object of possession (cf. the word "my," repeated eight times), the woman speaker does not simply reverse the gaze and turn the man into an object. The body is still female, and the female body is still poetry. But it is a self-asserting, self-inscribing female body that returns the male gaze upon itself. "The man," which is both the generic "man" and, in black American usage, the white man or policeman—that is, the representative of the whole existing patriarchal order—is about to become incomprehensible to himself. He is told to "discover self" and "pray in tongues," to learn the experience of exclusion, alienation, dispossession. He must discover himself as *other*. Clifton's poem thus not only revises the male tradition, but invites the male tradition to re-vision itself. The intertextual house has many mansions, and each "New Thing" can teach us to rewrite its history all over again from the beginning.

IV

OTHER INFLECTIONS OF DIFFERENCE

12

Mallarmé as Mother

What do I mean by the notion of Mallarmé as mother?

I do not primarily mean Mallarmé as *would-be* mother, as an experiencer and overcomer of womb envy, although poems like "Don du poéme," in which poetic production is compared somewhat unfavorably to natural reproduction, or letters in which Mallarmé describes his daughter Genevieve and his poem "Hérodiade" as rival siblings, or sonnets like "Une dentelle s'abolit," in which Mallarmé invents a new and linguistico-musical method of birth, would seem to suggest that such an idea would not be completely without foundation.

I do not mean Mallarmé as *woman*, although the fact that he produced a fashion magazine which he signed with a variety of feminine pseudonyms, and that in his address to the "Modern Muse of Impotence" he described himself as "une âme purement passive qui n'est que femme encore" ("a purely passive soul who is yet but a woman") would suggest that his preoccupation with impotence on the one hand and with jewels, decoration, and finery on the other might play a transexuating role.

And I do not mean Mallarmé as occupying a female *social* position, although his concern with domesticity, his stance beside the hearth in his apartment on the rue de Rome, his role as host in a poetic "salon," his low-prestige job as a high school English teacher, and his self-ironic remarks about his life's lack of adventure or anecdote, would suggest that such a view would unify many of the existential stances of his social self.

All three of these possible ways of seeing Mallarmé as mother, although interesting and not contradictory to what I have in mind, would locate Mallarmé's maternity in a feminine *persona*. In contrast, I would like to situate what is maternal in Mallarmé as a *function* or *structure*, defined not in terms of a female *figure* but in terms of a specific set of interactions and transactions that structure the relation between the earliest parent and the child.

First, let me sketch out the context in which the notion of Mallarmé as mother came to seem useful. What, in other words, was the *question* on which Mallarmé-as-mother seemed to shed light? The question might be formulated as follows: What is it about Mallarmé's writing that is capable of exerting intense fascination in some cases and intense discomfort or rejection in others? What is the nature of the appeal, and of the threat? What sorts of unconscious wishes or fears does Mallarmé's poetry evoke in the reader?

The characteristics of Mallarmé most often cited for admiration or rejection are

1. Obscurity, difficulty;
2. Lack of determinable meaning: undecidability, ambiguity, plays of the signifier;
3. Impersonality, distance, negativity;
4. Inseparability of a poem's significance from the reading or writing process: poems seem to be about their own production or interpretation.

It is doubtless no accident that it is these same characteristics that exert attraction or repulsion in the writings of certain contemporary theorists for whose work Mallarmé is, in fact, fundamental—Derrida, Kristeva, Lacan, de Man. Hence, behind this exploration of Mallarmé's maternal role in *literary* history lies a possible thought about the role of those Mallarmé-inspired theorists within the history of criticism. But that thought will remain implicit for the time being.

It was while pondering the strange attraction-repulsion of the concept of *undecidability* that I came across the writings of the American psychoanalyst Margaret Mahler on the pre-oedipal development of the child. While Mahler can easily be criticized on many counts from a Lacanian or feminist point of view, her differentiations among various subphases of the processes of separation and individuation in the pre-oedipal period provide texture and temporality to patterns that have received small attention from either Freud or Lacan.

The separation-individuation process described by Mahler moves from mother-child symbiosis toward greater and greater autonomy, through four subphases. The child is followed from the age of four or five months to about three years, from "lap-babyhood" to "toddlerhood." Since the mother in these structures is defined not in terms of womb or breast but in terms of emotional and physical proximity, it is not structurally necessary that she be a woman, although Mahler never considers this. The four subphases are described as follows:

1. *Differentiation:* "hatching" from symbiotic oneness or lack of differentiation between child and mother; decrease of complete bodily dependence, increase of sensorimotor investigations, peek-a-boo games.
2. *Practicing:* great narcissistic investment of the child in his own functions, his own body, as well as in the objects and objectives of his expanding reality testing; relatively great imperviousness to knocks and falls and other frustrations. The child alternates between obliviousness to mother and periodic return to mother for emotional refueling.
3. *Rapprochement:* increased motor and communicative activity is accompanied, paradoxically, by a greater concern for mother's presence, a greater tendency to separation anxiety. The child passes from vocal affective expressions through the ability to use "no!" toward verbal communication. Both separation and active approach behavior increase: the child is both more dependent and more demanding; his "pleasure in independent functioning . . . seems to be proportionate to . . . his success in eliciting the mother's interest and participation" (p. 39).
4. *Object constancy:* greater tolerance for separation from mother and for delayed gratification; development of role-playing and make-believe. The absent mother is libidinally available because she is internalized as an image, not experienced as loss.[1]

It is the third, or rapprochement, phase that seems to me most fruitful to an understanding of the workings of Mallarmé's poetry. In that phase, the forces of separation and the forces of merger work in tandem yet against each other, and they do so at a moment when the preverbal slides into the verbal through the word "no".

As far as the verbal development is concerned, it is easy to see that in emphasizing the negative (*aboli bibelot, nul ptyx, rien n'aura eu lieu,* etc.) and in silencing or musicalizing the verbal as structure or sonority while rediscovering the properties of words as such, Mallarmé's poetry manages to make simultaneous the three linguistic steps involved in the rapprochement phase—affective gesture or vocalization, negativity, and the newness of verbal communication.[2] For the remainder of this paper I will concentrate on the attendant problematics of separation and rapprochement per se.

Mallarmé's poems would seem to be characterized by a high degree of separation from anything outside themselves. *Le Livre* was to be impersonal and anonymous ("le Texte y parlant de lui-même et sans voix d'auteur," ["the Text there speaking on its own and without the voice of an author"]). The author, in the very act of writing, is cut off from the work ("Sait-on ce que c'est qu'écrire? . . . Qui l'accomplit, intégralement, se retranche" ["Does anyone know what writing is? . . . Whoever accomplishes it, integrally, cuts himself off"]). The work is cut off from reference as well: the word *flower* can name only "what is absent from any bouquet." The poem is detached and autonomous like the beautiful, sterile, solitary Hérodiade, who is of course a figure for the poem's aspiration toward separation.

There are two ways in which this thrust toward separation is countered by an equal and opposite force of attachment and indifferentiation. On the one hand, these poetic prodigies of separation envisaged by Mallarmé never achieve separation as finished works. "Igitur," "Hérodiade," *Le Livre, Pour un Tombeau d'Anatole* all remain unfinished and, hence, unable to perform the separations they depict. Mallarmé as mother of his poems would be playing out the maternal ambivalence toward separation: on the one hand, he directs his poems toward an idealized *image* of autonomy; on the other hand, he cannot let them go. A mother's self-effacement is never done. Concomitant to this is Mallarmé's tendency to devalue the works that he does finish: they are "cartes de visite," "études en vue de mieux," "des riens." The back-and-forth working-through of separation is denied in either case: either the dice never leave the enclosing hand, or they are tossed out into nothingness.

Separation is differently resisted *within* the completed, seemingly autonomous texts. Here, the text plays the role of mother; the reader, that of child. The text of a Mallarmé poem works out a complex pattern of undecidability, ambiguity, and obscurity through which the reader, who attempts to separate and differentiate meanings, can only find himself or herself further and further entangled with the text, less and less able to separate and differentiate. The desire for separation and the desire for merger are thus simultaneously satisfied on two different levels: the text proclaims its autonomy and individuality, but that individualty is itself composed of structures of indifferentiation and entanglement. The reader's separation from the text is never done.

The most condensed version of the simultaneity of separation and merger in Mallarmé is the functioning of the *blancs* in his texts. In Mallarmé's writing, whiteness functions both as spacing and as image, both as syntactical, material articulation and as semantic, thematic reference. On the one hand, the blank spaces cut up the text: separation functions within the textual body; the text is explicitly articulated as spacing, absence, incompletion, not as an organic whole. On the other hand, whiteness itself, as image, stands within Mallarmé's imagery, within the traditional Western imagery of the blank page, within certain strands of psychoanalytic theory, as a figure for the female body and, ultimately, for the maternal breast.[3] In Mallarmé's clearest depiction of the parallel between the poet-poem relation and the mother-child relation, "Don du poème," Mallarmé asks the woman to accept his poetic "child":

O la berceuse, avec ta fille et l'innocence
De vos pieds froids, accueille une horrible naissance:
Et ta voix rappelant viole et clavecin,
Avec le doigt fané presseras-tu le sein
Par qui coule en blancheur sibylline la femme
Pour les lèvres que l'air du vierge azur affame?

O cradler, with your daughter and the innocence
Of your cold feet, welcome a horrible birth:
And your voice recalling viol and harpsichord,
With faded finger will you press the breast
Through which in sibylline whiteness woman flows
For lips half starved by virgin azure air?

It is this forever undecipherable yet somehow maternal sibylline whiteness—or undecidability *as* maternity—that flows and is articulated through the poetry of Mallarmé. *Les blancs* sketch out presence and absence, pure semantic flux and pure syntactic division, separation and reunion. But the blanks in the text do not simply make the mother present; they recreate the drama of the simultaneity of attachment and detachment that defines the maternal *function*.

Hence, it could be said that the unconscious desires and fears tapped by Mallarmé's writing—the reasons readers are both attracted and repelled by it—have to do with its ability to recreate the simultaneous forces of separation and indifferentiation of the pre-oedipal period. The desire to separate is satisfied by the poem's free-standingness. The desire to merge is satisfied by the poem's absorption of the reader into its structures of obscurity and undecidability. And the fear of separation is evoked by the abyss of nonreferentiality or impersonality, while the fear of merger is evoked by the loss of the ability to control or master meaning.

How can it be said that a male poet comes to play a maternal role in literary *history*? Why is the mother's part not taken by a woman? One answer might run as follows: Everyone can believe that men are powerful. Everyone can believe that mothers are powerful. But we are not taught to believe that *women* are powerful. Hence, a man whose work consists of questioning certain assumptions and structures of phallogocentrism—the determinability of meaning, the separability of binary opposites, the search for self-identity—would somehow appear to fill the maternal role better, more effectively, than a woman. To the extent that a critique of the paternal position involves a privileging of ambiguity, undecidability, and deferral—the deferral of both separation and merger—that critique is operating from the arena of the pre-oedipal mother. But the fact that the maternal function is wielded by men— indeed, that literature is one of the ways in which men have elaborated the maternal position—means that the silence of actual women is all the more effectively enforced. With men playing all the parts, the drama appears less incomplete than it really is. Were women to take over the critique of the paternal position, they might not remain content with the maternal role.

What remains to be discussed is the value assigned to the maternal position in developmental narratives like Mahler's. By situating Mallarmé's power as that of the pre-oedipal mother, am I not implicitly considering it as regressive, something to be outgrown, as a critique that is actually a defense?

According to prevailing developmental schemes, this would indeed be the case. For although the mother is seen as powerful, her power, viewed exclusively through the eyes of the child, is a power that must be overcome, outgrown, escaped. Whether that power is nurturing or smothering, it is seen as a threat to autonomy. And autonomy comes to stand as the very structure of maturity. Any theory that sees maturity as the achievement of separation is bound to see the mother's power as inferior—as less desirable—than the father's. If the father stands for distance and the world and the mother stands for closeness and the home, then the more like the father one is, the more mature one is considered to be. According to this hierarchy of development, a woman would almost by definition never achieve full maturity, especially since she is constantly in danger of falling into symbiosis by becoming a mother herself. But a model of maturation that measures development by the standard of only one gender is clearly inadequate. This is the point of Carol Gilligan's book *In a Different Voice*, in which gender bias is analyzed in existing models of ethical development.

I would like to end by outlining three directions in which one might move to displace existing paradigms of maturation and gender, so that pre-oedipal structures could be recognized as permanent and pervasive rather than simply regressive.

1. Through an analysis of gender bias in models of human psychology and development, it should be possible to rethink the notion of maturity to include more of the spectrum of relationships than an idealized version of autonomy. At the very least, the capacity for mothering should, for example, stand as

one of several maturational models for people of both sexes. A tolerance for incomplete separation could be seen as differently mature from an insistence on total independence.

2. The function of mother—or of nurturing parent of either sex— should be analyzed otherwise than through the eyes of a child—indeed, implicitly, a male child—a child-theorist whose wishful anticipation of a free, self-identical needlessness has always dreamed human maturity as the completion of a separation that in fact can be achieved only in death.

3. The figure of the mother should be analyzed as the subject of discourse rather than as the source of life or the object of desire and anger. Recent writings—particularly Adrienne Rich's *Of Woman Born* and essays by Susan Suleiman and Marianne Hirsch[4]—have opened up extremely rich directions for an analysis of the mother as writer.

Finally, where does this leave Mallarmé? To the extent that it now seems urgent to question the claims to universality and the forces of exclusion that have gone into the making of the European literary canon, it may perhaps leave him silent. But any attempt to move away from that canon, to go beyond Mallarmé's maternity to a more feminist critique of the structures he both questioned and reinforced, would necessarily place Mallarmé and others like him in the role of primal parent, pre-oedipal mother, source of the earliest *literary* training and nourishment. It remains to be seen whether the feminist drama of separation from the canon can avoid the fallacies of autonomy without losing the differentiations that may, perhaps, ultimately, make a difference.

13

My Monster/My Self

To judge from recent trends in scholarly as well as popular literature, three crucial questions can be seen to stand at the forefront of today's preoccupations: the question of mothering, the question of the woman writer, and the question of autobiography. Although these questions and current discussions of them often appear unrelated to each other, it is my intention here to explore some ways in which the three questions *are* profoundly interrelated. To attempt to shed some new light on each by approaching it via the others, I shall base my remarks upon two twentieth-century theoretical studies—Nancy Friday's *My Mother/My Self* and Dorothy Dinnerstein's *The Mermaid and the Minotaur*—and one nineteenth-century gothic novel, *Frankenstein; or, The Modern Prometheus,* written by Mary Shelley, whose importance for literary history has until quite recently been considered to arise not from her own writings but from the fact that she was the second wife of poet Percy Bysshe Shelley and the daughter of the political philosopher William Godwin and the pioneering feminist Mary Wollstonecraft.[1]

All three of these books, in strikingly diverse ways, offer a critique of the institution of parenthood. *The Mermaid and the Minotaur* is an analysis of the damaging effects of the fact that human infants are cared for almost exclusively by women. "What the book's title as a whole is meant to connote," writes Dinnerstein, "is both (*a*) our longstanding general awareness of our uneasy, ambiguous position in the animal kingdom, and (*b*) a more specific awareness: that until we grow strong enough to renounce the pernicious forms of collaboration between the sexes, both man and woman will remain semi-human, monstrous" (p. 5). Even as Dinnerstein describes convincingly the types of imbalance and injustice the prevailing asymmetry in gender relations produces, she also analyzes the reasons for our refusal to abandon the very modes of monstrousness from which we suffer most. Nancy Friday's book, which is subtitled "A Daughter's Search for Identity," argues that the mother's repression of herself necessitated by the myth of maternal love creates a heritage of self-rejection, anger, and duplicity that makes it difficult for the daughter to seek any emotional satisfaction other than the state of idealized symbiosis that both mother and daughter continue to punish themselves for never having been able to achieve. Mary Shelley's *Frankenstein* is an even more elaborate and unsettling formulation of the relation between parenthood and monstrousness. It is the story of two antithetical modes of parenting that give rise to two increasingly parallel lives—the life of Victor Frankenstein, who is the beloved child of two doting parents, and the life of the monster he single-handedly creates but immediately spurns and abandons. The fact that in the end both characters reach an equal degree of alienation and self-torture and indeed become indistinguishable as they pursue each other across the frozen polar wastes indicates that the novel is, among other things, a study of the impossibility of finding an adequate model for what a parent should be.

All three books agree, then, that in the existing state of things there is something inherently monstrous about the prevailing parental arrangements. While Friday and Dinnerstein, whose analyses directly address the problem of sexual difference, suggest that this monstrousness is curable, Mary Shelley, who does not explicitly locate the self's monstrousness in its gender arrangements, appears to dramatize divisions within the human being that are so much a part of being human that no escape from monstrousness seems possible.

What I will try to do here is to read these three books not as mere studies of the monstrousness of selfhood, not as mere accounts of human monsterdom in general, but as autobiographies in their own right, as textual dramatizations of the very problems with which they deal. None of the three books, of course, presents itself explicitly as autobiography. Yet each includes clear instances of the auto-biographical—not the purely authorial—first-person pronoun. In each case the autobiographical reflex is triggered by the resistance and am-bivalence involved in the act of writing the book. What I shall argue here is that what is specifically feminist in each book is directly related to this struggle for female authorship.

The notion that *Frankenstein* can somehow be read as the auto-biography of a woman would certainly appear at first sight to be lu-dicrous. The novel, indeed, presents not one but three autobiographies of men. Robert Walton, an arctic explorer on his way to the North Pole, writes home to his sister of his encounter with Victor Frankenstein, who tells Walton the story of his painstaking creation and unexplained aban-donment of a nameless monster who suffers excruciating and fiendish loneliness, and who tells Frankenstein *his* life story in the middle pages of the book. The three male autobiographies motivate themselves as follows:

> [Walton, to his sister:] "You will rejoice to hear that no disaster has accompanied the commencement of an enterprise which you have regarded with such evil forebodings. I arrived here yesterday, and my first task is to assure my dear sister of my welfare." (P. 15)

> [Frankenstein, with his hands covering his face, to Walton, who has been speaking of his scientific ambition:] "Unhappy man! Do you share my madness? Have you drunk also of the intoxicating draught? Hear me; let me reveal my tale, and you will dash the cup from your lips!" (P. 26)

> [Monster, to Frankenstein:] "I entreat you to hear me before you give vent to your hatred on my devoted head." [Frankenstein:] "Begone! I will not hear you. There can be no community between you and me." [Monster places his hands before Frankenstein's eyes:] "Thus I take from thee a sight which you abhor. Still thou canst listen to me and grant me thy compassion. . . . God, in pity, made man beautiful and alluring, after his own image; but my form is a filthy type of yours, more horrid even from the very resemblance." (Pp. 95, 96, 97, 125)

All three autobiographies here are clearly attempts at persuasion rather than simple accounts of facts. They all depend on a presupposition of resemblance between teller and addressee: Walton assures his sister that he has not really left the path she would wish for him, that he still resembles *her*. Frankenstein recognizes in Walton an image of himself and rejects in the monster a resemblance he does not wish to acknowledge. The teller is in each case speaking into a mirror of his own transgression. The tale is designed to reinforce the resemblance between teller and listener so that somehow transgression can be eliminated. Yet the desire for resemblance, the desire to create a being like oneself—which is the autobiographical desire par excellence—is also the central transgression in Mary Shelley's novel. What is at stake in Frankenstein's workshop of filthy creation is precisely the possibility of shaping a life in one's own image: Frankenstein's monster can thus be seen as a figure for autobiography as such. Victor Frankenstein, then, has twice obeyed the impulse to construct an image of himself: on the first occasion he creates a monster, and on he second he tries to explain to Walton the causes and consequences of the first. *Frankenstein* can be read as the story of autobiography as the attempt to neutralize the monstrosity of autobiography. Simultaneously a revelation and a cover-up, autobiography would appear to constitute itself as in some way a repression of autobiography.

These three fictive male autobiographies are embedded within a thin introductory frame, added in 1831, in which Mary Shelley herself makes the repression of her own autobiographical impulse explicit:

> The publishers of the standard novels, in selecting *Frankenstein* for one of their series, expressed a wish that I should furnish them with some account of the origin of the story. . . . It is true that I am very averse to bringing myself forward in print, but as my account will only appear as an appendage to a former production, and as it will be confined to such topics as have connection with my authorship alone, I can scarcely accuse myself of a personal intrusion. (P. vii)

Mary Shelley, here, rather than speaking into a mirror, is speaking as an appendage to a text. It might perhaps be instructive to ask whether this change of status has anything to do with the problem of specifically feminine autobiography. In a humanistic tradition in which *man* is the measure of all things, how does an appendage go about telling the story of her life?

Before pursuing this question further, I would like to turn to a more explicit version of surreptitious feminine autobiography. Of the three books under discussion, Nancy Friday's account of the mother/daughter relationship relies the most heavily on the facts of the author's life in order to demonstrate its thesis. Since the author grew up without a father, she shares with Frankenstein's monster some of the problems of coming from a single-parent household. The book begins with a chapter entitled "Mother Love," of which the first two sentences are "I have always lied to my mother. And she to me" (p. 19). Interestingly, the book carries the following dedication: "When I stopped seeing my mother with the eyes of a child, I saw the woman who helped me give birth to myself. This book is for Jane Colbert Friday Scott." How then, can we be sure that this huge book is not itself another lie to the mother it is dedicated to? Is autobiography somehow always in the process of symbolically killing the mother off by telling her the lie that we have given birth to ourselves? On page 460, Nancy Friday is still not sure what kind of lie she has told. She writes: "I am suddenly afraid that the mother I have depicted throughout this book is false." Whose life is this, anyway? This question cannot be resolved by a book that sees the "daughter's search for identity" as the necessity of choosing *between* symbiosis and separation, *between* the mother and the autonomous self. As long as this polarity remains unquestioned, the autobiography of Nancy Friday becomes the drawing and redrawing of the portrait of Jane Colbert Friday Scott. The most truly autobiographical moments occur not in expressions of triumphant separation but in descriptions of the way the book itself attempts to resist its own writing. At the end of the chapter on loss of virginity, Nancy Friday writes:

> It took me twenty-one years to give up my virginity. In some similar
> manner I am unable to let go of this chapter. . . .
>
> It is no accident that wrestling with ideas of loss of virginity
> immediately bring me to a dream of losing my mother. This chapter
> has revealed a split in me. Intellectually, I think of myself as a sexual
> person, just as I had intellectually been able to put my ideas for this
> chapter down on paper. Subjectively, I don't want to face what I have
> written: that the declaration of full sexual independence is the decla-
> ration of separation from my mother. As long as I don't finish this
> chapter, as long as I don't let myself understand the implication of
> what I've written, I can maintain the illusion, at least, that I can be
> sexual and have my mother's love and approval too. (Pp. 331–33)

As long as sexual identity and mother's judgment are linked as antithetical and exclusive poles of the daughter's problem, the "split" she describes will prevent her from ever completing her declaration of sexual
independence. "Full sexual independence" is shown by the book's own
resistance to be as illusory and as mystifying an ideal as the notion of
"mother love" that Friday so lucidly rejects.

Dinnerstein's autobiographical remarks are more muted, although her way of letting the reader know that the book was written
partly in mourning for her husband subtly underlies its persuasive seriousness. In her gesture of rejecting more traditional forms of scholarship, she pleads not for the validity but for the urgency of her message:

> Right now, what I think is that the kind of work of which this is an
> example is centrally necessary work. Whether our understanding
> makes a difference or not, we must try to understand what is threat-
> ening to kill us off as fully and clearly as we can. . . . What [this book]
> is, then, is not a scholarly book: it makes no effort to survey the
> relevant literature. Not only would that task be (for me) unmanagea-
> bly huge. It would also be against my principles. I *believe* in reading
> unsystematically and taking notes erratically. Any effort to form a
> rational policy about what to take in, out of the inhuman flood of
> printed human utterance that pours over us daily, feels to me like a
> self-deluded exercise in pseudomastery. (Pp. viii–ix)

The typographical form of this book bears out this belief in renouncing
the appearance of mastery: there are two kinds of notes, some at the foot
of the page and some at the back of the book; there are sections between
chapters with unaligned right-hand margins which are called "Notes
toward the next chapter." And there are boldface inserts which carry on
a dialogue with the controversial points in the main exposition. Clearly,

great pains have been taken to let as many seams as possible show in the fabric of the argument. The preface goes on:

> I mention these limitations in a spirit not of apology but of warning. To the extent that it succeeds in communicating its point at all, this book will necessarily enrage the reader. What it says is emotionally threatening. *(Part of why it has taken me so long to finish it is that I am threatened by it myself.)* (P. ix; emphasis mine)

My book is roughly sutured, says Dinnerstein, and it is threatening. This description sounds uncannily like a description of Victor Frankenstein's monster. Indeed, Dinnerstein goes on to warn the reader not to be tempted to avoid the threatening message by pointing to superficial flaws in its physical makeup. The reader of *Frankenstein*, too, would be well advised to look beyond the monster's physical deformity, both for his fearsome power and for his beauty. There are indeed numerous ways in which *The Mermaid and the Minotaur* can be seen as a modern rewriting of *Frankenstein*.

Dinnerstein's book situates its plea for two-sex parenting firmly in an apparently twentieth-century double bind: the realization that the very technological advances that make it possible to change the structure of parenthood also threaten to extinguish earthly life altogether. But it is startling to note that this seemingly contemporary pairing of the question of parenthood with a love-hate relation to technology is already at work in Mary Shelley's novel, where the spectacular scientific discovery of the secrets of animation produces a terrifyingly vengeful creature who attributes his evil impulses to his inability to find or to become a parent. Subtitled "The Modern Prometheus," *Frankenstein* itself indeed refers back to a myth that already links scientific ambivalence with the origin of mankind. Prometheus, the fire bringer, the giver of both creation and destruction, is also said by some accounts to be the father of the human race. Ambivalence toward technology can thus be seen as a displaced version of the love-hate relation we have toward our own children.

It is only recently that critics have begun to see Victor Frankenstein's disgust at the sight of his creation as a study of postpartum depression, as a representation of maternal rejection of a newborn infant, and to relate the entire novel to Mary Shelley's mixed feelings about motherhood.[2] Having lived through an unwanted pregnancy from a man married to someone else only to see that baby die, followed by a second baby named William—which is the name of the monster's first murder victim—Mary Shelley, at the age of only eighteen, must have had excruciatingly divided emotions. Her own mother, indeed, had died upon giving birth to her. The idea that a mother can loathe,

fear, and reject her baby has until recently been one of the most repressed of psychoanalytical insights, although it is of course already
implicit in the story of Oedipus, whose parents cast him out as an infant
to die. What is threatening about each of these books is the way in which
its critique of the *role* of the mother touches on primitive terrors of the
mother's rejection of the child. Each of these women writers does in her
way reject the child as part of her coming to grips with the untenable
nature of mother love: Nancy Friday decides not to have children, Dorothy Dinnerstein argues that men as well as women should do the mothering, and Mary Shelley describes a parent who flees in disgust from the
repulsive being to whom he has just given birth.

Yet it is not merely in its depiction of the ambivalence of motherhood that Mary Shelley's novel can be read as autobiographical. In the
introductory note added in 1831, she writes:

> The publishers of the standard novels, in selecting *Frankenstein* for
> one of their series, expressed a wish that I should furnish them with
> some account of the origin of the story. I am the more willing to
> comply because I shall thus give a general answer to the question so
> very frequently asked me—how I, then a young girl, came to think of
> and to *dilate* upon so very hideous an idea. (P. vii; emphasis mine)

As this passage makes clear, readers of Mary Shelley's novel had frequently expressed the feeling that a young girl's fascination with the
idea of monstrousness was somehow monstrous in itself. When Mary
ends her introduction to the reedition of her novel with the words,
"And now, once again, I bid my hideous progeny go forth and prosper,"
the reader begins to suspect that there may perhaps be meaningful
parallels between Victor's creation of his monster and Mary's creation of
her book.

Such parallels are indeed unexpectedly pervasive. The impulse to
write the book and the desire to search for the secret of animation both
arise under the same seemingly trivial circumstances: the necessity of
finding something to read on a rainy day. During inclement weather on
a family vacation, Victor Frankenstein happens upon the writings of
Cornelius Agrippa and is immediately fired with the longing to penetrate the secrets of life and death. Similarly, it was during a wet, un-
genial summer in Switzerland that Mary, Shelley, Byron, and several
others picked up a volume of ghost stories and decided to write a collection of spine-tingling tales of their own. Moreover, Mary's discovery of
the subject she would write about is described in almost exactly the
same words as Frankenstein's discovery of the principle of life: "Swift as
light and as cheering was the idea that broke in upon me" (p. xi), writes
Mary in her introduction, while Frankenstein says: "From the midst of

this darkness a sudden light broke in upon me" (p. 51). In both cases the sudden flash of inspiration must be supported by the meticulous gathering of heterogeneous, ready-made materials: Frankenstein collects bones and organs; Mary records overheard discussions of scientific questions that lead her to the sudden vision of monstrous creation. "Invention," she writes of the process of writing, but her words apply equally well to Frankenstein's labors, "Invention . . . does not consist in creating out of the void, but out of chaos; the materials must, in the first place, be afforded: it can give form to dark, shapeless substances but cannot bring into being the substance itself" (p. x). Perhaps the most revealing indication of Mary's identification of Frankenstein's activity with her own is to be found in her use of the word "artist" on two different occasions to qualify the "pale student of unhallowed arts": "His success would terrify the artist" (p. xi), she writes of the catastrophic moment of creation, while Frankenstein confesses to Walton: "I appeared rather like one doomed by slavery to toil in the mines, or any other unwholesome trade than an artist occupied by his favorite employment" (p. 55).

Frankenstein, in other words, can be read as the story of the experience of writing *Frankenstein*. What is at stake in Mary's introduction as well as in the novel is the description of a primal scene of creation. *Frankenstein* combines a monstrous answer to two of the most fundamental questions one can ask: Where do babies come from? and Where do stories come from? In both cases, the scene of creation is described, but the answer to these questions is still withheld.

But what can Victor Frankenstein's workshop of filthy creation teach us about the specificity of *female* authorship? At first sight, it would seem that *Frankenstein* is much more striking for its avoidance of the question of femininity than for its insight into it. All the interesting, complex characters in the book are male, and their deepest attachments are to other males. The females, on the other hand, are beautiful, gentle, selfless, boring nurturers and victims who never experience inner conflict or true desire. Monstrousness is so incompatible with femininity that Frankenstein cannot even complete the female companion that his creature so eagerly awaits.

On the other hand, the story of Frankenstein is, after all, the story of a man who usurps the female role by physically giving birth to a child. It would be tempting, therefore, to conclude that Mary Shelley, surrounded as she then was by the male poets Byron and Shelley, and mortified for days by her inability to think of a story to contribute to their ghost-story contest, should have fictively transposed her own frustrated female pen envy into a tale of catastrophic male womb envy. In this perspective, Mary's book would suggest that a woman's desire to write and a man's desire to give birth would both be capable only of producing monsters.

Yet clearly things cannot be so simple. As the daughter of a famous feminist whose *Vindication of the Rights of Women* she was in the process of rereading during the time she was writing *Frankenstein*, Mary Shelley would have no conscious reason to believe that writing was not proper for a woman. Indeed, as she says in her introduction, Mary was practically born with ink flowing through her veins. "It is not singular that, as the daughter of two persons of distinguished literary celebrity, I should very early in life have thought of writing. . . . My husband . . . was from the first very anxious that I should prove myself worthy of my parentage and enroll myself on the page of fame" (pp. vii–viii). In order to prove herself worthy of her parentage, Mary, paradoxically enough, must thus usurp the parental role and succeed in giving birth to *herself* on paper. Her declaration of existence as a writer must therefore figuratively repeat the matricide that her physical birth all too literally entailed. The connection between literary creation and the death of a parent is in fact suggested in the novel by the fact that, immediately after the monster's animation, Victor Frankenstein dreams that he holds the corpse of his dead mother in his arms. It is also suggested by the juxtaposition of two seemingly unrelated uses of italics in the novel: Mary's statement that she had *"thought of a story"* (which she inexplicably italicizes twice) and the monster's promise to Frankenstein, *"I will be with you on your wedding night,"* which is repeatedly italicized. Both are eliminations of the mother, since the story Mary writes is a tale of motherless birth, and the wedding night marks the death of Frankenstein's bride, Elizabeth. Indeed, Mary herself was in fact the unwitting murderous intruder present on her own parents' wedding night: their decision to marry was due to the fact that Mary Wollstonecraft was already carrying the child that was to kill her. When Mary, describing her waking vision of catastrophic creation, affirms that "his success would terrify the artist," she is not giving vent to any ordinary fear-of-success syndrome. Rather, what her book suggests is that what is at stake behind what is currently being banalized under the name of female fear of success is nothing less than the fear of somehow effecting the death of one's own parents.

It is not, however, the necessary murderousness of any declaration of female subjectivity that Mary Shelley's novel is proposing as its most troubling message of monsterdom. For, in a strikingly contemporary sort of predicament, Mary had not one but *two* mothers, each of whom consisted in the knowledge of the unviability of the other. After the death of Mary Wollstonecraft, Mary's father, William Godwin, married a woman as opposite in character and outlook as possible, a staunch, housewifely mother of two who clearly preferred her own children to Godwin's. Between the courageous, passionate, intelligent, and suicidal mother Mary knew only through her writings and the vulgar, repressive "pustule of vanity" whose dislike she resented and returned, Mary must have known at first hand a whole gamut of feminine contradictions, impasses, and options. For the complexities of the demands, desires, and sufferings of Mary's life as a woman were staggering. Her father, who had once been a vehement opponent of the institution of marriage, nearly disowned his daughter for running away with Shelley, an already married disciple of Godwin's own former views. Shelley himself, who believed in multiple love objects, amicably fostered an erotic correspondence between Mary and his friend Thomas Jefferson Hogg, among others. For years, Mary and Shelley were accompanied everywhere by Mary's stepsister Claire, whom Mary did not particularly like, who had a child by Byron, and who maintained an ambiguous relation with Shelley. During the writing of *Frankenstein*, Mary learned of the suicide of her half-sister Fanny Imlay, her mother's illegitimate child by an American lover, and the suicide of Shelley's wife Harriet, who was pregnant by a man other than Shelley. By the time she and Shelley married, Mary had had two children; she would have two more by the time of Shelley's death and watch as all but one of the children died in infancy. Widowed at age twenty-four, she never remarried. It is thus indeed perhaps the very hiddenness of the question of femininity in *Frankenstein* that somehow proclaims the painful message not of female monstrousness but of female contradictions. For it is the fact of self-contradiction that is so vigorously repressed in women. While the story of a man who is haunted by his own contradictions is representable as an allegory of monstrous doubles, how indeed would it have been possible for Mary to represent feminine contradiction *from the point of view of its repression* otherwise than precisely in the *gap* between angels of domesticity and an uncompleted monsteress, between the murdered Elizabeth and the dismembered Eve?

It is perhaps because the novel does succeed in conveying the unresolvable contradictions inherent in being female that Percy Shelley himself felt compelled to write a prefatory disclaimer in Mary's name before he could let loose his wife's hideous progeny upon the world. In a series of denials jarringly at odds with the daring negativity of the novel, Shelley places the following words in Mary's mouth:

> I am by no means indifferent to the manner in which whatever moral tendencies exist in the sentiments or characters it contains shall affect the reader; yet my chief concern in this respect has been limited

to . . . the exhibition of the amiableness of domestic affection, and the excellence of universal virtue. The opinions which naturally spring from the character and situation of the hero are by no means to be conceived as existing always in my own conviction; nor is any inference justly to be drawn from the following pages as prejudicing any philosophical doctrine of whatever kind. (Pp. xiii–xiv)

How is this to be read except as a gesture of repression of the very specificity of the power of feminine contradiction, a gesture reminiscent of Frankenstein's destruction of his nearly completed female monster? What is being repressed here is the possibility that a woman can write anything that would *not* exhibit "the amiableness of domestic affection," the possibility that for women as well as for men the home can be the very site of the *unheimlich*.

It can thus be seen in all three of the books we have discussed that the monstrousness of selfhood is intimately embedded within the question of female autobiography. Yet how could it be otherwise, since the very notion of a self, the very shape of human life stories, has always, from Saint Augustine to Freud, been modeled on the man? Rousseau's—or any man's—autobiography consists in the story of the difficulty of conforming to the standard of what a *man* should be. The problem for the female autobiographer is, on the one hand, to resist the pressure of masculine autobiography as the only literary genre available for her enterprise, and, on the other, to describe a difficulty in conforming to a female ideal which is largely a fantasy of the masculine, not the feminine, imagination. The fact that these three books deploy a *theory* of autobiography as monstrosity within the framework of a less overtly avowed struggle with the raw materials of the authors' own lives and writing is perhaps, in the final analysis, what is most autobiographically fertile and *telling* about them.

14

Metaphor, Metonymy, and Voice in
Their Eyes Were Watching God

Not so very long ago, metaphor and metonymy burst into prominence as the salt and pepper, the Laurel and Hardy, the Yin and Yang, and often the Scylla and Charybdis of literary theory. Then, just as quickly, this cosmic couple passed out of fashion again. How did it happen that such an arcane rhetorical opposition was able to acquire the brief but powerful privilege of dividing and naming the whole of human reality, from Mommy and Daddy or Symptom and Desire all the way to God and Country or Beautiful Lie and Sober Lucidity?[1]

The contemporary sense of the opposition between metaphor and metonymy was first formulated by Roman Jakobson in an article entitled "Two Aspects of Language and Two Types of Aphasic Disturbances."[2] That article, first published in English in 1956, derives much of its celebrity from the central place accorded by the French structuralists to the 1963 translation of a selection of Jakobson's work entitled *Essais de linguistique générale*, which included the aphasia study. The words *metaphor* and *metonymy* are not, of course, twentieth-century coinages: they are classical tropes traditionally defined as the substitution of a figurative expression for a literal or proper one. In metaphor, the substitution is based on resemblance or analogy; in metonymy, it is based on a relation or association other than that of similarity (cause and effect, container and contained, proper name and qualities or works associated with it, place and event or institution, instrument and user, etc.). The use of the name "Camelot" to refer to King Arthur's world is a metonymy (of place), while the same word applied to John Kennedy's Washington is a metaphor, since it implies an analogy between Kennedy's world and King Arthur's.

Jakobson's use of the two terms is an extension and polarization of their classical definitions. Jakobson found that patterns of aphasia (speech dysfunction) fell into two main categories: similarity disorders and contiguity disorders. In the former, grammatical contexture and lateral associations remain while synonymity drops out; in the latter, heaps of word substitutes are kept while grammar and connectedness vanish. Jakobson concludes:

> The development of a discourse may take place along two different semantic lines: one topic may lead to another either through their similarity or through their contiguity. The metaphoric way would be the most appropriate term for the first case and the metonymic way for the second, since they find their most condensed expression in metaphor and metonymy respectively. In aphasia one or the other of these two processes is restricted or totally blocked—an effect which makes the study of aphasia particularly illuminating for the linguist. In normal verbal behavior both processes are continually operative, but careful observation will reveal that under the influence of a cultural pattern, personality, and verbal style, preference is given to one of the two processes over the other.
>
> In a well-known psychological test, children are confronted with some noun and told to utter the first verbal response that comes into their heads. In this experiment two opposite linguistic predilections are invariably exhibited: the response is intended either as a substitute for, or as a complement to the stimulus. In the latter case the stimulus and the response together form a proper syntactic construction, most usually a sentence. These two types of reaction have been labeled substitutive and predicative.
>
> To the stimulus *hut* one response was *burnt out;* another, *is a poor little house.* Both reactions are predicative; but the first creates a purely narrative context, while in the second there is a double connection with the subject *hut:* on the one hand, a positional (namely, syntactic) contiguity, and on the other a semantic similarity.
>
> The same stimulus produced the following substitutive reactions: the tautology *hut;* the synonyms *cabin* and *hovel;* the autonym *palace;* and the metaphors *den* and *burrow.* The capacity of two words to replace one another is an instance of positional similarity, and, in addition, all these responses are linked to the stimulus by semantic similarity (or contrast). Metonymical responses to the same stimulus, such as *thatch, litter,* or *poverty,* combine and contrast the positional similarity with semantic contiguity.
>
> In manipulating these two kinds of connection (similarity and contiguity) in both their aspects (positional and semantic)—selecting, combining, and ranking them—an individual exhibits his personal style, his verbal predilections and preferences. (Pp. 76–77)

Two problems immediately arise that render the opposition between metaphor and metonymy at once more interesting and more problematic than at first appears. The first is that there are not two poles here, but four: similarity, contiguity, semantic connection, and syntactic connection. A more adequate representation of these oppositions can be schematized (see figure 1). Jakobson's contention that poetry is a syntactic extension of metaphor ("The poetic function projects the principle of equivalence from the axis of selection into the axis of combination"),[3] while realist narrative is an extension of metonymy, can be added to the graph (see figure 2).

The second problem that arises in any attempt to apply the metaphor/metonymy distinction is that it is often very hard to tell the two apart. In Ronsard's poem "Mignonne, allons voir si la rose," the speaker invites the lady to go for a walk with him (the walk being an example of contiguity) to see a rose which, once beautiful (like the lady), is now withered (as the lady will eventually be): the day must therefore be seized. The metonymic proximity to the flower is designed solely to reveal the metaphoric point of the poem: enjoy life while you still bloom. The tendency of contiguity to become overlaid by similarity, and vice versa, may be summed up in the proverb "Birds of a feather flock together"—"qui se ressemble s'assemble." One has only to think of the applicability of this proverb to the composition of neighborhoods in America to realize that the question of the separability of similarity from contiguity may have considerable political implications. The controversy surrounding the expression "Legionnaires' disease" provides a more comical example: while the name of the disease derives solely from the contingent fact that its first victims were at an American Legion Convention, and is thus a metonymy, the fear that it will take on a metaphoric color—that a belief in some natural connection or similarity may thereby be propagated between Legionnaires and the disease—has led spokesmen for the Legionnaires to attempt to have the malady renamed. And finally, in the sentence "the White House denied the charges," one might ask whether the place name is a purely contiguous metonymy for the presidency, or whether the whiteness of the house isn't somehow metaphorically connected to the whiteness of its inhabitant.

One final prefatory remark about the metaphor/metonymy distinction: far from being a neutral opposition between equals, these two tropes have always stood in hierarchical relation to each other. From Aristole to George Lakoff, metaphor has always, in the Western tradition, had the privilege of revealing unexpected truth.[4] As Aristotle puts it, "Midway between the unintelligible and the commonplace, it is a

Figure 1

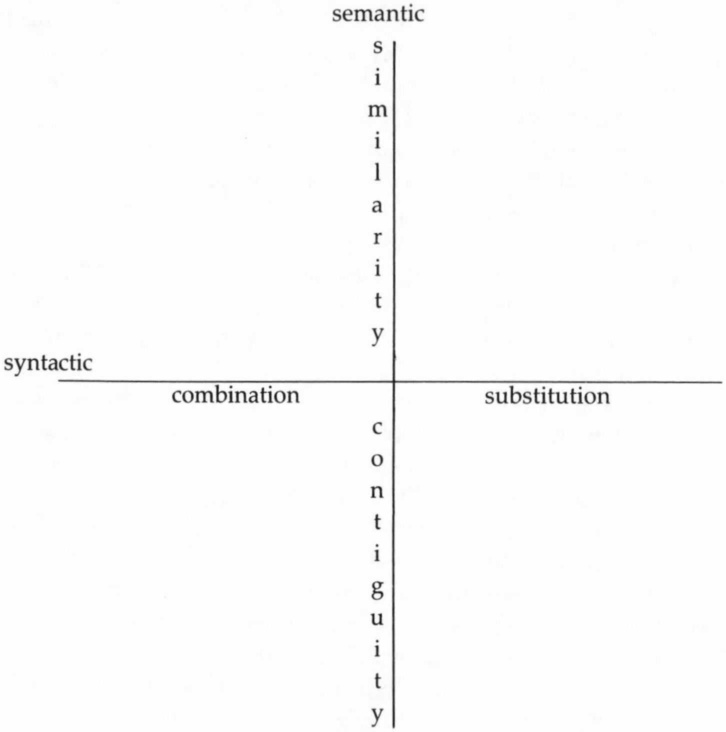

```
                         semantic
                            s │
                            i │
                            m │
                            i │
                            l │
                            a │
                            r │
                            i │
                            t │
                            y │
  syntactic                    │
  ───────────────────────────────────────────────────────
          combination          │       substitution
                            c │
                            o │
                            n │
                            t │
                            i │
                            g │
                            u │
                            i │
                            t │
                            y │
```

metaphor which most produces knowledge" (*Rhetoric* 3.1410). Paul de Man summarizes the preference for metaphor over metonymy by aligning analogy with necessity and contiguity with chance: "The inference of identity and totality that is constitutive of metaphor is lacking in the purely relational metonymic contact: an element of truth is involved in taking Achilles for a lion but none in taking Mr. Ford for a motor car."[5] De Man then goes on to reveal this "element of truth" as the product of a purely rhetorical—and ultimately metonymical—sleight of hand, thus overturning the traditional hierarchy and deconstructing the very basis for the seductiveness and privilege of metaphor.

I would like now to turn to the work of an author acutely conscious of, and superbly skilled in, the seductiveness and complexity of metaphor as privileged trope and trope of privilege. Zora Neale Hurston—novelist, folklorist, essayist, anthropologist, and Harlem Renaissance per-

Figure 2

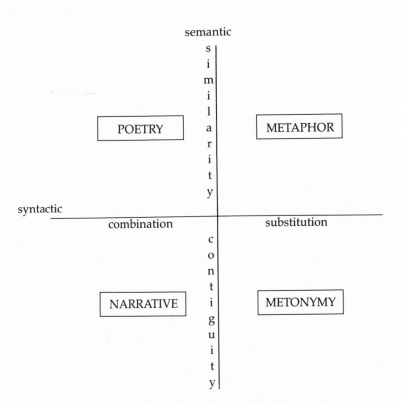

sonality—cut her teeth on figurative language during the tale-telling, or "lying," sessions that took place on a store porch in the all-black town of Eatonville, Florida, where she was born around 1901.[6] She devoted her life to the task of recording, preserving, novelizing, and analyzing the patterns of speech and thought of the rural black South and related cultures. At the same time, she deplored the appropriation, dilution, and commodification of black culture (through spirituals, jazz, etc.) by the pre-Depression white world, and she constantly tried to explain the difference between a reified "art" and a living culture in which the distinctions between spectator and spectacle, rehearsal and performance, experience and representation, are not fixed. "Folklore," she wrote, "is the arts of the people before they find out that there is such a thing as art."

Folklore does not belong to any special area, time, nor people. It is a world and an ageless thing, so let us look at it from that viewpoint. It is the boiled down juice of human living and when one phase of it passes another begins which shall in turn give way before a successor. Culture is a forced march on the near and the obvious. . . . The intelligent mind uses up a great part of its lifespan trying to awaken its consciousness sufficiently to comprehend that which is plainly there before it. Every generation or so some individual with extra keen perception grasps something of the obvious about us and hitches the human race forward slightly by a new "law." Millions of things had been falling on men for thousands of years before the falling apple hit Newton on the head and he saw the law of gravity.[7]

Through this strategic description of the folkloric heart of scientific law, Hurston dramatizes the predicament not only of the anthropologist but also of the novelist: both are caught between the (metaphorical) urge to universalize or totalize and the knowledge that it is precisely "the near and the obvious" that will never be grasped once and for all, but only (metonymically) named and renamed as different things successively strike different heads. I will return to this problem of universality at the end of this essay, but first I would like to take a close look at some of the figurative operations at work in Hurston's best-known novel, *Their Eyes Were Watching God*.[8]

The novel presents, in a combination of first- and third-person narration, the story of Janie Crawford and her three successive husbands. The first, Logan Killicks, is chosen by Janie's grandmother for his sixty acres and as a socially secure harbor for Janie's awakening sexuality. When Janie realizes that love does not automatically follow upon marriage and that Killicks completely lacks imagination, she decides to run off with ambitious, smart-talking, stylishly dressed Joe Starks, who is headed for a new all-black town, where he hopes to become what he calls a "big voice." Later, as store owner and mayor of the town, he proudly raises Janie to a pedestal of property and propriety. Because this involves her submission to his idea of what a mayor's wife should be, Janie soon finds her pedestal to be a straitjacket, particularly when it involves her exclusion—both as speaker and as listener—from the tale-telling sessions on the store porch and at the mock funeral of a mule. Little by little, Janie begins to talk back to Joe, finally insulting him so profoundly that, in a sense, he dies of it. Some time later, into Janie's life walks Tea Cake Woods, whose first act is to teach Janie how to play checkers. "Somebody wanted her to play," says the text in free indirect discourse; "Somebody thought it natural for her to play" (p. 146). Thus begins a joyous liberation from the rigidities of status, image, and property—one of the most beautiful and convincing love stories in any literature. In a series of courtship dances, appearances, and disappearances, Tea Cake succeeds in fulfilling Janie's dream of "a bee for her blossom" (p. 161). Tea Cake, unlike Joe and Logan, regards money and work as worth only the amount of play and enjoyment they make possible. He gains and loses money unpredictably until he and Janie begin working side by side picking beans on "the muck" in the Florida everglades. This idyll of pleasure, work, and equality ends dramatically with a hurricane, during which Tea Cake, while saving Janie's life, is bitten by a rabid dog. When Tea Cake's subsequent hydrophobia transforms him into a wild and violent animal, Janie is forced to shoot him in self-defense. Acquitted of murder by an all-white jury, Janie returns to Eatonville, where she tells her story to her friend Phoeby Watson.

The passage on which I would like to concentrate both describes and dramatizes, in its figurative structure, a crucial turning point in Janie's relation to Joe and to herself. The passage follows an argument over what Janie has done with a bill of lading, during which Janie shouts, "You sho loves to tell me whut to do, but Ah can't tell you nothin' Ah see!"

> "Dat's 'cause you need tellin'," he rejoined hotly. "It would be pitiful if Ah didn't. Somebody got to think for women and chillun and chickens and cows. I god, they sho don't think none theirselves."
>
> "Ah knows uh few things, and womenfolks thinks sometimes too!"
>
> "Aw naw they don't. They just think they's thinkin'. When Ah see one thing Ah understands ten. You see ten things and don't understand one."
>
> Times and scenes like that put Janie to thinking about the inside state of her marriage. Time came when she fought back with her tongue as best she could, but it didn't do her any good. It just made Joe do more. He wanted her submission and he'd keep on fighting until he felt he had it.
>
> So gradually, she pressed her teeth together and learned how to hush. The spirit of the marriage left the bedroom and took to living in the parlor. It was there to shake hands whenever company came to visit, but it never went back inside the bedroom again. So she put something in there to represent the spirit like a Virgin Mary image in a church. The bed was no longer a daisy-field for her and Joe to play in. It was a place where she went and laid down when she was sleepy and tired.
>
> She wasn't petal-open anymore with him. She was twenty-four and seven years married when she knew. She found that out one day when he slapped her face in the kitchen. It happened over one of those dinners that chasten all women sometimes. They plan and they

fix and they do, and then some kitchen-dwelling fiend slips a scrochy, soggy, tasteless mess into their pots and pans. Janie was a good cook, and Joe had looked forward to his dinner as a refuge from other things. So when the bread didn't rise and the fish wasn't quite done at the bone, and the rice was scorched, he slapped Janie until she had a ringing sound in her ears and told her about her brains before he stalked on back to the store.

Janie stood where he left her for unmeasured time and thought. She stood there until something fell off the shelf inside her. Then she went inside there to see what it was. It was her image of Jody tumbled down and shattered. But looking at it she saw that it never was the flesh and blood figure of her dreams. Just something she had grabbed up to drape her dreams over. In a way she turned her back upon the image where it lay and looked further. She had no more blossomy openings dusting pollen over her man, neither any glistening young fruit where the petals used to be. She found that she had a host of thoughts she had never expressed to him, and numerous emotions she had never let Jody know about. Things packed up and put away in parts of her heart where he could never find them. She was saving up feelings for some man she had never seen. She had an inside and an outside now and suddenly she knew how not to mix them. (Pp. 110–13)

This opposition between an inside and an outside is a standard way of describing the nature of a rhetorical figure. The vehicle, or surface meaning, is seen as enclosing an inner tenor, or figurative meaning. This relation can be pictured somewhat facetiously as a gilded carriage—the vehicle—containing Luciano Pavarotti, the tenor. Within the passage cited from *Their Eyes Were Watching God*, I would like to concentrate on the two paragraphs that begin respectively "So gradually . . ." and "Janie stood where he left her . . ." In these two paragraphs Hurston plays a number of interesting variations on the inside/outside opposition.

In both paragraphs, a relation is set up between an inner "image" and outward, domestic space. The parlor, bedroom, and store full of shelves already exist in the narrative space of the novel: they are figures drawn metonymically from the familiar contiguous surroundings. Each of these paragraphs recounts a little narrative of, and within, its own figurative terms. In the first, the inner spirit of the marriage moves outward from the bedroom to the parlor, cutting itself off from its proper place, and replacing itself with an image of virginity, the antithesis of marriage. Although Joe is constantly exclaiming, "I god, Janie," he will not be as successful as his namesake in uniting with the Virgin Mary.

Indeed, it is his godlike self-image that forces Janie to retreat to virginity. The entire paragraph is an externalization of Janie's feelings onto the outer surroundings in the form of a narrative of movement from private to public space. While the whole of the figure relates metaphorically, analogically, to the marital situation it is designed to express, it reveals the marriage space to be metonymical, a movement through a series of contiguous rooms. It is a narrative not of union but of separation, centered on an image not of conjugality but of virginity.

In the second passage, just after the slap, Janie is standing, thinking, until something "fell off the shelf inside her." Janie's "inside" is here represented as a store that she then goes in to inspect. While the former paragraph was an externalization of the inner, here we find an internalization of the outer: Janie's inner self resembles a store. The material for this metaphor is drawn from the narrative world of contiguity: the store is the place where Joe has set himself up as lord, master, and proprietor. But here, Jody's image is broken and reveals itself never to have been a metaphor, but only a metonymy, of Janie's dream: "Looking at it she saw that it never was the flesh and blood figure of her dreams. Just something she had grabbed up to drape her dreams over."

What we find in juxtaposing these two figural mininarratives is a kind of chiasmus, or crossover, in which the first paragraph presents an externalization of the inner, a metaphorically grounded metonymy, while the second paragraph presents an internalization of the outer, or a metonymically grounded metaphor. In both cases, the quotient of the operation is the revelation of a false or discordant "image." Janie's image, as Virgin Mary, acquires a new intactness, while Joe's lies shattered on the floor. The reversals operated by the chiasmus map out a reversal of the power relations between Janie and Joe. Henceforth, Janie will grow in power and resistance, while Joe deteriorates both in his body and in his public image.

The moral of these two figural tales is rich with implications: "She had an inside and an outside now and suddenly she knew how not to mix them." On the one hand, this means that she knew how to keep the inside and the outside separate without trying to blend or merge them into one unified identity. On the other hand it means that she has stepped irrevocably into the necessity of figurative language, where inside and outside are never the same. It is from this point on in the novel that Janie, paradoxically, begins to speak. And it is by means of a devastating figure—"You look like the change of life"—that she wounds Jody to the quick. Janie's acquisition of the power of voice thus grows not out of her identity but out of her division into inside and outside. Knowing how not to mix them is knowing that articulate language requires the co-presence of two distinct poles, not their collapse into oneness.

This, of course, is what Jakobson concludes in his discussion of metaphor and metonymy. For it must be remembered that what is at stake in the maintenance of both sides—metaphor and metonymy, inside and outside—is the very possibility of speaking at all. The reduction of a discourse to oneness, identity—in Janie's case, the reduction of woman to mayor's wife—has as its necessary consequence aphasia, silence, the loss of the ability to speak: "She pressed her teeth together and learned to hush."

What has gone unnoticed in theoretical discussions of Jakobson's article is that behind the metaphor/metonymy distinction lies the much more serious distinction between speech and aphasia, between silence and the capacity to articulate one's own voice. To privilege either metaphor or metonymy is thus to run the risk of producing an increasingly aphasic *critical* discourse. If both, or all four, poles must be operative in order for speech to function fully, then the very notion of an "authentic voice" must be redefined. Far from being an expression of Janie's new wholeness or identity as a character, Janie's increasing ability to speak grows out of her ability not to mix inside with outside, not to pretend that there is no difference, but to assume and articulate the incompatible forces involved in her own division. The sign of an authentic voice is thus not self-identity but self-difference.

The search for wholeness, oneness, universality, and totalization can nevertheless never be put to rest. However rich, healthy, or lucid fragmentation and division may be, narrative seems to have trouble resting content with it, as though a story could not recognize its own end as anything other than a moment of totalization—even when what is totalized is loss. The ending of *Their Eyes Were Watching God* is no exception:

> Of course [Tea Cake] wasn't dead. He could never be dead until she herself had finished feeling and thinking. The kiss of his memory made pictures of love and light against the wall. Here was peace. She pulled in her horizon like a great fish-net. Pulled it from around the waist of the world and draped it over her shoulder. So much of life in its meshes! She called in her soul to come and see.

The horizon, with all of life caught in its meshes, is here pulled into the self as a gesture of total recuperation and peace. It is as though self-division could be healed over at last, but only at the cost of a radical loss of the other.

This hope for some ultimate unity and peace seems to structure the very sense of an ending as such, whether that of a novel or that of a work of literary criticism. At the opposite end of the "canonical" scale, one finds it, for example, in the last chapter of Erich Auerbach's *Mimesis*, perhaps the greatest of modern monuments to the European literary canon. That final chapter, entitled "The Brown Stocking" after the stocking that Virginia Woolf's Mrs. Ramsay is knitting in *To the Lighthouse*, is a description of certain narrative tendencies in the modern novel: "multipersonal representation of consciousness, time strata, disintegration of the continuity of exterior events, shifting of narrative viewpoint," and so on.[9] "Let us begin with a tendency which is particularly striking in our text from Virginia Woolf. She holds to minor, unimpressive, random events: measuring the stocking, a fragment of a conversation with the maid, a telephone call. Great changes, exterior turning points, let alone catastrophes, do not occur" (p. 483). Auerbach concludes his discussion of the modernists' preoccupation with the minor, the trivial, and the marginal by saying:

> It is precisely the random moment which is comparatively independent of the controversial and unstable orders over which men fight and despair. . . . The more numerous, varied, and simple the people are who appear as subjects of such random moments, the more effectively must what they have in common shine forth. . . . So the complicated process of dissolution which led to fragmentation of the exterior action, to reflection of consciousness, and to stratification of time seems to be tending toward a very simple solution. Perhaps it will be too simple to please those who, despite all its dangers and catastrophes, admire and love our epoch for the sake of its abundance of life and the incomparable historical vantage point which it affords. But they are few in number, and probably they will not live to see much more than the first forewarnings of the approaching unification and simplification. (P. 488)

Never has the desire to transform fragmentation into unity been expressed so succinctly and authoritatively—indeed, almost prophetically. One cannot help but wonder, though, whether the force of this desire has not been provoked by the fact that the primary text it wishes to unify and simplify was written by a woman. What Auerbach calls "minor, unimpressive, random events"—measuring a stocking, conversing with the maid, answering the phone—can all be identified as conventional *women's* activities. "Great changes, exterior turning points," and "catastrophes" have been the stuff of heroic *male* literature. Even plot itself—up until *Madame Bovary*, at least—has been conceived as the doings of those who do *not* stay at home, in other words, men. Auerbach's urge to unify and simplify is an urge to resubsume female difference under the category of the universal, which has always been unavowedly male. The random, the trivial, and the marginal will simply be added to the list of things all *men* have in common.

If "unification and simplification" is the privilege and province of the male, it is also, in America, the privilege and province of the white. If the woman's voice, to be authentic, must incorporate and articulate division and self-difference, so, too, has Afro-American literature always had to assume its double-voicedness. As Henry Louis Gates, Jr., puts it in "Criticism in the Jungle":

> In the instance of the writer of African descent, her or his texts occupy spaces in at least two traditions—the individual's European or American literary tradition, and one of the three related but distinct black traditions. The "heritage" of each black text written in a Western language, then, is a double heritage, two-toned, as it were. . . . Each utterance, then, is double-voiced. [10]

This is a reformulation of W.E.B. Dubois's famous image of the "veil" that divides the black American in two:

> The Negro is a sort of seventh son, born with a veil, and gifted with second sight in this American world, —a world which yields him no true self-consciousness, but only lets him see himself through the revelation of the other world. It is a peculiar sensation, this double-consciousness, this sense of always looking at one's self through the eyes of others, of measuring one's soul by the tape of a world that looks on in amused contempt and pity. One ever feels his twoness— an American, a Negro; two souls, two thoughts, two unreconciled strivings; two warring ideals in one dark body, whose dogged strength alone keeps it from being torn asunder.
>
> The history of the American Negro is the history of this strife, — this longing to attain self-conscious manhood, to merge his double self into a better and truer self. [11]

James Weldon Johnson, in his *Autobiography of an Ex-Colored Man*, puts it this way:

> This is the dwarfing, warping, distorting influence which operates upon each and every colored man in the United States. He is forced to take his outlook on all things, not from the view-point of a citizen, or a man, or even a human being, but from the view-point of a *colored* man. . . . This gives to every colored man, in proportion to his intellectuality, a sort of dual personality. [12]

What is striking about the above two quotations is that they both assume without question that the black subject is male. The black woman is totally invisible in these descriptions of the black dilemma. Richard

Wright, in his review of *Their Eyes Were Watching God*, makes it plain that for him, too, the black female experience is nonexistent. The novel, says Wright, lacks "a basic idea or theme that lends itself to significant interpretation. . . . [Hurston's] dialogue manages to catch the psychological movements of the Negro folk-mind in their pure simplicity, but that's as far as it goes. . . . The sensory sweep of her novel carries no theme, no message, no thought."[13]

No message, no theme, no thought: the full range of questions and experiences of Janie's life are as invisible to a mind steeped in maleness as Ellison's Invisible Man is to minds steeped in whiteness. If the black *man*'s soul is divided in two, what can be said of the black woman's? Here again, what is constantly seen exclusively in terms of a binary opposition—black versus white, man versus woman—must be redrawn at least as a tetrapolar structure (see figure 3). What happens in the case of a black woman is that the four quadrants are constantly being collapsed into two. Hurston's work is often called nonpolitical simply because readers of Afro-American literature tend to look for confrontational *racial* politics, not sexual politics. If the black woman voices opposition to male domination, she is often seen as a traitor to the cause of racial justice. But if she sides with black men against white oppression, she often winds up having to accept her position within the Black Power movement as, in Stokely Carmichael's words, "prone." This impossible position between two oppositions is what I think Hurston intends when, at the end of the novel, she represents Janie as acquitted of the murder of Tea Cake by an all-white jury but condemned by her fellow blacks. This is not out of a "lack of bitterness toward whites," as one

Figure 3

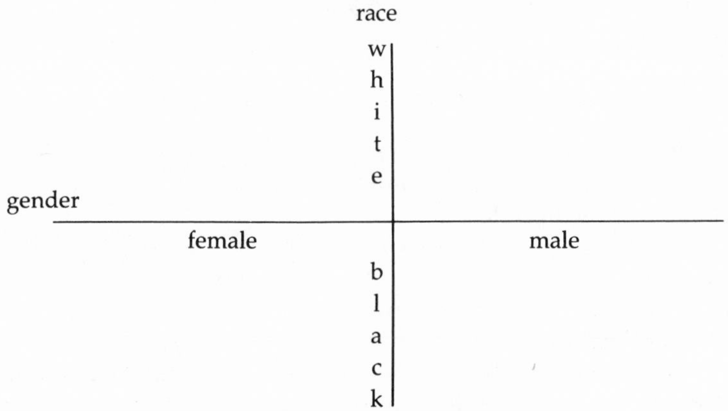

reader would have it,[14] but rather out of a knowledge of the standards of male dominance that pervade both the black and the white worlds. The black crowd at the trial murmurs: "Tea Cake was a good boy. He had been good to that woman. No nigger woman ain't never been treated no better" (p. 276). As Janie's grandmother puts it early in the novel:

> "Honey, de white man is de ruler of everything as fur as Ah been able tuh find out. Maybe it's some place way off in de ocean where de black man is in power, but we don't know nothin' but what we see. So de white man throw down de load and tell de nigger man tuh pick it up. He pick it up because he have to, but he don't tote it. He hand it to his womenfolks. De nigger woman is de mule uh de world so fur as Ah can see." (P. 29)

In a very persuasive book on black women and feminism entitled *Ain't I a Woman*, Bell Hooks (Gloria Watkins) discusses the ways in which black women suffer from both sexism and racism within the very movements whose ostensible purpose is to set them free. Watkins argues that "black woman" has never been considered a separate, distinct category with a history and complexity of its own. When a president appoints a black woman to a cabinet post, for example, he does not feel he is appointing a person belonging to the category "black woman"; he is appointing a person who belongs *both* to the category "black" *and* to the category "woman," and is thus killing two birds with one stone. Watkins says of the analogy often drawn—particularly by white feminists—between blacks and women:

> Since analogies derive their power, their appeal, and their very reason for being from the sense of two disparate phenomena having been brought closer together, for white women to acknowledge the overlap between the terms "blacks" and "women" (that is, the existence of black women) would render this analogy unnecessary. By continuously making this analogy, they unwittingly suggest that to them the term "women" is synonymous with "white women" and the term "blacks" synonymous with "black men."[15]

The very existence of black women thus disappears from an analogical discourse designed to express the types of oppression from which black women have the most to suffer.

In the current hierarchical view of things, this tetrapolar graph can be filled in as in figure 4. The black woman is both invisible and ubiquitous: never seen in her own right but forever appropriated by the others for their own ends.

Ultimately, though, this mapping of tetrapolar differences is itself a fantasy of universality. Are all the members of each quadrant the

Figure 4

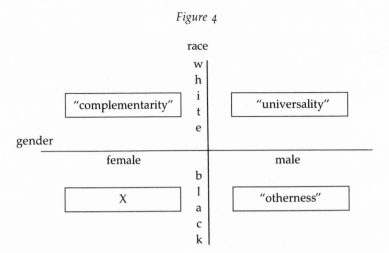

same? Where are the nations, the regions, the religions, the classes, the professions? Where are the other races, the interracial subdivisions? How can the human world be totalized, even as a field of divisions? In the following quotation from Zora Neale Hurston's autobiography, we see that even the same black woman can express self-division in two completely different ways:

Work was to be all of me, so I said. . . . I had finished that phase of research and was considering writing my first book, when I met the man who was really to lay me by the heels. . . .

He was tall, dark brown, magnificently built, with a beautifully modeled back head. His profile was strong and good. The nose and lips were especially good front and side. But his looks only drew my eyes in the beginning. I did not fall in love with him just for that. He had a fine mind and that intrigued me. When a man keeps beating me to the draw mentally, he begins to get glamorous. . . . His intellect got me first for I am the kind of woman that likes to move on mentally from point to point, and I like for my man to be there way ahead of me. . . .

His great desire was to do for me. *Please* let him be a *man!* . . .

That very manliness, sweet as it was, made us both suffer. My career balked the completeness of his ideal. I really wanted to conform, but it was impossible. To me there was no conflict. My work was one thing, and he was all the rest. But I could not make him see that. Nothing must be in my life but himself. . . . We could not leave each other alone, and we could not shield each other from hurt. . . . In the midst of this, I received my Guggenheim Fellowship. This was my chance to release him, and fight myself free from my obsession. He would get over me in a few months and go on to be a very big man. So I sailed off to Jamaica [and] pitched in to work hard on my research to smother my feelings. But the thing would not down. The plot was far from the circumstances, but I tried to embalm all the tenderness of my passion for him in *Their Eyes Were Watching God*.[16]

The plot is indeed far from the circumstances, and, what is even more striking, it is lived by what seems to be a completely different woman. While Janie struggles to attain equal respect *within* a relation to a man, Zora readily submits to the pleasures of submission yet struggles to establish the legitimacy of a professional life *outside* the love relation. The female voice may be universally described as divided, but it must be recognized as divided in a multitude of ways.

There is no point of view from which the universal characteristics of the human, or of the woman, or of the black woman, or even of Zora Neale Hurston, can be selected and totalized. Unification and simplification are fantasies of domination, not understanding.

The task of the writer, then, would seem to be to narrate both the appeal and the injustice of universalization, in a voice that assumes and articulates its own, ever-differing self-difference. In the opening pages of *Their Eyes Were Watching God* we find, indeed, a brilliant and subtle transition from the seduction of a universal language through a progressive de-universalization that ends in the exclusion of the very protagonist herself. The book begins:

> Ships at a distance have every man's wish on board. For some they come in with the tide. For others they sail forever on the horizon, never out of sight, never landing until the Watcher turns his eyes away in resignation, his dreams mocked to death by Time. That is the life of men.
>
> Now, women forget all those things they don't want to remember, and remember everything they don't want to forget. The dream is the truth. Then they act and do things accordingly.
>
> So the beginning of this was a woman, and she had come back from burying the dead. Not the dead of sick and ailing with friends at the pillow and the feet. She had come back from the sodden and the bloated; the sudden dead, their eyes flung wide open in judgment.
>
> The people all saw her come because it was sundown. (P. 9)

At this point Janie crosses center stage and goes out, while the people, the "bander log," pass judgment on her. The viewpoint has moved from "every man" to "men" to "women" to "a woman" to an absence commented on by "words without masters," the gossip of the front porch. When Janie begins to speak, even the universalizing category of standard English gives way to the careful representation of dialect. The narrative voice in this novel expresses its own self-divison by shifts between first and third person, standard English and dialect. This self-division culminates in the frequent use of free indirect discourse, in which, as Henry Louis Gates, Jr., points out, the inside/outside boundaries between narrator and character, between standard and individual, are both transgressed and preserved, making it impossible to identify and totalize either the subject or the nature of discourse.[17]

Narrative, it seems, is an endless fishing expedition with the horizon as both the net and the fish, the big one that always gets away. The meshes continually enclose and let escape, tear open and mend up again. Mrs. Ramsay never finishes the brown stocking.[18] A woman's work is never done. Penelope's weaving is nightly re-unraveled. The porch never stops passing the world through its mouth. The process of de-universalization can never, universally, be completed.

15

Thresholds of Difference

Structures of Address in Zora Neale Hurston

In preparing to write this chapter, I found myself repeatedly stopped by conflicting conceptions of the structure of address into which I was inserting myself. It was not clear to me what I, a white deconstructor, was doing talking about Zora Neale Hurston, a black novelist and anthropologist, or to *whom* I was talking. Was I trying to convince white establishment scholars who long for a return to Renaissance ideals that the study of the Harlem Renaissance is not a trivialization of their humanistic pursuits? Was I trying to contribute to the attempt to adapt the textual strategies of literary theory to the analysis of Afro-American literature? Was I trying to rethink my own previous work and to re-referentialize the notion of difference so as to move the conceptual operations of deconstruction out of the realm of abstract linguistic universality? Was I talking to white critics, black critics, or myself?

Well, all of the above. What finally struck me was the fact that what I was analyzing in Hurston's writings was precisely, again and again, her strategies and structures of problematic address. It was as though I were asking Zora Neale Hurston for answers to questions I did not even know I was unable to formulate. I had a lot to learn, then, from Hurston's way of dealing with multiple agendas and heterogeneous implied readers. I will here focus on three texts that play interesting variations on questions of identity and address: two short essays— "How It Feels to Be Colored Me" and "What White Publishers Won't Print"—and a book-length collection of folk tales, songs, and hoodoo practices entitled *Mules and Men*.[1]

One of the presuppositions with which I began was that Hurston's work was situated "outside" the mainstream literary canon and that I, by implication, was an institutional "insider." I soon came to see, however, not only that the insider becomes an outsider the minute she steps out of the inside, but also that Hurston's work itself was constantly dramatizing and undercutting just such inside/outside oppositions, transforming the plane geometry of physical space into the complex transactions of discursive exchange. In other words, Hurston could be read not just as an example of the "noncanonical" writer, but as a commentator on the dynamics of any encounter between an inside and an outside, any attempt to make a statement about difference.

One of Hurston's most memorable figurations of the inside/outside structure is her depiction of herself as a threshold figure mediating between the all-black town of Eatonville, Florida, and the big road traveled by passing whites:

> The front porch might seem a daring place for the rest of the town, but it was a gallery seat for me. My favorite place was atop the gate-post. Proscenium box for a born first-nighter. Not only did I enjoy the show, but I didn't mind the actors knowing that I liked it. 1 usually spoke to them in passing. . . . They liked to hear me "speak pieces" and sing and wanted to see me dance the parse-me-la, and gave me generously of their small silver for doing these things. . . . The colored people gave no dimes. They deplored any joyful tendencies in me, but I was their Zora nevertheless.

The inside/outside opposition here opens up a reversible theatrical space in which proscenium box becomes center stage and small silver passes to the boxholder-turned-actor.

Hurston's joyful and sometimes lucrative gatepost stance between black and white cultures was very much a part of her Harlem Renaissance persona, and was indeed often deplored by fellow black · artists. Langston Hughes, who for a time shared with Hurston the problematic patronage of the wealthy Charlotte Mason, wrote of Hurston:

> Of the "niggerati," Zora Neale Hurston was certainly the most amusing. Only to reach a wider audience, need she ever write books—because she was the perfect book of entertainment in herself. In her youth she was always getting scholarships and things from wealthy white people, some of whom simply paid her just to sit around and represent the Negro race for them, she did it in such a racy fashion. . . . To many of her white friends, no doubt, she was a perfect "darkie."[2]

"Representing the Negro race for whites" was nevertheless in many ways the program of the Harlem Renaissance. While Hurston has often been read and judged on the basis of personality alone, her "racy" adoption of the "happy darkie" stance, which was a successful strategy for survival, does not by any means exhaust the representational strategies of her *writing*.

Questions of identity, difference, and race representation are interestingly at issue in the 1928 essay entitled "How It Feels to Be Colored Me," from which the gatepost passage was taken. Published in a white journal sympathetic to Harlem Renaissance writers, the essay is quite clearly a response to the unspoken question inevitably asked by whites of the black artist. Since any student of literature trained in the European tradition and interested in Hurston out of a concern for the noncanonical is implicitly asking her that question, a close reading of that essay is likely to shed light on what is at stake in such an encounter.

The essay is divided into a series of vignettes, each of which responds to the question differently. The essay begins, "I am colored but I offer nothing in the way of extenuating circumstances except the fact that I am the only Negro in the United States whose grandfather on the mother's side was *not* an Indian chief." Collapsed into this sentence are two myths of black identity, the absurdity of whose juxtaposition sets the tone for the entire essay. On the one hand, it implies that being colored is a misdemeanor, for which some extenuation must be sought. On the other, it implies that among the stories Negroes tell about themselves the story of Indian blood is a common extenuation, dilution, and hence effacement of the crime of coloredness. By making *lack* of Indian blood into an extenuating circumstance and by making explicit the absurdity of seeking extenuating circumstances for something over which one has no control, Hurston is shedding an ironic light both on the question ("How does it feel to be colored you?") and on one possible answer ("I'm not 100% colored"). Hurston is saying in effect, "I am colored, but I am different from other members of my race in that I am not different from my race."[3]

While the first paragraph thus begins, "I am colored," the second starts, "I remember the very day that I *became* colored" (italics mine). The presuppositions of the question are again undercut. If one can become colored, then one is not born colored, and the definition of "colored" shifts. Hurston goes on to describe her precolored childhood, spent in the all-black town of Eatonville, Florida. "During this period," she writes, "white people differed from colored to me only in that they rode through town and never lived there." It was not that there was no difference; it was that difference needed no extenuation.

> But changes came in the family when I was thirteen, and I was sent to school in Jacksonville. I left Eatonville, the town of the oleanders, as Zora. When I disembarked from the river-boat at Jacksonville, she was

no more. It seemed that I had suffered a sea change. I was not Zora of Orange County any more, I was now a little colored girl. I found it out in certain ways. In my heart as well as in the mirror, I became a fast brown—warranted not to rub nor run.

In this sea change, the acquisition of color is a *loss* of identity: the "I" is no longer Zora, and "Zora" becomes a "she." "Everybody's Zora" had been constituted not by *an* other but by the system of otherness itself, the ability to role-play rather than the ability to play any particular role. Formerly an irrepressible speaker of pieces, she now becomes a speaker of withholdings: "I found it out in certain ways."

The acquisition of color, which is here a function of motion (from Eatonville to Jacksonville), ends up entailing the fixity of a correspondence between inside and outside: "In my heart as well as in the mirror, I became a fast brown—warranted not to rub nor run." But the speed hidden in the word "fast," which belies its claim to fixity, is later picked up to extend the color = motion equation and to transform the question of race into the image of a road race: "The terrible struggle that made an American out of a potential slave said 'On the line!' The Reconstruction said 'Get set!'; and the generation before said 'Go!' I am off to a flying start and I must not halt in the stretch to look behind and weep." Later, however, "I am a dark rock surged upon," a stasis in the midst of motion.

The remainder of the essay is dotted with sentences playing complex variations on the title words "feel," "color," and "me."

But I am not tragically colored.

I do not always feel colored.

I feel most colored when I am thrown against a sharp white background.

At certain times I have no race, I am *me.*

I have no separate feeling about being an American citizen and colored.

The feelings associated with coloredness are, on the one hand, the denial of sorrow and anger ("There is no great sorrow dammed up in my soul"; "Sometimes I feel discriminated against, but it does not make me angry") and, on the other, the affirmation of strength and excitement ("I have seen that the world is to the strong regardless of a little pigmentation more or less"; "It is quite exciting to hold the center of the national stage"). Each case involves a reversal of implicit white expectations: I am not pitiful but powerful; being colored is not a liability but an advantage. "No one on earth ever had a greater chance for glory. . . . The position of my white neighbor is much more difficult."

There is one point in the essay, however, when Hurston goes out of her way to conform to a stereotype very much in vogue in the 1920s. The passage bears citing in its entirety:

> Sometimes it is the other way around. A white person is set down in our midst, but the contrast is just as sharp for me. For instance, when I sit in the drafty basement that is The New World Cabaret with a white person, my color comes. We enter chatting about any little nothing that we have in common and are seated by the jazz waiters. In the abrupt way that jazz orchestras have, this one plunges into a number. It loses no time in circumlocutions, but gets right down to business. It constricts the thorax and splits the heart with its tempo and narcotic harmonies. This orchestra grows rambunctious, rears on its hind legs and attacks the tonal veil with primitive fury, rending it, clawing it until it breaks through to the jungle beyond. I follow those heathen— follow them exultingly. I dance wildly inside myself; I yell within, I whoop; I shake my assegai above my head, I hurl it true to the mark *yeeeeooww!* I am in the jungle and living in the jungle way. My face is painted red and yellow and my body is painted blue. My pulse is throbbing like a war drum. I want to slaughter something—give pain, give death to what, I do not know. But the piece ends. The men of the orchestra wipe their lips and rest their fingers. I creep back slowly to the veneer we call civilization with the last tone and find the white friend sitting motionless in his seat, smoking calmly.
>
> "Good music they have here," he remarks, drumming the table with his fingertips.
>
> Music. The great blobs of purple and red emotion have not touched him. He has only heard what I felt. He is far away and I see him but dimly across the ocean and the continent that have fallen between us. He is so pale with his whiteness then and I am *so* colored.

"Feeling" here, instead of being a category of which "colored" is one example, becomes instead a *property* of the category "colored" ("He has only heard what I felt"). While the passage as a whole dramatizes the image of the exotic primitive, its relation to expectations and presuppositions is not as simple as it first appears. Having just described herself as feeling "most colored when . . . thrown against a sharp white background," Hurston's announcement of having it "the other way around" leads one to expect something other than a description of feeling "most colored." Yet there is no other way around. The moment there is a juxtaposition of black and white, what "comes" is color. But the colors that come in the passage are skin *paint*, not skin complexion:

red, yellow, blue—primary colors for primal experiences—plus the color purple. The "tonal veil" is rent indeed, on the level at once of color, of sound, and of literary style. The move into the jungle is a move into mask; the return to civilization is a return to veneer. Either way, what is at stake is an artificial, ornamental surface.

Hurston undercuts the absoluteness of the opposition between white and black in another way as well. In describing the white man as "drumming the table with his fingertips," Hurston places in his body a counterpart to the "war drum" central to the jungle. If the jungle represents the experience of the body as such, the surge of bodily life external to conscious knowledge ("give pain, give death to what, I do not know"), then the nervous gesture is an alienated synecdoche for such bodily release.

In an essay entitled "What White Publishers Won't Print," written for *Negro Digest* in 1950, twenty-two years after "How It Feels to Be Colored Me," Hurston again takes up this "jungle" stereotype, this time to disavow it. The contrast between the two essays is significant:

> This insistence on defeat in a story where upperclass Negroes are portrayed, perhaps says something from the subconscious of the majority. Involved in western culture, the hero or heroine, or both, must appear frustrated and go down to defeat, somehow. Our literature reeks with it. It is the same as saying, "You can translate Virgil, and fumble with the differential calculus, but can you really comprehend it? Can you cope with our subtleties?"
>
> That brings us to the folklore of "reversion to type." This curious doctrine has such wide acceptance that it is tragic. One has only to examine the huge literature on it to be convinced. No matter how high we may *seem* to climb, put us under strain and we revert to type, that is, to the bush. Under a superficial layer of western culture, the jungle drums throb in our veins.

There are many possible explanations for Hurston's changed use of this image. For one thing, the exotic primitive was in vogue in 1928 while this was no longer the case in 1950. For another, she was addressing a white readership in the earlier essay and a black readership here. But the most revealing difference lies in the way the image is embedded in a structure of address. In the first essay, Hurston describes the jungle feeling as an art, an *ability* to feel, not a reversion. In the second, the jungle appears as a result of "strain." In the first, Hurston can proclaim "I am this," but when the image is repeated as "you are that," it changes completely. The content of the image may be the same, but its interpersonal use is different. The study of Afro-American literature as a whole poses a similar problem of address: any attempt to lift out of a text an image or essence of blackness is bound to violate the interlocutionary strategy of its formulation.

"What White Publishers Won't Print" is a complex meditation on the possibility of representing difference in order to erase it. Lamenting the fact that "the average, struggling, non-morbid Negro is the best-kept secret in America," Hurston explains the absence of a black *Main Street* by the majority's "indifference, not to say scepticism, to the internal life of educated minorities." The revelation to the public of the Negro who is "just like everybody else" is "the thing needed to do away with that feeling of difference which inspires fear and which ever expresses itself in dislike." The thing that prevents the publication of such representations of Negroes is thus said to be the public's *indifference* to finding out that there *is* no difference. Difference is a misreading of sameness, but it must be represented in order to be erased. The resistance to finding out that the other is the same springs out of the reluctance to admit that the same is other. If the average man could recognize that the Negro was "just like him," he would have to recognize that he was just like the Negro. Difference disliked is identity affirmed. But the difficulty of pleading for a representation of difference *as* sameness is exemplified by the almost unintelligible distinction in the following sentence: "As long as the majority cannot conceive of a Negro or a Jew feeling and reacting inside just as they do, the majority will keep right on believing that people who do not feel like them cannot possibly feel as they do." The difference between difference and sameness can barely be said. It is as small and as vast as the difference between "like" and "as."

Hurston ends "How It Feels to Be Colored Me," too, with an attempt to erase difference. She describes herself as "a brown bag of miscellany" whose contents are as different from each other as they are similar to those of other bags, "white, red, and yellow." The outside is no guarantee of the nature of the inside. The last sentence of the article, which responds distantly to the title, is "Who knows?"

By the end of the essay, then, Hurston has conjugated a conflicting and ironic set of responses to her title. Far from answering the question of "how it feels to be colored me," she deconstructs the very grounds of an answer, replying, "Compared to what? As of when? Who is asking? In what context? For what purpose? With what interests and presuppositions?" What Hurston rigorously shows is that questions of difference and identity are always a function of a specific interlocutionary situation—and the answers, matters of strategy rather than truth. In its rapid passage from image to image and from formula to formula, Hurston's *text* enacts the question of identity as a process of *self*-difference that Hurston's *persona* often explicitly denies.

It is precisely that self-difference that Hurston will assert, however, as the key to her anthropological enterprise in *Mules and Men*. In discussing Hurston's folktale anthology, I will focus less on the tales themselves than on Hurston's multilayered envelope of address, in which such self-differentiations are most obvious and functional. In the opening lines of her introduction to the volume, Hurston writes:

> I was glad when somebody told me, "You may go and collect Negro folk-lore." In a way it would not be a new experience for me. When I pitched headforemost into the world I landed in a crib of negroism. . . . But it was fitting me like a tight chemise. I couldn't see it for wearing it. It was only when I was off in college, away from my native surroundings, that I could see myself like somebody else and stand off and look at my garment. Then I had to have the spy-glass of Anthropology to look through at that. (P. 3)

The journey away to school does not confer color and fixed identity as it did in the 1928 essay but rather sight and self-division. "Seeing" and "wearing" (significantly, not seeing and being) cannot coincide, and we cannot always be sure which side of the spyglass our narrator is standing on. The ambiguity of the inside/outside opposition involved in "see[ing] myself like somebody else" is dramatized in many ways in Hurston's collection of folk tales, songs, and hoodoo practices, resulting in a complex interaction between the authority of her spyglass and the rhetorical nature of her material.

Mules and Men is a book with multiple frames: it begins with a preface by Franz Boas, Hurston's teacher, and ends with a glossary and appendix. As we have seen, Hurston's own introduction begins with a paraphrase of the 122d Psalm which replaces the biblical "they" with an unnamed "somebody," and it ends by placing itself geographically just outside the town line of Eatonville: "So I rounded Park Lane and came speeding down the straight stretch into Eatonville. . . . Before I enter the township, I wish to make acknowledgments to Mrs. R. Osgood Mason of New York City. She backed my falling in a hearty way, in a spiritual way, and in addition, financed the whole expedition in the manner of the Great Soul that she is" (p. 6). And Part One begins: "As I crossed the Maitland-Eatonville township line . . ." (p. 9). That line is the line between the two ends of the spyglass, but it is also supposed to stand as the line between the theoretical introduction and the tales. Yet Hurston has already told the first tale, a folk tale she remembers as she drives, a tale of creation and of the unequal distribution of "Soul." Hence, not only does the first tale subvert the opposition between theory and material, but the tale itself comments doubly upon the acknowledgment to Mrs. Mason: what Mrs. Mason backed is called a "falling"—

both a postcreational Fall and a losing hand in the "Georgia Skin Game" often referred to in the text. And since the story is about God's promise to redistribute "soul" more equally in the future, it sheds an ironic light on the designation of Hurston's wealthy patron as a "Great Soul."

Hurston does, however, offer some theoretical remarks in her introduction:

> Folk-lore is not as easy to collect as it sounds. The best source is where there are the least outside influences and these people, being usually under-privileged, are the shyest. They are most reluctant at times to reveal that which the soul lives by. And the Negro, in spite of his open-faced laughter, his seeming acquiescence, is particularly eva-sive. You see we are a polite people and we do not say to our ques-tioner, "Get out of here!" We smile and tell him or her something that satisfies the white person because, knowing so little about us, he doesn't know what he is missing. The Indian resists curiosity by a stony silence. The Negro offers a feather-bed resistance. That is, we let the probe enter, but it never comes out. It gets smothered under a lot of laughter and pleasantries.
>
> The theory behind our tactics: "The white man is always trying to know into somebody else's business. All right, I'll set something outside the door of my mind for him to play with and handle. He can read my writing but he sho' can't read my mind. I'll put this play toy in his hand, and he will seize it and go away. Then I'll say my say and sing my song." (Pp. 4–5)

The shifts and reversals in this passage are multiple. Hurston begins as an outsider, a scientific narrative voice that refers to "these people" in the third person, as a group whose inner lives are difficult to penetrate. Then, suddenly, she leaps into the picture she has just painted, includ-ing herself in a "we" that addresses a "you"—the white reader, the new implied outsider. The structure of address changes from description to direct address. From that point on it is impossible to tell whether Hurston the narrator is *describing* a strategy or *employing* one. Is her book something set "outside the door" for the white man to "play with and handle," or is the difficulty of penetrating the featherbed resistance being described in order to play up her own privileged skill and access to its inner secrets? In any event, theory is here on the side of the with-holder.

The text itself is a frame narrative recounting Hurston's quest for folk tales along with the folk tales themselves. It is a tale of the gathering of tales, or "lies," as they are called by the tellers. Hurston puts herself in a position to hear the tales only to the extent that she herself "lies." When she tells the townspeople that she has come to collect their "lies," one of them exclaims, "Shucks, Zora, don't you come here and tell de biggest lie first thing. Who you reckon want to read all them old-time tales about Brer Rabbit and Brer Bear?" Later, when Hurston leaves Eatonville to gather more tales elsewhere, she is snubbed as an outsider because of her car and expensive dress until she lies and says that she is a bootlegger fleeing from justice. With her loss of difference comes a flood of tales. The strategy to obtain the material becomes indistinguishable from the material obtained.

This is not to say that the anthropological frame is entirely adequate to its task of accurate representation. The following tale can be read as a questioning of the framing activity:

Ah know another man wid a daughter.
The man sent his daughter off to school for seben years, den she come home all finished up. So he said to her, "Daughter, git yo' things and write me a letter to my brother!" So she did.
He says, "Head it up," and she done so.
"Now tell 'im, 'Dear Brother, our chile is done come home from school and all finished up and we is very proud of her.' "
Then he ast de girl "Is you got dat?"
She tole 'im "yeah."
"Now tell him some mo'. 'Our mule is dead but Ah got another mule and when Ah say (clucking sound of tongue and teeth) he moved from de word.' "
"Is you got dat?" he ast de girl.
"Naw suh," she tole 'im.
He waited a while and ast her again, "You got that down yet?"
"Naw suh, Ah ain't got it yet."
"Now come you ain't got it?"
"Cause Ah can't spell (clucking sound)."
"You mean to tell me you been off to school seben years and can't spell (clucking sound)? Why Ah could spell dat myself and Ah ain't been to school a day in mah life. Well jes' say (clucking sound) he'll know what yo' mean and go on wid de letter." (Pp. 43–44)

The daughter in the tale is in a situation analogous to that of Hurston: the educated student returns home to transcribe what her forebears utter orally. She has learned a notation system that considers itself complete, but that turns out to lack a sign for (clucking sound). The "inside" is here commenting on the "outside," the tale commenting on the book as a whole. It is not by chance that this should be a tale precisely about mules and men. The non-coextensiveness of oral signs and written signs is a problem very much at the heart of Hurston's enterprise. But lest one fall into a simple opposition between the tale's orality and the transcriber's literacy, it is well to note that the orality/literacy relation is the very *subject* of the tale, which cannot be appreciated by those who, like the father *in* the tale, cannot write. Its irony is directed both ways.

Despite Boas's prefatory claim that Hurston has made "an unusual contribution to our knowledge of the true inner life of the Negro," the nature of such "knowledge" cannot be taken for granted. Who does Boas mean by "we"? Like Hurston's representation of "colored me," her collection of folk tales forces us to ask not whether an "inside" has been accurately represented but what is the nature of the dialogic situation into which the representation has been called. Since this is always specific, always a play of specific desires and expectations, it is impossible to conceive of a pure inside. There is no universalized other for the self to reveal itself *to*. Inside the chemise is the other side of the chemise: the side on which the observer can read the nature of his or her own desire to see.

Mules and Men ends, unexpectedly, with one final tale. Hurston has just spent 150 pages talking not about folk tales but about hoodoo practices. Suddenly, after a break but without preamble, comes the following tale:

> Once Sis Cat got hungry and caught herself a rat and set herself down to eat 'im. Rat tried and tried to git loose but Sis Cat was too fast and strong. So jus' as de cat started to eat 'im he says "Hol' on dere, Sis Cat! Ain't you got no manners atall? You going set up to de table and eat 'thout washing yo' face and hands?"
>
> Sis Cat was mighty hongry but she hate for de rat to think she ain't got no manners, so she went to de water and washed her face and hands and when she got back de rat was gone.
>
> So de cat caught herself a rat again and set down to eat. So de Rat said, "Where's yo' manners at, Sis Cat? You going to eat 'thout washing yo' face and hands?"
>
> "Oh, Ah, got plenty manners," de cat told 'im. "But Ah eats mah dinner and washes mah face and uses mah manners afterwards." So she et right on 'im and washed her face and hands. And cat's been washin' after eatin' ever since.
>
> I'm sitting here like Sis Cat, washing my face and usin' my manners. (Pp. 251–52)

So ends the book. But what manners is she using? Upon reading this strange, uncommented-upon final story, one cannot help wondering who, in the final analysis, has swallowed what. The reader? Mrs. Mason? Franz Boas? Hurston herself? As Nathan Huggins writes, after an attempt to determine the sincerity of Hurston's poses and self-representations, "It is impossible to tell from reading Miss Hurston's autobiography who was being fooled."[4] If, as Hurston often implies, the essence of telling "lies" is the art of conforming a narrative to existing structures of address while gaining the upper hand, then Hurston's very ability to fool us—or to fool us into *thinking* we have been fooled—is itself the only effective way of conveying the rhetoric of the "lie." To turn one's own life into a trickster tale of which even the teller herself might be the dupe certainly goes far in deconstructing the possibility of representing the truth of identity.

If I initially approached Hurston out of a desire to re-referentialize difference, what Hurston gives me back seems to be difference as a suspension of reference. Yet the terms *black* and *white*, *inside* and *outside*, continue to matter. Hurston suspends the certainty of reference not by erasing these differences but by foregrounding the complex dynamism of their interaction.

16

Apostrophe, Animation, and Abortion

The abortion issue is as alive and controversial in the body politic as it is in the academy and the courtroom.
—Jay L. Garfield, *Abortion: Moral and Legal Perspectives*

Although rhetoric can be defined as something politicians often accuse each other of, the political dimensions of the scholarly study of rhetoric have gone largely unexplored by literary critics. What, indeed, could seem more dry and apolitical than a rhetorical treatise? What could seem farther away from budgets and guerrilla warfare than a discussion of anaphora, antithesis, prolepsis, and preterition? Yet the notorious CIA manual on psychological operations in guerrilla warfare ends with just such a rhetorical treatise: an appendix on techniques of oratory which lists definitions and examples for these and many other rhetorical figures.[1] The manual is designed to set up a Machiavellian campaign of propaganda, indoctrination, and infiltration in Nicaragua, underwritten by the visible display and selective use of weapons. Shoot softly, it implies, and carry a big schtick. If rhetoric is defined as language that says one thing and means another, then the manual is in effect attempting to maximize the collusion between deviousness in language and accuracy in violence, again and again implying that targets are most effectively hit when most indirectly aimed at. Rhetoric, clearly, has everything to do with covert operations. But are the politics of violence already encoded in rhetorical figures as such? In other words, can the very essence of a political issue—an issue like, say, abortion—hinge on the structure of a figure? Is there any *inherent* connection between figurative language and questions of life and death, of who will wield and who will receive violence in a given human society?

As a way of approaching this question, I will begin in a much more traditional way by discussing a rhetorical device that has come to seem almost synonymous with the lyric voice: the figure of apostrophe. In an essay in *The Pursuit of Signs,* Jonathan Culler indeed sees apostrophe as an embarrassingly explicit emblem of procedures inherent, but usually better hidden, in lyric poetry as such.[2] Apostrophe in the sense in which I will be using it involves the direct address of an absent, dead, or inanimate being by a first-person speaker: "O wild West Wind, thou breath of Autumn's being." Apostrophe is thus both direct and indirect: based etymologically on the notion of turning aside, of digressing from straight speech, it manipulates the I/thou structure of direct address in an indirect, fictionalized way. The absent, dead, or inanimate entity addressed is thereby made present, animate, and anthropomorphic. Apostrophe is a form of ventriloquism through which the speaker throws voice, life, and human form into the addressee, turning its silence into mute responsiveness.

Baudelaire's poem "Moesta et Errabunda,"[3] whose Latin title means "sad and vagabond," raises questions of rhetorical animation through several different grades of apostrophe. Inanimate objects like trains and ships or abstract entities like perfumed paradises find themselves called upon to attend to the needs of a plaintive and restless lyric speaker. Even the poem's title poses questions of life and death in linguistic terms: the fact that Baudelaire here temporarily resuscitates a dead language prefigures the poem's attempts to function as a finder of lost loves. But in the opening lines of the poem, the direct-address structure seems straightforwardly *un*figurative: "Tell me, Agatha." This could be called a minimally fictionalized apostrophe, although that is of course its fiction. Nothing at first indicates that Agatha is any more dead, absent, or inanimate than the poet himself.

The poem's opening makes explicit the relation between direct address and the desire for the *other*'s voice: "Tell me: *you* talk." But something strange soon happens to the face-to-face humanness of this conversation. What Agatha is supposed to talk about starts a process of dismemberment that might have something to do with a kind of reverse anthropomorphism: "Does your heart sometimes take flight?" Instead of conferring a human shape, this question starts to undo one. Then, too, why the name Agatha? Baudelaire scholars have searched in vain for a biographical referent, never identifying one, but always presuming that one exists. In the Pléiade edition of Baudelaire's complete works, a footnote sends the reader to the only other place in Baudelaire's oeuvre where the name Agathe appears—a page in his *Carnets* where he is listing debts and appointments. This would seem to indicate that Agathe was indeed a real person. What do we know about her? A footnote to the *Carnets* tells us she was probably a prostitute. Why? See the poem "Moesta et Errabunda." This is a particularly stark example of the inevitable circularity of biographical criticism.

If Agathe is finally only a proper name written on two different pages in Baudelaire, then the name itself must have a function *as* a name. The name is a homonym for the word *agate*, a semiprecious stone. Is Agathe really a stone? Does the poem express the Orphic hope of getting a stone to talk?

In a poem about wandering, taking flight, getting away from "here," it is surprising to find that, structurally, each stanza acts out, not a departure, but a return to its starting point, a repetition of its first line. The poem's structure is at odds with its apparent theme. But we soon see that the object of the voyage is precisely to return—to return to a prior state, planted in the first stanza as virginity, in the second as motherhood (through the image of the nurse and the pun on *mer/mère*), and finally as childhood love and furtive pleasure. The voyage outward in space is a figure for the voyage backward in time. The poem's structure of address backs up, too, most explicitly in the third stanza. The cry apostrophizing train and ship to carry the speaker off leads to a seeming reprise of the opening line, but by this point the inanimate has entirely taken over: instead of addressing Agatha directly, the poem asks whether Agatha's heart ever speaks the line the poet himself has spoken four lines earlier. Agatha is replaced by one of her parts, which itself replaces the speaker. Agatha herself now drops out of the poem, and direct address is temporarily lost too in the grammar of the sentence ("Est-il vrai que . . ."). The poem is as if emptying itself of all its human characters and voices. It seems to be acting out a *loss* of animation—which is in fact its subject: the loss of childhood aliveness brought about by the passage of time. The poem thus enacts in its own temporality the loss of animation it situates in the temporality of the speaker's life.

At this point it launches into a new apostrophe, a new direct address to an abstract, lost state: "Comme vous êtes loin, paradis parfumé." The poem reanimates, addresses an image of fullness and wholeness and perfect correspondence ("Où tout ce que l'on aime est digne d'être aimé"). This height of liveliness, however, culminates strangely in an image of death. The heart that formerly kept trying to fly away now drowns in the moment of reaching its destination ("Où dans la volupté pure le coeur se noie!"). There may be something to gain, therefore, by deferring arrival, as the poem next seems to do by interrupting itself before grammatically completing the fifth stanza. The poem again ceases to employ direct address and ends by asking two drawn-out, self-interrupting questions. Is that paradise now farther away than India or China? Can one call it back and animate it with a silvery voice? This last question—"Peut-on le rappeler avec des cris plaintifs / Et l'animer encore d'une voix argentine?"—is a perfect description of apostrophe itself: a trope which, by means of the silvery voice of rhetoric, calls up and animates the absent, the lost, and the dead. Apostrophe itself, then, has become not just the poem's mode but also the poem's theme. In other words, what the poem ends up wanting to know is not how far away childhood is, but whether its own rhetorical strategies can be effective. The final question becomes: Can this gap be bridged? Can this loss be healed, through language alone?

Shelley's "Ode to the West Wind," which is perhaps the ultimate apostrophaic poem, makes even more explicit the relation between apostrophe and animation. Shelley spends the first three sections demonstrating that the west wind is a figure for the power to animate: it is described as the breath of being, moving everywhere, blowing movement and energy through the world, waking it from its summer dream, parting the waters of the Atlantic, uncontrollable. Yet the wind animates by bringing death, winter, destruction. How do the rhetorical strategies of the poem carry out this program of animation through the giving of death?

The apostrophe structure is immediately foregrounded by the interjections, four times spelled "O" and four times spelled "oh." One of the bridges this poem attempts to build is the bridge between the "O" of the pure vocative, Jakobson's conative function, or the pure presencing of the second person, and the "oh" of pure subjectivity, Jakobson's emotive function, or the pure presencing of the first person.

The first three sections are grammatical amplifications of the sentence "O thou, hear, oh, hear!" All the vivid imagery, all the picture painting, comes in clauses subordinate to this obsessive direct address. But the poet addresses, gives animation, gives the capacity of responsiveness, to the wind, not in order to make it speak but in order to make it listen to him—in order to make it listen to him doing nothing but address *it*. It takes him three long sections to break out of this intense near-tautology. As the fourth section begins, the "I" starts to inscribe itself grammatically (but not thematically) where the "thou" has been. A power struggle starts up for control over the poem's grammar, a struggle which mirrors the rivalry named in such lines as "If even/I were as in my boyhood . . . /. . . I would ne'er have *striven / As thus with thee* in prayer in my sore need." This rivalry is expressed as a comparison: "less free than thou," but then, "one *too like* thee." What does it mean to be "too like"? Time has created a loss of similarity, a loss of animation that has made the sense of similarity even more hyperbolic. In other words, the poet, in becoming less than, less like the wind, somehow becomes more like the wind in his rebellion against the loss of likeness.

In the final section the speaker both inscribes and reverses the structure of apostrophe. In saying "be thou me," he is attempting to restore metaphorical exchange and equality. If apostrophe is the giving of voice, the throwing of voice, the giving of animation, then a poet using it is always in a sense saying to the addressee, "Be thou me." But this implies that a poet has animation to give. And *that* is what this poem is saying is not, or no longer, the case. Shelley's speaker's own sense of animation is precisely what is in doubt, so that he is in effect saying to the wind, "I will animate you so that you will animate, or reanimate, me." "Make me thy lyre . . ."

Yet the wind, which is to give animation, is also the giver of death. The opposition between life and death has to undergo another reversal, another transvaluation. If death could somehow become a positive force for animation, then the poet would thereby create hope for his own "dead thoughts." The animator that will blow his words around the world will also instate the power of their deadness, their deadness *as* power, the place of maximum potential for renewal. This is the burden of the final rhetorical question. Does death necessarily entail rebirth? If winter comes, can spring be far behind? The poem is attempting to appropriate the authority of natural logic—in which spring always does follow winter—in order to claim the authority of cyclic reversibility for its own prophetic powers. Yet because this clincher is expressed in the form of a rhetorical question, it expresses natural certainty by means of a linguistic device that mimics no natural structure and has no stable one-to-one correspondence with a meaning. The rhetorical question, in a sense, leaves the poem in a state of suspended animation. But that, according to the poem, is the state of maximum potential.

Both the Baudelaire and the Shelley, then, end with a rhetorical question that both raises and begs the question of rhetoric. It is as though the apostrophe is ultimately directed toward the reader, to whom the poem is addressing Mayor Koch's question: "How 'm I doing?" What is at stake in both poems is, as we have seen, the fate of a lost child—the speaker's own former self—and the possibility of a new birth or reanimation. In the poems that I will discuss next, these structures of apostrophe, animation, and lost life will take on a very different cast through the foregrounding of the question of motherhood and the premise that the life that is lost may be someone else's.

In Gwendolyn Brooks' poem "The Mother," the structures of address are shifting and complex. In the first line ("Abortions will not let you forget"), there is a "you" but there is no "I." Instead, the subject of the sentence is the word "abortions," which thus assumes a position of grammatical control over the poem. As entities that disallow forgetting, the abortions are not only controlling but animate and anthropomorphic, capable of treating persons as objects. While Baudelaire and Shelley addressed the anthropomorphized other in order to repossess their lost selves, Brooks is representing the self as eternally addressed and possessed by the lost, anthropomorphized other. Yet the self that is possessed here is itself already a "you," not an "I." The "you" in the opening lines can be seen as an "I" that has become alienated, distanced from itself, and combined with a generalized other, which includes and feminizes the reader of the poem. The grammatical I/thou starting point of traditional apostrophe has been replaced by a structure in which the speaker is simultaneously eclipsed, alienated, and confused with the addressee. It is already clear that something has happened to the possibility of establishing a clear-cut distinction in this poem between subject and object, agent and victim.

The second section of the poem opens with a change in the structure of address. "I" takes up the positional place of "abortions," and there is temporarily no second person. The first sentence narrates: "I have heard in the voices of the wind the voices of my dim killed children." What is interesting about this line is that the speaker situates the children's voices firmly in a traditional romantic locus of lyric apostrophe—the voices of the wind, Shelley's west wind, say, or Wordsworth's "gentle breeze."[4] Gwendolyn Brooks, in other words, is here rewriting the male lyric tradition, textually placing aborted children in the spot formerly occupied by all the dead, inanimate, or absent entities previously addressed by the lyric. And the question of animation and anthropomorphism is thereby given a new and disturbing twist. For if apostrophe is said to involve language's capacity to give life and human form to something dead or inanimate, what happens when those questions are literalized? What happens when the lyric speaker assumes responsibility for producing the death in the first place, but without being sure of the precise degree of human animation that existed in the entity killed? What is the debate over abortion about, indeed, if not the question of when, precisely, a being assumes a human form?

It is not until line 14 that Brooks' speaker actually addresses the dim killed children. And she does so not directly, but in the form of a self-quotation: "I have said, Sweets, if I sinned . . ." This embedding of the apostrophe appears to serve two functions here, just as it did in Baudelaire: a self-distancing function, and a foregrounding of the question of the adequacy of language. But whereas in Baudelaire the distance between the speaker and the lost childhood is what is being lamented, and a restoration of vividness and contact is what is desired, in Brooks the vividness of the contact is precisely the source of the pain. While Baudelaire suffers from the dimming of memory, Brooks suffers from an inability to forget. And while Baudelaire's speaker actively seeks a fusion between present self and lost child, Brooks' speaker is attempting to fight her way out of a state of confusion between self and other. This confusion is indicated by the shifts in the poem's structures of address. It is never clear whether the speaker sees herself as an "I" or a "you," an addressor or an addressee. The voices in the wind are not created *by* the lyric apostrophe; they rather initiate the need for one. The initiative of speech seems always to lie in the other. The poem continues to struggle to clarify the relation between "I" and "you," but in the end it succeeds only in expressing the inability of its language to do so. By not closing the quotation in its final line, the poem, which began by confusing the reader with the aborter, ends by implicitly including the reader among those aborted—and loved. The poem can no more distinguish between "I" and "you" than it can come up with a proper definition of life.

In line 28, the poem explicitly asks, "Oh, what shall I say, how is the truth to be said?" Surrounding this question are attempts to make impossible distinctions: got/did not get, deliberate/not deliberate, dead/never made. The uncertainty of the speaker's control as a subject mirrors the uncertainty of the children's status as an object. It is interesting that the status of the human subject here hinges on the word "deliberate." The association of deliberateness with human agency has a long (and very American) history. It is deliberateness, for instance, that underlies that epic of separation and self-reliant autonomy, Thoreau's *Walden*. "I went to the woods," writes Thoreau, "because I wished to live deliberately, to front only the essential facts of life."[5] Clearly, for Thoreau, pregnancy was not an essential fact of life. Yet for him as well as for every human being that has yet existed, someone else's pregnancy is the very *first* fact of life. How might the plot of human subjectivity be reconceived (so to speak) if pregnancy rather than autonomy is what raises the question of deliberateness?

Much recent feminist work has been devoted to the task of rethinking the relations between subjectivity, autonomy, interconnectedness, responsibility, and gender. Carol Gilligan's book *In a Different Voice* (and this focus on "voice" is not irrelevant here) studies gender differences in patterns of ethical thinking. The central ethical question analyzed by Gilligan is precisely the decision whether to have, or not to have, an abortion. The first time I read the book, this struck me as strange. Why, I wondered, would an investigation of gender *differences* focus on one of the questions about which an even-handed comparison of the male and the female points of view is impossible? Yet this, clearly, turns out to be the point: there is difference *because* it is not always possible to make symmetrical oppositions. As long as there is symmetry, one is not dealing with difference but rather with versions of the same. Gilligan's difference arises out of the impossibility of maintaining a rigorously logical binary model for ethical choices. Female logic, as she defines it, is a way of rethinking the logic of choice in a situation in which none of the choices are good. "Believe that even in my deliberateness I was not deliberate": believe that the agent is not entirely autonomous, believe that I can be subject and object of violence at the same time, believe that I have not chosen the conditions under which I must choose. As Gilligan writes of the abortion decision, "The occurrence of the dilemma itself precludes nonviolent resolution."[6] The choice is not between violence and nonviolence, but between simple violence to a fetus and complex, less determinate violence to an involuntary mother and/or an unwanted child.

Readers of Brooks' poem have often read it as an argument against abortion. And it is certainly clear that the poem is not saying that abortion is a good thing. But to see it as making a simple case for the embryo's right to life is to assume that a woman who has chosen abortion does not have the right to mourn. It is to assume that no case *for* abortion can take the woman's feelings of guilt and loss into consideration, that to take those feelings into account is to deny the right to choose the act that produced them. Yet the poem makes no such claim: it attempts the impossible task of humanizing both the mother and the aborted children while presenting the inadequacy of language to resolve the dilemma without violence.

What I would like to emphasize is the way in which the poem suggests that the arguments for and against abortion are structured through and through by the rhetorical limits and possibilities of something akin to apostrophe. The fact that apostrophe allows one to animate the inanimate, the dead, or the absent implies that whenever a being is apostrophized, it is thereby automatically animated, anthropomorphized, "person-ified." (By the same token, the rhetoric of calling makes it difficult to tell the difference between the animate and the inanimate, as anyone with a telephone answering machine can attest.) Because of the ineradicable tendency of language to animate whatever it addresses, rhetoric itself can always have already answered "yes" to the question of whether a fetus is a human being. It is no accident that the antiabortion film most often shown in the United States should be entitled *The Silent Scream*. By activating the imagination to believe in the anthropomorphized embryo's mute responsiveness in exactly the same way that apostrophe does, the film (which is of course itself a highly rhetorical entity) is playing on rhetorical possibilities that are inherent in all linguistically based modes of representation.

Yet the function of apostrophe in the Brooks poem is far from simple. If the fact that the speaker addresses the children at all makes them human, then she must pronounce herself guilty of murder—but only if she discontinues her apostrophe. As long as she addresses the children, she can keep them alive, can keep from finishing with the act of killing them. The speaker's attempt to absolve herself of guilt depends on never forgetting, never breaking the ventriloquism of an apostrophe through which she cannot define her identity otherwise than as the mother eaten alive by the children she has never fed. Who, in the final analysis, exists by addressing whom? The children are a rhetorical extension of the mother, but she, as the poem's title indicates, has no existence apart from her relation to them. It begins to be clear that the speaker has written herself into a poem that she cannot get out of without violence. The violence she commits in the end is to her own language: as the poem ends, the vocabulary shrinks away, words are repeated, nothing but "all" rhymes with "all." The speaker has written herself into silence. Yet hers is not the only silence in the poem: earlier she has said, "You will never . . . silence or buy with a sweet." If sweets are for silencing, then by beginning her apostrophe, "Sweets, if I sinned . . . ," the speaker is already saying that the poem, which exists to memorialize those whose lack of life makes them eternally alive, is also attempting to silence once and for all the voices of the children in the wind. It becomes impossible to tell whether language is what gives life or what kills.

> *Women have said again and again "This is* my *body!" and they have reason to feel angry, reason to feel that it has been like shouting into the wind.*
> —Judith Jarvis Thompson, "A Defense of Abortion"

It is interesting to note the ways in which legal and moral discussions of abortion tend to employ the same terms as those we have been using to describe the figure of apostrophe. Thus, Justice Blackmun, in *Roe v. Wade:* "These disciplines [philosophy, theology, and civil and canon law] variously approached the question in terms of the point at which the embryo or fetus became "formed" or recognizably human, or in terms of when a "person" came into being, that is, infused with a "soul" or "animated.""[7] The issue of "fetal personhood" (Garfield and Hennessey, p. 55) is of course a way of bringing to a state of explicit uncertainty the fundamental difficulty of defining personhood in general.[8] Even if the question of defining the nature of "persons" is restricted to the question of understanding what is meant by the word "person" in the United States Constitution (since the Bill of Rights guarantees the rights only of "persons"), there is not at present, and probably will never be, a stable legal definition. Existing discussions of the legality and morality of abortion almost invariably confront, leave unresolved, and detour around the question of the nature and boundaries of human life. As Justice Blackmun puts it in *Roe v. Wade:* "We need not resolve the difficult question of when life begins. When those trained in the respective disciplines of medicine, philosophy, and theology are unable to arrive at any consensus, the judiciary, at this point in the development of man's knowledge, is not in a position to speculate as to the answer" (Garfield and Hennessey, p. 27).

In the case of *Roe v. Wade,* the legality of abortion is derived from the right to privacy—an argument which, as Catherine MacKinnon argues in *"Roe vs. Wade: A Study in Male Ideology"* (Garfield and Hennessey, pp. 45–54), is itself problematic for women, since by protecting "privacy" the courts also protect the injustices of patriarchal sexual arrangements. When the issue is an unwanted pregnancy, some sort of privacy has already, in a sense, been invaded. In order for the personal to avoid being reduced once again to the nonpolitical, privacy, like deliberateness, needs to be rethought in terms of sexual politics. Yet even the attempt to re-gender the issues surrounding abortion is not simple. As Kristin Luker convincingly demonstrates, the debate turns around the claims not only of woman versus fetus or woman versus patriarchal state, but also of woman versus woman:

> Pro-choice and pro-life activists live in different worlds, and the scope of their lives, as both adults and children, fortifies them in their belief that their views on abortion are the more correct, more moral and more reasonable. When added to this is the fact that should "the other side" win, one group of women will see the very real devaluation of their lives and life resources, it is not surprising that the abortion debate has generated so much heat and so little light. . . .
> . . . Are pro-life activists, as they claim, actually reaching their cherished goal of "educating the public to the humanity of the unborn child"? As we begin to seek an answer, we should recall that motherhood is a topic about which people have very complicated feelings, and because abortion has become the battleground for different definitions of motherhood, neither the pro-life nor the pro-choice movement has ever been "representative" of how most Americans feel about abortion. More to the point, all our data suggest that *neither of these groups will ever be able to be representative.* (Pp. 215, 224)

It is often said, in literary-theoretical circles, that to focus on undecidability is to be apolitical. Everything I have read about the abortion controversy in its present form in the United States leads me to suspect that, on the contrary, the undecidable *is* the political. There is politics precisely because there is undecidability.

And there is also poetry. There are striking and suggestive parallels between the "different voices" involved in the abortion debate and the shifting address-structures of poems like Gwendolyn Brooks' "The Mother." A glance at several other poems suggests that there tends indeed to be an overdetermined relation between the theme of abortion and the problematization of structures of address. In Anne Sexton's "The Abortion," six 3-line stanzas narrate, in the first person, a trip to Pennsylvania where the "I" has obtained an abortion. Three times the poem is interrupted by the italicized lines:

> *Somebody who should have been born*
> *is gone.*

Like a voice-over narrator taking superegoistic control of the moral bottom line, this refrain (or "burden," to use the archaic term for both "refrain" and "child in the womb") puts the first-person narrator's authority in question without necessarily constituting the voice of a separate entity. Then, in the seventh and final stanza, the poem extends and intensifies this split:

> Yes, woman, such logic will lead
> to loss without death. Or say what you meant,
> you coward . . . this baby that I bleed.

Self-accusing, self-interrupting, the narrating "I" turns on herself (or is it someone else?) as "you," as "woman." The poem's speaker becomes as split as the two senses of the word "bleed." Once again, "saying what one means" can be done only by ellipsis, violence, illogic, transgression, silence. The question of who is addressing whom is once again unresolved.

As we have seen, the question of "when life begins" is complicated partly because of the way in which language blurs the boundary between life and death. In "Menstruation at Forty," Sexton sees menstruation itself as the loss of a child ("two days gone in blood")—a child that exists *because* it can be called:

> I was thinking of a son . . .
> You! . . .
> Will you be the David or the Susan?
> .   .   .   .
> my carrot, my cabbage,
> I would have possessed you before all women,

calling your name,
calling you mine.

The political consequences and complexities of addressing—of "calling"—are made even more explicit in a poem by Lucille Clifton entitled "The Lost Baby Poem." By choosing the word "dropped" ("i dropped your almost body down"), Clifton renders it unclear whether the child has been lost through abortion or through miscarriage. What is clear, however, is that that loss is both mourned and rationalized. The rationalization occurs through the description of a life of hardship, flight, and loss: the image of a child born into winter, slipping like ice into the hands of strangers in Canada, conflates the scene of Eliza's escape in *Uncle Tom's Cabin* with the exile of draft resisters during the Vietnam War. The guilt and mourning occur in the form of an imperative in which the notion of "stranger" returns in the following lines:

if i am ever less than a mountain
for your definite brothers and sisters

.   .   .   .

. . . let black men call me stranger
always for your never named sake.

The act of "calling" here correlates a lack of name with a loss of membership. For the sake of the one that cannot be called, the speaker invites an apostrophe that would expel *her* into otherness. The consequences of the death of a child ramify beyond the mother-child dyad to encompass the fate of an entire community. The world that has created conditions under which the loss of a baby becomes desirable must be resisted, not joined. For a black woman, the loss of a baby can always be perceived as a complicity with genocide. The black mother sees her own choice as one of being either a stranger or a rock. The humanization of the lost baby addressed by the poem is thus carried out at the cost of dehumanizing, even rendering inanimate, the calling mother.

Yet each of these poems exists, finally, *because* a child does not.[9] In Adrienne Rich's poem "To a Poet," the rivalry between poems and children is made quite explicit. The "you" in the poem is again aborted, but here it is the mother herself who could be called "dim and killed" by the fact not of abortion but of the institution of motherhood. And again, the structures of address are complex and unstable. The deadness of the "you" cannot be named: not suicide, not murder. The question of the life or death of the addressee is raised in an interesting way through Rich's rewriting of Keats' sonnet on his mortality. While Keats writes, "When I have fears that *I* will cease to be," Rich writes, "and I have fears

196 / Other Inflections of Difference

that *you* will cease to be." If poetry is at stake in both intimations of mortality, what is the significance of this shift from "I" to "you"? On the one hand, the very existence of the Keats poem indicates that the pen *has* succeeded in gleaning something before the brain has ceased to be. No such grammatical guarantee exists for the "you." Death in the Keats poem is as much a source as it is a threat to writing. Hence death, for Keats, could be called the mother of poetry, while motherhood, for Rich, is precisely the death of poetry. The Western myth of the conjunction of word and flesh implied by the word "incarnate" is undone by images of language floating and vanishing in the bowl of the toilet of real fleshly needs. The word is not made flesh; rather, flesh unmakes the mother-poet's word. The difficulty of retrieving the "you" as poet is enacted by the structures of address in the following lines:

> I write this   not for you
> who fight to write your own
> words fighting up the falls
> but for another woman   dumb

In saying "I write this not for you," Rich seems almost to be excluding as addressee anyone who could conceivably be reading this poem. The poem is setting aside both the I and the you—the pronouns Benveniste associates with personhood—and reaches instead toward a "she," which belongs in the category of "nonperson." The poem is thus attempting the impossible task of directly addressing not a second person but a third person—a person who, if she is reading the poem, cannot be the reader the poem has in mind. The poem is trying to include what is by its own grammar excluded from it, to animate through language the nonperson, the "other woman." This poem, too, therefore, is bursting the limits of its own language, inscribing a logic that it itself reveals to be impossible—but necessary. Even the divorce between writing and childbearing is less absolute than it appears: in comparing the writing of words to the spawning of fish, Rich's poem reveals itself to be trapped between the inability to combine and the inability to separate the woman's various roles.

In each of these poems, then, a kind of competition is implicitly instated between the bearing of children and the writing of poems. Something unsettling has happened to the analogy often drawn by male poets between artistic creation and procreation. For it is not true that literature contains no examples of male pregnancy. Sir Philip Sidney, in the first sonnet from Astrophel and Stella, describes himself as "great with child to speak," but the poem is ultimately produced at the expense of no literalized child. Sidney's labor pains are smoothed away by a midwifely apostrophe (" 'Fool,' said my Muse to me, 'look in thy heart, and write!' "), and by a sort of poetic Caesarian section, out springs the poem we have, in fact, already finished reading.[10] Mallarmé, in "Don du poème," describes himself as an enemy father seeking nourishment for his monstrous poetic child from the woman within apostrophe-shot who is busy nursing a literalized daughter.[11] But since the woman presumably has two breasts, there seems to be enough to go around. As Shakespeare assures the fair young man, "But were some child of yours alive that time, / You should live twice in it and in my rhyme" (sonnet 17). Apollinaire, in his play *Les Mamelles de Tirésias*, depicts woman as a de-maternalized neo-Malthusian leaving the task of childbearing to a surrealistically fertile husband. But again, nothing more disturbing than Tiresian cross-dressing seems to occur. Children are alive and well, and far more numerous than ever. Indeed, in one of the dedicatory poems, Apollinaire indicates that his drama represents a return to health from the literary reign of the *poète maudit:*

> La féconde raison a jailli de ma fable,
> Plus de femme stérile et non plus d'avortons.[12]

> [Fertile reason springs out of my fable,
> No more sterile women, no aborted children]

This dig at Baudelaire, among others, reminds us that in the opening poem to *Les Fleurs du mal* ("Bénédiction"), Baudelaire represents the poet himself as an abortion *manqué,* cursed by the poisonous words of a rejecting mother. The question of the unnatural seems more closely allied with the bad mother than with the pregnant father.

Even in the seemingly more obvious parallel provided by poems written to dead children by male poets, it is not really surprising to find that the substitution of poem for child lacks the sinister undertones and disturbed address exhibited by the abortion poems we have been discussing. Jonson, in "On my First Son," calls his dead child "his best piece of poetry," while Mallarmé, in an only semiguilty *Aufhebung,* transfuses the dead Anatole to the level of an idea. More recently, Jon Silkin has written movingly of the death of a handicapped child ("something like a person") as a change of silence, not a splitting of voice. And Michael Harper, in "Nightmare Begins Responsibility," stresses the powerlessness and distrust of a black father leaving his dying son to the care of a "white-doctor-who-breathed-for-him-all-night."[13] But again, whatever the complexity of the voices in that poem, the speaker does not split self-accusingly or infra-symbiotically in the ways we have noted in the abortion/motherhood poems. While one could undoubtedly find counterexamples on both sides, it is not surprising that the substitution of art for children should not be inherently transgressive for the male poet. Men have in a sense always had no choice but to substitute something for the literal process of birth. That, at least, is the belief that has long been encoded into male poetic conventions. It is as though male writing were by nature procreative, while female writing is somehow by nature infanticidal.

It is, of course, as problematic as it is tempting to draw general conclusions about differences between male and female writing on the basis of these somewhat random examples. Yet it is clear that a great many poetic effects may be colored according to *expectations* articulated through the gender of the poetic speaker. Whether or not men and women would "naturally" write differently about dead children, there is something about the connection between motherhood and death that refuses to remain comfortably and conventionally figurative. When a woman speaks about the death of children in any sense other than that of pure loss, a powerful taboo is being violated. The indistinguishability of miscarriage and abortion in the Clifton poem indeed points to the notion that *any* death of a child is perceived as a crime committed by the mother, something a mother ought by definition to be able to prevent. That these questions should be inextricably connected to the figure of apostrophe, however, deserves further comment. For there may be a deeper link between motherhood and apostrophe than we have hitherto suspected.

The verbal development of the infant, according to Lacan, begins as a demand addressed to the mother, out of which the entire verbal universe is spun. Yet the mother addressed is somehow a personification, not a person—a personification of presence or absence, of Otherness itself.

> Demand in itself bears on something other than the satisfactions it calls for. It is demand of a presence or of an absence—which is what is manifested in the primordial relation to the mother, pregnant with that Other to be situated *within* the needs that it can satisfy. . . . Insofar as [man's] needs are subjected to demand, they return to him alienated. This is not the effect of his real dependence . . . , but rather the turning into signifying form as such, from the fact that it is from the locus of the Other that its message is emitted.[14]

If demand is the originary vocative, which assures life even as it inaugurates alienation, then it is not surprising that questions of animation inhere in the rhetorical figure of apostrophe. The reversal of apostrophe we noted in the Shelley poem ("animate me") would be no reversal at all, but a reinstatement of the primal apostrophe in which, despite Lacan's disclaimer, there is precisely a link between demand and animation, between apostrophe and life-and-death dependency.[15] If apostrophe is structured like demand, and if demand articulates the primal relation to the mother as a relation to the Other, then lyric poetry itself— summed up in the figure of apostrophe—comes to look like the fantastically intricate history of endless elaborations and displacements of the single cry, "Mama!" The question these poems are asking, then, is what happens when the poet is speaking *as* a mother, a mother whose cry arises out of—and is addressed to—a dead child?

It is no wonder that the distinction between addressor and addressee should become so problematic in poems about abortion. It is also no wonder that the debate about abortion should refuse to settle into a single voice. Whether or not one has ever been a mother, everyone participating in the debate has once been a child. Psychoanalysis, too, is a theory of development from the child's point of view. Rhetorical, psychoanalytical, and political structures are profoundly implicated in one another. The difficulty in all three would seem to reside in the attempt to achieve a full elaboration of any discursive position other than that of child.

Appendix to Chapter 7

News in Brief
by Stéphane Mallarmé

Apart from truths the poet can extract and keep secretly for himself, away from the talk of the day, pondering their production for the opportune moment, with transfiguration, nothing about this collapse of Panama interested me through the mere glitter of sensationalism. By the light of phantasmagorical sunsets, when clouds alone are sinking (with whatever, unbeknownst to him, man probably has lent them of his dreams), a treasure-liquefaction flows, spreads, gleams on the horizon. I thereby gain an impression of what such sums might be, millions by the hundreds and beyond, equal to those whose enumeration, in the statement by the prosecution and in the superb defense by the lawyers, during the trial, leaves me, as far as their existence is concerned, incredulous. And yet, it is, this gold, and even a bit all over! but the inability of figures, however grandiloquent, to translate it, truly springs out of a case; in which no one has taken the pains to see. Nothing in me can explain it; though one gets a hint from the fact that the more a sum increases or backs up, as far as the simple man in the street is concerned, toward the improbable, it includes, as it inscribes itself, more and more zeros; signifying that its total is equal to nothing, almost. What is it that is hidden in this lack of resplendence revealed by the discussion of financial interests, by far the vastest of the century, if not, perhaps, that to elect a god is not so as to confine him in the inner shadows of iron safes and pockets. Hence his lack of splendor, when the time comes or when the shining ought to take place. Everything does him a disservice, right down to those notorious checks and, in particular, the care taken by the recipient to truncate and render unreadable his own signature. The whole thing has been gray, contemptible, monochromatic: at the very moment when what was at stake was that which alone sheds light— on the conscience or in consciousness. The terrible precision instrument leads to utter vagueness. Billion has ended; I'm back to Pactolus. This refusal—plausible enough under ordinary circumstances, on the part of business, where the object is rather to keep things veiled—to betray any sumptuousness can cease, in despair and if light shines suddenly from without. Then, a magnificence like that of a ship setting itself afire and celebrating sea and sky with its heroism. The onlooker ought to ascertain, from this dull effacement of gold, under theatrical circumstances in which it should appear, blinding, bright, cynical, the indifference everyone feels toward money when it is not a matter of grabbing some. The highly vain universal deity, with neither circumstance nor pomp. I raise no complaint in my disappointment, thinking, to myself, that perhaps it is this phenomenon and no other that is the reason it falls to the writer, the gift of amassing radiant spots of clarity with the sole words that he proffers; such as those well-placed words, for example, Truth and Beauty.

Abstention from any show of fireworks on the part of that monster for whose sake little by little the once human individual is abdicating: light nevertheless cannot help but fall on the intense, poignant figure of an old man long acclaimed by the public, the fallen athlete, Ferdinand de Lesseps. I'm not sure it is possible to say whether his advanced age, marking him as with a stupor at the approach of events that remain foreign to him, and consenting that they escape his destiny, has not conferred upon him a kind of superiority among his contemporaries. He will remain forever ignorant of the disaster that has befallen a portion of national pride adjoining his own. Custom indeed has it that one cannot apprehend a man condemned in his absence, as here, until one has signified to him the nature of the sentence: now, since he would never understand, it will be forever deferred.

Such are the facts.

As an example of imagination coming up with the perfect noble, suffering hero, you have to admit that this isn't bad, as far as modernity goes, which rather drowns and erases, covering each edifice with a cloud, the marble statues. No era has combined these elements of tragedy better than our own, involuntarily. It seemed to me important to single out the main character, since he too easily confirms, as an exception, the indisputable remark prompted by this trial. Or the inaptitude of Justice in certain cases to make its judgment stick. I must add that I by no means reject its intervention nor, to go further, as soon as its action is underway, its result, the sentence. It is necessary, in order to conclude one of those extraordinary enterprises which, in finance, import some of what is left over from the war, that one be covered, by the tyrant: or misfortune: governmental anonymity can, nay, must, intervene and stop everything short. Suez succeeded, dishonestly. Nevertheless one must not lose sight of the fact that the function of Justice is a fiction, owing to the simple fact that it doesn't give the money back. Never will a man be negated by a machine, however one might know it to be clean, impartial, and correct. I don't even ask the legal profession for its account of this, that legality is not felicitous in its words, and, for example, indicates the calamitous end inflicted upon the promoter of one of the most grandiose of contemporary adventures with the word "fraud." I understand that Justice is duty-bound to simplify, in function of the fact that a multiplicity of epithets is not needed to enumerate all men; when they are outside the elite. I do not blame it a bit, say I, and I bow down before the case judged, as it suffices; and also before the terms, because I know them to be false and that through their sinister generality can come salvation, for this or that condemned man. Who will be struck, to show that it cannot touch him or that fine heads are carried high whatever happens. Thus, out of this strange hour, one of the saddest that can be experienced by a nation (on that subject I promised myself to not write or it's hardly my business) this remark, which springs up, in spite of all and myself. Except for the rabble of souls turned on by the sight of an overturned statue, there is no one that this conviction satisfied, in the mysterious quibbles of its equity. A sentence remains a gross, crude thing, precisely because it becomes the mouthpiece for too many people; in addition to all the appeals and cassations, it leaves an out for the mind, which retains its sovereignty. A formality that is respectable or necessary for the maintenance of order and common good, playing the role of a prompt, insistant tap on the shoulder, "Cease and desist, Sirs, I won't permit": without the old mark of the branding iron. Some point of view follows any public commotion, and predominates for years. This glimmering takes on, as soon as it is properly noted, the value, inappreciable among us, in an embryonic democracy that the lie wants to obscure, vomited up out of who know what throat! of a weapon capable of destroying the individual, in everyone's name; or certainly at least to take away his honor. An idea has by chance sprung out of what is called "the world," connected with that sharpness in taste and emotion derived from the French past. The salons spoke justly. So many hands, in a sense anarchistic, of otherwise conventionally proper people, holding themselves back for fear of seeming to protest the sentence that had just been read, went on to shake the hands of those who had been convicted, with dignity, spontaneity, and gravity, as if nothing had happened, thus erasing the ignominious traces of their shackles: those hands signified something unconscious and supreme. Judges, pronounce your verdict: but for us, a tribute imprudently paid, to remit the punishment, no: at least, intimate and superior consequences. I do not know, to tie in with the order of facts this new, imprecise, yet certain feeling that has come to light, or that seemed to determine this article, the intentions of the European cabinets and of our own chancellery relative to the most honor-bedecked, beribboned, and bemedalled poor octogenarian who ever existed: and whether it will be agreed that he should be stripped of such honors on the immanent occasion of his solitary funeral. A doubt remains whether the French Academy, that scrupulous guardian of all formalism (it represents Letters), will vote the eradication [*la radiation*] of old Mr. de Lesseps, who was once rashly admitted through some extraliterary consideration.

—From the *National Observer*, February 18, 1893

Gold

The highly vain universal deity with neither exterior nor pomp—

This refusal to betray any brightness must perhaps cease, in despair and if light shines from without: then, sumptuousness like a ship that sinks, does not give up, and celebrates sky and sea as it burns.

Not, when the time comes for show—

At the crash of a Bank; vague, mediocre, gray.

Currency, the terrible precision instrument, clean to the conscience, loses even its meaning.

By the light of phantasmagorical sunsets when clouds alone are sinking, with whatever man surrenders up to them of dreams, a treasure liquefaction crawls, gleams on the horizon: I thereby gain a notion of what sums can be, by the hundreds and beyond, equal to those whose enumeration, in the closing arguments during a trial involving high finance, leaves one, as far as their existence goes, cold. The inability of figures, however grandiloquent, to translate, here springs out of a case; one searches, with this hint that, if a number increases and backs up, toward the improbable, it inscribes more and more zeros: signifying that its total is spiritually equal to nothing, almost.

Mere smoke, those billions, outside the moment to grab some: or, the lack of resplendence or even interest shows that to elect a god is not so as to confine him to the shadow of iron safes and pockets.

No complaint from my curiosity disappointed by the effacement of gold under theatrical circumstances in which to appear blinding, bright, cynical: to myself thinking that, no doubt, because of money's incapacity to shine abstractly, the gift occurs, in the writer, of amassing radiant clarity with the words he proffers, such as Truth and Beauty.

—From Mallarmé, *Divagations* (1897)

Appendix to Chapter 16

Moesta et Errabunda
by Charles Baudelaire

> Dis-moi, ton coeur s'envole-t-il, Agathe,
> Loin du noir océan de l'immonde cité,
> Vers un autre océan où la splendeur éclate,
> Bleu, clair, profond, ainsi que la virginité?
> Dis-moi, ton coeur parfois s'envole-t-il, Agathe?
>
> La mer, la vaste mer, console nos labeurs!
> Quel démon a doté la mer, rauque chanteuse
> Qu'accompagne l'immense orgue des vents grondeurs,
> De cette fonction sublime de berceuse?
> La mer, la vaste mer, console nos labeurs!
>
> Emporte-moi, wagon! enlève-moi, frégate!
> Loin, loin! ici la boue est faite de nos pleurs!
> —Est-il vrai que parfois le triste coeur d'Agathe
> Dise: Loin des remords, des crimes, des douleurs,
> Emporte-moi, wagon, enlève-moi, frégate?
>
> Comme vous êtes loin, paradis parfumé,
> Où sous un clair azur tout n'est qu'amour et joie,
> Où tout ce que l'on aime est digne d'être aimé,
> Où dans la volupté pure le coeur se noie!
> Comme vous êtes loin, paradis parfumé!
>
> Mais le vert paradis des amours enfantines,
> Les courses, les chansons, les baisers, les bouquets,
> Les violons vibrant derrière les collines,
> Avec les brocs de vin, le soir, dans les bosquets,
> —Mais le vert paradis des amours enfantines,

L'innocent paradis, plein de plaisirs furtifs,
Est-il déjà plus loin que l'Inde et que la Chine?
Peut-on le rappeler avec des cris plaintifs,
Et l'animer encor d'une voix argentine,
L'innocent paradis plein de plaisirs furtifs?

Moesta et Errabunda

Tell me, Agatha, does your heart take flight
Far from the city's black and filthy sea
Off to another sea of splendid light,
Blue, bright, and deep as virginity?
Tell me, Agatha, does your heart take flight?

Seas, unending seas, console our trials!
What demon gave the sea this raucous voice
With organ music from the rumbling skies,
And made it play the role of sublime nurse?
Seas, unending seas, console our trials!

Carry me off, engines! lift me, bark!
Far, far away! our tears here turn to mud!
—Can it be true that sometimes Agatha's heart
Says: far from the crimes, remorse, distress, and dread
Carry me off, engines, lift me, bark!

How far away you are, sweet paradise,
Where what we love is worthy of our loves,
Where all is pleasure under azure skies,
Where hearts are drowned in pure voluptuous floods!
How far away you are, sweet paradise!

That verdant paradise of childhood loves,
The songs and games and kisses and bouquets,
The trembling violins in wooded groves,
The wine behind the hills as evening grays,
—That verdant paradise of childhood loves,

That paradise of blameless, furtive joys—
Does it lie farther off than China lies?
Can it be called back with a silvery voice
And animated again with plaintive cries,
That paradise of blameless, furtive joys?

Ode to the West Wind
by Percy Bysshe Shelley

I

O wild West Wind, thou breath of Autumn's being,
Thou, from whose unseen presence the leaves dead
Are driven, like ghosts from an enchanter fleeing,

Yellow, and black, and pale, and hectic red,
Pestilence-stricken multitudes: O thou,
Who chariotest to their dark wintry bed

The wingéd seeds, where they lie cold and low,
Each like a corpse within its grave, until
Thine azure sister of the Spring shall blow

Her clarion o'er the dreaming earth, and fill
(Driving sweet buds like flocks to feed in air)
With living hues and odors plain and hill:

Wild Spirit, which art moving everywhere;
Destroyer and preserver; hear, oh, hear!

II

Thou on whose stream, mid the steep sky's commotion,
Loose clouds like earth's decaying leaves are shed,
Shook from the tangled boughs of Heaven and Ocean,

Angels of rain and lightning: there are spread
On the blue surface of thine aëry surge,
Like the bright hair uplifted from the head

Of some fierce Maenad, even from the dim verge
Of the horizon to the zenith's height,
The locks of the approaching storm. Thou dirge

Of the dying year, to which this closing night
Will be the dome of a vast sepulcher,
Vaulted with all thy congregated might

Of vapors, from whose solid atmosphere
Black rain, and fire, and hail will burst: oh, hear!

III

Thou who didst waken from his summer dreams
The blue Mediterranean, where he lay,
Lulled by the coil of his crystálline streams,

Besides a pumice isle in Baiae's bay,
And saw in sleep old palaces and towers
Quivering within the wave's intenser day,

All overgrown with azure moss and flowers
So sweet, the sense faints picturing them! Thou
For whose path the Atlantic's level powers

Cleave themselves into chasms, while far below
The sea-blooms and the oozy woods which wear
The sapless foliage of the ocean, know

Thy voice, and suddenly grow gray with fear,
And tremble and despoil themselves: oh, hear!

IV

If I were a dead leaf thou mightest bear;
If I were a swift cloud to fly with thee;
A wave to pant beneath thy power, and share

The impulse of thy strength, only less free
Than thou, O uncontrollable! If even
I were as in my boyhood, and could be

The comrade of thy wanderings over Heaven,
As then, when to outstrip thy skyey speed
Scarce seemed a vision; I would ne'er have striven

As thus with thee in prayer in my sore need.
Oh, lift me as a wave, a leaf, a cloud!
I fall upon the thorns of life! I bleed!

A heavy weight of hours has chained and bowed
One too like thee: tameless, and swift, and proud.

V

Make me thy lyre, even as the forest is:
What if my leaves are falling like its own!
The tumult of thy mighty harmonies

Will take from both a deep, autumnal tone,
Sweet though in sadness. Be thou, Spirit fierce,
My spirit! Be thou me, impetuous one!

Drive my dead thoughts over the universe
Like withered leaves to quicken a new birth!
And, by the incantation of this verse,

Scatter, as from an unextinguished hearth
Ashes and sparks, my words among mankind!
Be through my lips to unawakened earth

The trumpet of a prophecy! O Wind,
If Winter comes, can Spring be far behind?

The Abortion
by Anne Sexton

> *Somebody who should have been born*
> *is gone*

Just as the earth puckered its mouth,
each bud puffing out from its knot,
I changed my shoes, and then drove south.

Up past the Blue Mountains, where
Pennsylvania humps on endlessly,
wearing, like a crayoned cat, its green hair,

its roads sunken in like a gray washboard;
where, in truth, the ground cracks evilly,
a dark socket from which the coal has poured,

> *Somebody who should have been born*
> *is gone.*

the grass as bristly and stout as chives,
and me wondering when the ground would break,
and me wondering how anything fragile survives;

up in Pennsylvania, I met a little man,
not Rumpelstiltskin, at all, at all . . .
he took the fullness that love began.

Returning north, even the sky grew thin
like a high window looking nowhere.
The road was as flat as a sheet of tin.

> *Somebody who should have been born*
> *is gone*

Yes, woman, such logic will lead
to loss without death. Or say what you meant,
you coward . . . this baby that I bleed.

the lost baby poem
by Lucille Clifton

the time i dropped your almost body down
down to meet the waters under the city
and run one with the sewage to the sea
what did i know about waters rushing back
what did i know about drowning
or being drowned

you would have been born into winter
in the year of the disconnected gas
and no car   we would have made the thin
walk over Genesee hill into the Canada wind
to watch you slip like ice into strangers' hands
you would have fallen naked as snow into winter
if you were here i could tell you these
and some other things

if i am ever less than a mountain
for your definite brothers and sisters
let the rivers pour over my head
let the sea take me for a spiller
of seas   let black men call me stranger
always   for your never named sake

To a Poet
by Adrienne Rich

Ice splits   under the metal
shovel   another day
hazed light off fogged panes
cruelty of winter   landlocked   your life
wrapped round you   in your twenties
an old bathrobe   dragged down
with milkstains   tearstains   dust

Scraping eggcrust from the child's
dried dish   skimming the skin
from cooled milk   wringing diapers
Language floats at the vanishing-point
incarnate   breathes the fluorescent bulb
primary   states the scarred grain of the floor
and on the ceiling in torn plaster laughs   *imago*

and I have fears that you will cease to be
before your pen has glean'd your teeming brain

for you are not a suicide
but no-one calls this murder
Small mouths, needy, suck you: *This is love*

I write this   not for you
who fight to write your own
words   fighting up the falls
but for another woman   dumb
with loneliness   dust   seeping plastic bags
with children   in a house
where language floats and spins
abortion   in
the bowl

Notes

Introduction

1. Barbara Johnson, *The Critical Difference* (Baltimore: Johns Hopkins University Press, 1980), pp. x–xi.
2. Duncan Kennedy, *Legal Education and the Reproduction of Hierarchy* (Cambridge, Mass.: Afar, 1983), p. 30.
3. I would like to thank John Schilb for calling these differences to my attention.
4. Paul de Man, *Allegories of Reading* (New Haven: Yale University Press, 1979), p. 299.

Chapter 1. Nothing Fails Like Success

This chapter was originally written for a session at the 1980 MLA Convention organized by the Society for Critical Exchange on the topic "The Future of Deconstruction." While I would want to argue some of the points a bit differently now (and perhaps with different examples), the basic thrust of the essay seems to me to be, if anything, even more relevant today. In the years since this essay was written, many more critiques of deconstruction have appeared, both from the left and from the right, but I leave the references as they were in 1980. Some of the later material will present itself in this book in dialogue with other chapters.

1. Peter Shaw, "Degenerate Criticism," *Harper's*, October 1979, p. 97; M. H. Abrams, "The Deconstructive Angel," *Critical Inquiry*, Spring 1977, p. 434; Gerald Graff, *Literature against Itself* (Chicago: University of Chicago Press, 1979), p. 39; Shaw, "Degenerate Criticism," p. 93; and Denis Donoghue, "Deconstructing Deconstruction," *New York Review of Books*, June 12, 1980, p. 37.
2. Jacques Derrida, *Dissemination*, trans. Barbara Johnson (Chicago: University of Chicago Press, 1981), p. 207.
3. Paul de Man, "The Purloined Ribbon," in *Glyph 1: John Hopkins Textual Studies* (Baltimore: Johns Hopkins University Press, 1977). (Reprinted as "Excuses" in *Allegories of Reading* [New Haven: Yale University Press, 1979].)
4. Graff, *Literature against Itself*, p. 65.
5. Cf., for example, Jeffrey Mehlman, "Teaching Reading," *Diacritics*, Winter 1976; Gayatri Chakravorti Spivak and Michael Ryan, "Anarchism Revisited," *Diacritics*, Summer 1978; John Brenkman, "Deconstruction and the Social Text,"

Social Text 1 (Winter 1979); and Edward Said, "Reflections on Recent American 'Left' Literary Criticism," Boundary 2 8, no. 1 (1979), reprinted in The World, the Text, and the Critic (Cambridge: Harvard University Press, 1983).

Chapter 2. Rigorous Unreliability

This chapter was conceived as a contribution to a session of the 1983 MLA Convention organized by Barbara Herrnstein Smith and Dorrit Cohn entitled "Questions of Value." News of Paul de Man's death reached me as I was writing the final section of the essay.

1. Paul de Man, Allegories of Reading: Figural Language in Rousseau, Nietzsche, Rilke, and Proust (New Haven: Yale University Press, 1979), p. x; all further references to this work will be included in the text.

2. Geoffrey Hartman, Introduction to Deconstruction and Criticism, ed. Harold Bloom (New York: Continuum, 1979), p. viii.

3. The logic of de Man's reading runs as follows. In order to produce the impression that "the total spectacle of the summer" (the outside) has been captured within the darkened room (the inside), Marcel Proust has recourse to various figurative strategies. In one instance he explicitly states a preference for a figure formed by necessity over a figure formed by chance: "the chamber music of the flies," Proust writes, is "evocative not in the manner of a human tune that, heard perchance during the summer, afterwards reminds you of it, but connected to summer by a more necessary link: born from beautiful days, resurrecting only when they return, containing some of their essence, it does not only awaken their image in our memory; it guarantees their return, their actual, persistent, unmediated presence" (quoted by de Man, p. 13). De Man glosses: "The preference is expressed by means of a distinction that corresponds to the difference between metaphor and metonymy, necessity and chance being a legitimate way to distinguish between analogy and contiguity" (p. 14). Hence, by its own account, the Proust passage achieves its guilt-erasing totalization through metaphor (necessity). Yet later in the passage the insertion of heat into the coolness of the room (another aspect of the totalization) is accomplished by means of a linguistic accident—not by "necessity." The "dark coolness" of the room, says Marcel, "matched my repose which (thanks to the adventures told by my book and stirring my tranquility) supported, like the quiet of a motionless hand in the middle of a running brook the shock and the motion of a torrent of activity" (pp. 13–14). De Man here points out that the expression "torrent of activity" is able to reconcile heat and bustle with cool tranquility only through the double contingency of the fact that it is a cliché ("torrent" and "activity" do not each separately convey the property of heat, but as a cliché—through habitual contiguity—the expression works up a sweat) and that the sleeping water image in "torrent" is reawakened by mere proximity to the "running brook." The totalization of essence (metaphor) is thus dependent upon linguistic contiguity (metonymy), and the preference for metaphor preached by the passage is undercut by its own practice.

Chapter 3. Is Writerliness Conservative?

This chapter was conceived as a contribution to a session of the 1984 MLA Convention organized by Naomi Schor entitled "The Politics of Poetry."

1. For some recent examples, see Edward Said, The World, the Text, and the

Critic (Cambridge: Harvard University Press, 1983); Frank Lentricchia, *Criticism and Social Change* (Chicago: University of Chicago Press, 1983); Terry Eagleton, *Walter Benjamin; or, Toward a Revolutionary Criticism* (London: Verso Editions, 1981); and Barbara Foley, "The Politics of Deconstruction," in *Rhetoric and Form: Deconstruction at Yale*, ed. Robert Con Davis and Ronald Schliefer (Norman: University of Oklahoma Press, 1985).

2. Lentricchia seems to me a bit overoptimistic about how easy it might be for literary intellectuals to avoid falling into the category of "liberals." His own writing indeed sometimes exhibits patterns of grammatical resistance to his urge to get on with the process of social change. "My presiding contention," he writes, for example, "is that our potentially most powerful political work as university humanists must be carried out in what we do, what we are trained for" (p. 7). The words "potentially" and "must" defer the urgency of a "presiding contention" into the vague hypothetical imperative of an unformulated future. This happens again and again in Lentricchia's book, and doubtless also in mine. Another definition of *liberal* is someone who stands *for* something that will ultimately put in question what s/he is standing *on*.

3. Charles Sanders Pierce, "The Scientific Attitude and Fallibilism," in *Philosophical Writings*, ed. J. Butchler (New York: Dover, 1955), p. 58.

4. See Roland Barthes, *S/Z*, trans. Richard Miller (New York: Hill and Wang, 1974), p. 4.

5. Stéphane Mallarmé, *Oeuvres Complètes* (Paris: Pléiade, 1945), pp. 355–60.

6. Ibid., pp. 409–12.

7. Adrienne Rich, *On Lies, Secrets, and Silence* (New York: Norton, 1979), p. 193.

Chapter 4. Gender Theory and the Yale School

This chapter, as the text makes clear, is very much a cry of its occasion: a conference entitled "Genre Theory and the Yale School" held May 31–June 1, 1984, at the University of Oklahoma at Norman.

1. Jonathan Culler, *On Deconstruction* (Ithaca, N.Y.: Cornell University Press, 1982), p. 289.

2. Jacques Derrida, "The Law of Genre," in *Glyph 7: Johns Hopkins Textual Studies* (Baltimore: Johns Hopkins University Press, 1980), pp. 203–4.

3. Geoffrey Hartman, *The Fate of Reading* (Chicago: University of Chicago Press, 1975), p. 248, and *Beyond Formalism* (New Haven: Yale University Press, 1970), p. 351.

4. Hartman, "Words, Wish, Worth: Wordsworth," in *Deconstruction and Criticism*, ed. Harold Bloom (New York: Continuum, 1979), p. 215. Further references to this and other essays in the volume will be indicated in the text by the abbreviation *DC* followed by a page number.

5. Harold Bloom, *A Map of Misreading* (New York: Oxford University Press, 1975), p. 33. I would like to thank Susan Suleiman for calling this quotation to my attention.

6. The story of Jael is found in Judges 4. Jael invites Sisera, the commander of the Canaanite army, into her tent, gives him a drink of milk, and then, when he has fallen asleep, drives a tent peg through his head and kills him. Sima Godfrey suggested this pun.

7. Paul de Man, "The Epistemology of Metaphor," *Critical Inquiry* 5 (1978): 13–28.

8. Barbara Johnson, *The Critical Difference* (Baltimore: Johns Hopkins University Press, 1980).

Chapter 5. Deconstruction, Feminism, and Pedagogy

This chapter was conceived as a contribution to a session of the 1985 MLA Convention organized by Thaïs Morgan entitled "Postpedagogy."

1. Paul de Man, "The Resistance to Theory," in *The Pedagogical Imperative*, ed. Barbara Johnson (New Haven: Yale University Press, 1982), hereafter referred to as *PI*; *Gendered Subjects*, ed. Margo Culley and Catherine Portuges (Boston: Routledge & Kegan Paul, 1985), hereafter referred to as *GS*.

Chapter 6. A Hound, a Bay Horse, and a Turtle Dove: Obscurity in Walden

1. Henry David Thoreau, *Walden; or, Life in the Woods* (New York: Signet, 1960), p. 22. All page references to *Walden* are to this edition.

2. Walter Benn Michaels, "*Walden*'s False Bottoms," *Glyph 1: Johns Hopkins Textual Studies* (Baltimore: Johns Hopkins University Press, 1977), pp. 132–49.

3. For detailed bibliographical information on these and other readings of the passage, see *The Annotated Walden*, ed. Philip Van Doren Stern (New York: Clarkson N. Potter, 1970), pp. 157–58, and *The Variorum Walden*, ed. Walter Harding (New York: Twayne, 1962), pp. 270–72.

4. Stanley Cavell, *The Senses of Walden* (San Francisco: North Point, 1981), p. 51.

5. Ralph Waldo Emerson, *Selected Prose and Poetry* (New York: Holt, Rinehart, and Winston, 1964), p. 20.

Chapter 7. Erasing Panama: Mallarmé and the Text of History

1. For the complete texts of both "versions" of this article, see the Appendix to Chapter 7. Texts cited are from Mallarmé, *Oeuvres complètes* (Paris: Pléiade, 1945). All translations are my own.

2. Norman Paxton, *The Development of Mallarmé's Prose Style* (Geneva: Droz, 1968), pp. 42, 66.

3. For a fascinating recent study of the entire Panama Canal story, see David McCullough, *The Path between the Seas* (New York: Touchstone, 1977).

4. Ferdinand de Lesseps, *Souvenirs de quarante ans* (Paris: Nouvelle Revue, 1887), pp. 25–27.

5. D. W. Brogan, *France under the Republic (1870–1939)* (New York: Harper, 1940), p. 269; emphasis mine.

Chapter 8. Teaching Ignorance: L'Ecole des femmes

1. *The School for Wives*, 1.1. In quoting from *L'Ecole des femmes* and the *Critique de l'Ecole des femmes* in English, I have generally followed the Donald Frame translation (*Tartuffe and Other Plays by Molière* [New York: New American Library, 1967]); passages in which I have modified the translation will be marked "TM" (translation modified). All translations of other French texts are my own.

2. In French: "Il m'a . . . pris . . . le . . . ."

3. *L'Ecole des femmes*, ed. Pierre Cabanis (Paris: Bordas, 1963), p. 14. Henceforth referred to as "Bordas."

4. *L'Ecole des femmes*, ed. Gérard Sablayrolles (Paris: Larousse, 1965), p. 58. Henceforth referred to as "Larousse."

5. Fénelon, *De l'education des filles* (1687), ch. 11.

6. Gustave Fagnier, *La Femme et la société française dans la première moitié du XVIIe siècle* (Paris: J. Gamber, 1929), pp. 11–12.

7. For valuable recent analyses of *préciosité* and feminism, see Dorothy Anne Liot Backer, *Precious Women* (New York: Basic Books, 1974); Carolyn C. Lougee, *Le Paradis des femmes* (Princeton: Princeton University Press, 1976); and Ian Maclean, *Woman Triumphant* (Oxford: Clarendon, 1977).

8. Georges Mongredien, *La Querelle de "L'Ecole des femmes"* (Paris: Librarie Marcel Didier, 1971), p. xxviii.

9. Neil Hertz, "Two Extravagant Teachings," in *Yale French Studies* 63 (1982): 59.

10. Plato, *Phaedrus*, trans. W. C. Helmbold and W. G. Rabinowitz (Indianapolis: Library of Liberal Arts, 1956), pp. 70–71.

11. Plato, *Meno*, trans. G.M.A. Grube (Indianapolis: Hackett, 1976), p. 15.

12. Søren Kierkegaard, *The Concept of Irony*, trans. Lee M. Capel (Bloomington: Indiana University Press, 1965), p. 285.

Chapter 9. Strange Fits:
Poe and Wordsworth on the Nature of Poetic Language

1. I shall refer to the 1805 version of the preface, as printed in *Wordsworth's Literary Criticism*, ed. W. J. B. Owen (London: Routledge & Kegan Paul, 1974). The "Philosophy of Composition" appears in *The Unabridged Edgar Allan Poe* (Philadelphia: Running Press, 1983).

2. E.g.: "I hope that there is in these Poems little falsehood of description, and that my ideas are expressed in language *fitted* to their respective importance" (p. 75); "If the Poet's subject be judiciously chosen, it will naturally, and upon *fit* occasion, lead him to passions the language of which, if selected truly and judiciously, must necessarily be dignified and variegated, and live with metaphors and figures" (p. 77); "As it is impossible for the Poet to produce upon all occasions language as exquisitely *fitted for the passion* as that which the real passion suggests, it is proper that he should consider himself as in the situation of a translator" (p. 79). The question then becomes, "Is every fit that fits fit?"

3. In addition to its meaning of "outburst," *fit* can also refer to an arrest, a stroke, a hiatus. Silas Marner's strange fits, for example, freeze him in stop-action stillness while the rest of life continues around him. That the notion of "fits" carries with it a suggestion of the supernatural or the mysterious is indicated by George Eliot's report of folk belief: "Some said that Marner must have been in a 'fit,' a word which seemed to explain things otherwise incredible." *Silas Marner* (Penguin ed.), p. 55.

4. Cf. Geoffrey Hartman: "To take the moon's drop as the direct cause of the thought assumes that the lover has identified his beloved with the moon." *Wordsworth's Poetry* (New Haven: Yale University Press, 1964), p. 23. The imputation of a suppressed personification here implies that Lucy herself is a person. But is she? The long-standing and unresolved debate over the identity of Wordsworth's Lucy would suggest that Lucy is already in fact not a person but a personification. For a fascinating conceptualization of the question of rhetorically mediate, "naturalized" personifications (that is, those that are made to seem real, "found" rather than allegorically made) and their relation to eighteenth-

century allegory, see Steven Knapp, *Personification and the Sublime* (Cambridge: Harvard University Press, 1985). At one point Knapp essentially uses the notion of a "strange fit" to refer to the Wordsworthian sublime: "Sometimes—and most strikingly in episodes of naturalized personification—the gap between two moments is replaced by a *curious lack of fit* between two ways of perceiving a single object" (p. 108).

5. It might be objected that this is not the type of personification Wordsworth had in mind, that what he wished to avoid was personifications of abstract ideas, not celestial bodies. Yet the example of bad personification Wordsworth cites in the preface *does* in fact involve celestial bodies, not abstract ideas. In the sonnet by Gray in which Wordsworth italicizes only the parts he considers valuable, it is the personification of the sun and of the natural world ("reddening Phoebus lifts his golden fire," etc.) that Wordsworth does *not* italicize.

6. A very suggestive gloss on what is unsettling in Wordsworth's rejection of personification is given by Frances Ferguson: "The insistance of the cottage girl in 'We are Seven' that she and her dead siblings are not separated from one another by death involves a kind of personification, but it is personification pushed to such an extreme that it becomes a virtual anti-type to personification. This girl personifies *persons*, and the radically disquieting element in her remarks is the growing consciousness in the poem that persons should need to be personified, should need to be reclaimed from death by the imagination. Her version of personification revolves around death as the essential abstract idea behind personification. Persons and personifications become united members in the community of the living and the dead." Frances Ferguson, *Wordsworth: Language as Counter-Spirit* (New Haven: Yale University Press, 1977), pp. 26–27.

Chapter 10. Disfiguring Poetic Language

1. For a broader development of this perspective, see my *Défigurations du langage poétique* (Paris: Flammarion, 1979), from which, with considerable modification, the present essay is derived. All translations, both of my own original French and of that of others, are mine unless otherwise indicated.

2. Baudelaire, "Le Gâteau," in *Oeuvres complètes* (Paris: Pléiade, 1976), 1:297–99.

3. Baudelaire, "Le Galant Tireur," in *Oeuvres complètes*, 1:349–50.

4. Jean Cohen, "Théorie de la figure," *Communications* 16 (1970): 8.

5. The magical quality of this figural operation casts an unexpected light on the famous Baudelairean conception of "language and writing taken as magic operations, evocative sorcery" ("Fusées," in *Oeuvres complètes*, 1:658). Indeed, in describing magical operations in *Totem and Taboo*, Freud refers to this same scene: "One of the most widespread magical procedures for injuring an enemy is by making an effigy of him from any convenient material. . . . Whatever is then done to the effigy, the same thing happens to the detested original" (*Standard Edition*, 13:79). It is precisely in rhetorical terms—substitution, resemblance, contiguity—that Freud describes such magical operations. The much-vaunted "magic of art" may then perhaps be something more unsettling than the rhetorical prestidigitation that would create out of nothing some "absente de tous bouquets." One begins to suspect that beneath every bouquet of flowers of rhetoric, the "evocative sorcery" of poetry may be producing, somewhere, a severed head.

6. Michel Deguy, *Figurations* (Paris: Gallimard, 1969), p. 121.

7. Cohen, "Théorie," pp. 4–5..
8. Jacques Lacan, *The Four Fundamental Concepts of Psychoanalysis*, trans. Alan Sheridan (New York: Norton, 1977), p. 62.
9. Daniel Sibony, "L'Infini et la castration," *Scilicet* 4 (1973): 81, 120.
10. Pierre Fontanier, *Les Figures du discours* (Paris: Flammarion, 1968), p. 63.
11. Gérard Genette, *Figures I* (Paris: Seuil, 1966), p. 120.
12. Baudelaire, "Le Poème du haschisch," in *Oeuvres complètes*, 1:420.

Chapter 11. Les Fleurs du Mal Armé: Some Reflections on Intertextuality

This chapter is a translation, revision, and extension of an essay originally published in French in *Michigan Romance Studies* 2 (1982): 87–99. All translations from the French are my own.

The title, "Les Fleurs du Mal Armé," is designed to be read as a paradigm for the question of intertextuality under discussion here. On the one hand, it appears to posit a linear, developmental, slightly overlapping relation between a precursor text ("Les Fleurs du mal") and a disciple (Mallarmé) engendered out of it. On the other hand, the double function of the word *mal* renders Baudelaire's title and Mallarmé's name both inseparable from each other and different from themselves, creating new dividing lines not *between* the two oeuvres but *within* each of them. The proper names thereby lose their properness, and their free-floating parts can combine into new signifying possibilities.

1. Mallarmé, "Symphonie littéraire," in *Oeuvres complètes* (Paris: Pléiade, 1945), p. 261. Page numbers referring to this edition will henceforth be included parenthetically in the text.
2. Baudelaire, *Correspondance* (Paris: Pléiade, 1973), 2:625.
3. Guy Michaud, *Mallarmé* (Paris: Hatier, 1958), p. 25.
4. Interestingly enough, there is a sentence in a letter from Mallarmé to Cazalis that seems unexpectedly to confirm this reading. In discussing the composition of "L'Azur," Mallarmé writes, "I had a lot of trouble with it because, banishing a thousand lyrical turns and beautiful lines that incessantly *haunted* my brain, I wanted to stick implacably to my subject." January 1864, in *Correspondance, 1862–1871* (Paris: Gallimard, 1959), p. 103; italics mine.
5. Victor Hugo, *Oeuvres poétique* (Paris: Pléiade, 1967), 2:482.
6. Baudelaire, *Oeuvres complètes* (Paris: Pléiade, 1976), 2:831.
7. Susan Gubar, "'The Blank Page' and Female Creativity," in *Writing and Sexual Difference*, ed. Elizabeth Abel (Chicago: University of Chicago Press, 1982), pp. 75, 77.
8. It is curious to note that the word with which "Idumée" rhymes in Boileau is "alarmée," and that "alarmes" is the first rhyme in the overture to "Hérodiade," which follows and imagistically grows out of "Don du Poème." Mallarmé's anagrammatical signature seems to lurk just behind these citations of poetic history.
9. For a brilliantly sustained analysis of the functioning of such "feminine" spaces in contemporary theory, see Alice Jardine, *Gynesis* (Ithaca: Cornell University Press, 1985). And for a related, fundamental treatment of Mallarmé's role in literary history, see Julia Kristeva, *Revolution in Poetic Language* (New York: Columbia University Press, 1984). The present essay can indeed in many ways be seen as a "poor woman's Kristeva."
10. Clément Marot, "Le Beau Tétin," in *Les Poètes du XVIe siècle* (Paris: Editions J'ai lu, 1962), p. 150.

11. Edmund Spenser, "Epithalamion," lines 172–77, in *The Norton Anthology of English Literature* (New York: Norton, 1962), 1:531.

12. "The Breast," in *The Complete Poems of Anne Sexton* (Boston: Houghton Mifflin, 1981), pp. 175–76.

13. Lucille Clifton, *Good Times* (New York: Random House, 1969).

Chapter 12. Mallarmé as Mother

1. Condensed and adapted from Margaret Mahler, "Mother-Child Interaction during Separation-Individuation," in *The Selected Papers of Margaret S. Mahler* (New York: Aronson, 1979).

2. For a full treatment of this aspect of Mallarmé's exploration of pre-oedipal structures, see Julia Kristeva, *Revolution in Poetic Language* (New York: Columbia University Press, 1984).

3. For a fuller development of the implications of the blanks as female body, see Chapter 11, above.

4. Adrienne Rich, *Of Woman Born: Motherhood as Experience and Institution* (New York: Bantam, 1976); Susan Suleiman, "Writing and Motherhood," in *The (M)other Tongue*, ed. Garner, Kahane, and Sprengnether (Ithaca: Cornell University Press, 1985), pp. 352–77; and recent work by Marianne Hirsch.

Chapter 13. My Monster/My Self

1. Nancy Friday, *My Mother/My Self* (New York: Dell, 1977); Dorothy Dinnerstein, *The Mermaid and the Minotaur* (New York: Harper Colophon, 1976); Mary Shelley, *Frankenstein; or, The Modern Prometheus* (New York: Signet, 1965).

2. See Ellen Moers, "Female Gothic," and U. C. Knoepflmacher, "Thoughts on the Aggression of Daughters," in *The Endurance of Frankenstein*, ed. George Levine and U. C. Knoepflmacher (Berkeley and Los Angeles: University of California Press, 1979). Other related and helpful studies include S. M. Gilbert and S. Gubar, "Horror's Twin," in *The Madwoman in the Attic* (New Haven: Yale University Press, 1979), and Mary Poovey, "My Hideous Progeny: Mary Shelley and the Feminization of Romanticism," *PMLA* 95 (May 1980): 332–47.

Chapter 14. Metaphor, Metonymy, and Voice
    in Their Eyes Were Watching God

1. For an excellent discussion of the importance of the metaphor/metonymy distinction, see Maria Ruegg, "Metaphor and Metonymy: The Logic of Structuralist Rhetoric," in *Glyph 6: Johns Hopkins Textual Studies* (Baltimore: Johns Hopkins University Press, 1979).

2. Roman Jakobson, "Two Aspects of Language and Two Types of Aphasic Disturbances," in Roman Jakobson and Morris Halle, *Fundamentals of Language* (The Hague: Mouton, 1956).

3. Roman Jakobson, "Linguistics and Poetics," in *The Structuralists from Marx to Lévi-Strauss* (Garden City, N.Y.: Doubleday Anchor, 1972), p. 95.

4. See George Lakoff and Mark Johnson, *Metaphors We Live By* (Chicago: University of Chicago Press, 1980).

5. Paul de Man, *Allegories of Reading* (New Haven: Yale University Press, 1979), p. 14.

6. It now appears, according to new evidence uncovered by Professor Cheryl

Wall of Rutgers University, that Hurston was born as much as ten years earlier than she claimed. See Robert Hemenway's Introduction to the re-edition of *Dust Tracks on a Road* (Urbana: University of Illinois Press, 1984), pp. x–xi.

7. "Folklore Field Notes from Nora Neale Hurston," introduced by Robert Hemenway, *The Black Scholar* 7, no. 7 (1976): 41–42.

8. Zora Neale Hurston, *Their Eyes Were Watching God* (1937), Illini Book Edition (Urbana: University of Illinois Press, 1978).

9. Erich Auerbach, *Mimesis* (New York: Doubleday Anchor, 1957), pp. 482–83.

10. Henry Louis Gates, Jr., "Criticism in the Jungle," introduction to *Black Literature and Literary Theory* (New York: Methuen, 1984), pp. 4, 8.

11. W.E.B. DuBois, *The Souls of Black Folk*, in *Three Negro Classics* (New York: Avon, 1965), pp. 214–15.

12. James Weldon Johnson, *The Autobiography of an Ex-Colored Man*, in *Three Negro Classics*, p. 403.

13. Richard Wright, "Between Laughter and Tears," *New Masses*, October 5, 1937, pp. 25–26.

14. Arthur P. Davis, *From the Dark Tower* (Washington, D.C.: Howard University Press, 1974), p. 116.

15. Bell Hooks, *Ain't I a Woman* (Boston: South End Press, 1981), p. 8.

16. Zora Neale Hurston, *Dust Tracks on a Road*, pp. 252–60.

17. See Gates' discussion of *Their Eyes Were Watching God* as what he calls (à la Barthes) a "speakerly text," in *The Signifying Monkey* (forthcoming).

18. I wish to thank Patti Joplin of Stanford University for calling this fact to my attention.

Chapter 15. Thresholds of Difference:
Structures of Address in Zora Neale Hurston

1. Zora Neale Hurston, "How It Feels to Be Colored Me," *World Tomorrow*, May 1928, reprinted in *I Love Myself When I Am Laughing . . . : A Zora Neale Hurston Reader*, ed. Alice Walker (Old Westbury, N.Y.: Feminist Press, 1979), pp. 152–55; "What White Publishers Won't Print," *Negro Digest*, April 1950, reprinted ibid., pp. 169–73; *Mules and Men* (New York: Lippincott, 1935; rpt. Bloomington: Indiana University Press, 1978).

2. Langston Hughes, *The Big Sea* (New York: Hill & Wang, 1963), pp. 238–39.

3. This formulation was suggested to me by a student, Lisa Cohen.

4. Nathan Huggins, *Harlem Renaissance* (London: Oxford University Press, 1971), p. 133.

Chapter 16. Apostrophe, Animation, and Abortion

1. I would like to thank Tom Keenan of Yale University for bringing this text to my attention. The present essay has in fact benefitted greatly from the suggestions of others, among whom I would like particularly to thank Marge Garber, Rachel Jacoff, Carolyn Williams, Helen Vendler, Steven Melville, Ted Morris, Stamos Metzidakis, Steven Ungar, and Richard Yarborough.

2. Jonathan Culler, "Apostrophe," in *The Pursuit of Signs* (Ithaca: Cornell University Press, 1981), pp. 135–154. Cf. also Paul de Man: "Now it is certainly beyond question that the figure of address is recurrent in lyric poetry, to the point of constituting the generic definition of, at the very least, the ode (which can, in turn, be seen as paradigmatic for poetry in general." Paul de Man,

"Lyrical Voice in Contemporary Theory," in *Lyric Poetry: Beyond New Criticism*, ed. Chaviva Hosek and Patricia Parker (Ithaca: Cornell University Press, 1985).

3. For complete texts of the poems under discussion, see the Appendix to Chapter 16. The texts cited are taken from the following sources: Charles Baudelaire, *Oeuvres complètes* (Paris: Pléiade, 1976); *The Norton Anthology of Poetry* (New York: Norton, 1975), for Shelley; Anne Sexton, *The Complete Poems* (Boston: Houghton Mifflin, 1981); Lucille Clifton, *Good News about the Earth* (New York: Random House, 1972); and Adrienne Rich, *The Dream of a Common Language* (New York: Norton, 1978). The translation of Baudelaire's "Moesta et Errabunda" is my own. Gwendolyn Brooks refused permission to reprint "The Mother," which can be found in Gwendolyn Brooks, *Selected Poems* (New York: Harper & Row, 1963), or in *The Norton Anthology of Literature by Women* (New York: Norton, 1985), or in *The Black Poets* (New York: Bantam, 1971).

4. It is interesting to note that the "gentle breeze," apostrophized as "Messenger" and "Friend" in the 1805–6 *Prelude* (book 1, line 5), is significantly *not* directly addressed in the 1850 version. One might ask whether this change stands as a sign of the much-discussed waning of Wordsworth's poetic inspiration, or whether it is, rather, one of a number of strictly rhetorical shifts that *give the impression* of a wane.

5. Henry David Thoreau, *Walden* (New York: Signet, 1960), p. 66.

6. Carol Gilligan, *In a Different Voice* (Cambridge: Harvard University Press, 1982), p. 94.

7. Quoted in Jay L. Garfield and Patricia Hennessey, eds. *Abortion: Moral and Legal Perspectives* (Amherst: University of Massachusetts Press, 1984), p. 15.

8. Cf. Kristin Luker, *Abortion and the Politics of Motherhood* (Berkeley and Los Angeles: University of California Press, 1984), p. 6.

9. For additional poems dealing with the loss of babies, see the anthology *The Limits of Miracles* collected by Marion Deutsche Cohen (South Hadley, Mass.: Bergin and Garvey, 1985). Sharon Dunn, editor of the *Agni Review*, told me recently that she has in fact noticed that such poems have begun to form almost a new genre.

10. Poems cited here and on the following pages from Sidney, Jonson, and Silkin may be found in *The Norton Anthology of Poetry* (New York: Norton, 1975).

11. Mallarmé, *Oeuvres complètes* (Paris: Pléiade, 1945), p. 40.

12. Guillaume Apollinaire, *Les Mamelles de Tirésias*, in *L'Enchanteur pourrissant* (Paris: Gallimard, 1972), p. 101.

13. Michael Harper, title poem in *Nightmare Begins Responsibility* (Urbana: University of Illinois Press, 1975).

14. Jacques Lacan, *Ecrits*, trans. Alan Sheridan (New York: Norton, 1977), p. 286.

15. An interesting example of a poem in which an apostrophe confers upon the totally Other the authority to animate the self is Randall Jarrell's "A Sick Child," which ends: "All that I've never thought of—think of me!" In *The Voice That Is Great within Us*, ed. Hayden Carruth (Bantam, 1970), p. 402.

Index

Motherhood as a romance? We particularly. Women had to buy into it as a means of establishing self-worth.

Not just a case of being for or against abortion - but who will decide! church, state, medicine - no women!